SEX, CLASS AND REALISM

SEX, CLASS AND REALISM

British Cinema 1956–1963

John Hill

BFI PUBLISHING

First published in 1986 by the
British Film Institute
21 Stephen Street
London W1P 2LN

Reprinted 1995,1997

British Library Cataloguing in Publication Data

Hill, John
    Sex, class and realism: British cinema 1956–1963.
    1. Moving-pictures   Great Britain – History and criticism
    I. Title   II. British Film Institute
    791.43′0941   PN1993.5.G7
    ISBN 0–85170–132–9
    ISBN 0–85170–133–7 Pbk

Cover: *Violent Playground* (1958)

Cover Design: Peter Virgo

Typeset by W.S. Cowell Ltd., London and Ipswich
Printed and bound in Great Britain by
Antony Rowe Ltd, Chippenham, Wiltshire

Contents

Acknowledgments

I would like to thank a number of people for their help in the preparation of this book.

My special thanks to Andrew Tudor for his continuing support, advice and encouragement throughout a lengthy, and often interrupted, period of research and writing-up. Had it not been for his confidence in my work, I might not have finished the book at all. My thanks also to Ed Buscombe, Jim Cook and Moira Nevin for their helpful comments on the first draft, and to John Springhall for his advice on Chapter One. Thanks too to Jonathan Simmons for sending me a copy of his unpublished M.A. thesis, 'British Youth Problem Feature Films of the 1950s', and a useful discussion on some of the more arcane aspects of the British social problem film.

I am also indebted to Elaine Burrows of the National Film Archive and Joan Woodhead of the British Film Institute Education Department for their help with screenings; to the staff of the National Film Archive Stills Department; and to Rosemary McCollum and Pearl Walton for their invaluable help with typing. Finally, I would like to thank Lisa Hardy of BFI Publishing for her enthusiasm and hard work in preparing the manuscript for publication.

Stills are courtesy of Associated British, Beaver Films, British Lion, Bryanston/Weyland, Charter Films, Columbia Pictures Industries Inc., EMI, Gala Films, Godwin–Willis–Lee Thompson Productions, Independent Artists, Rank, Remus, Romulus, Sheldrake, Vic Films/Waterhall, Woodfall.

Introduction

'Every sustained period of success of the British film has seemed to be based in a realist approach to contemporary life,' observes David Robinson. He then concludes his short survey of the British cinema with a welcome for the 'renaissance' of the British film and 'its new urge towards realism' as exemplified by such late 1950s films as *Look Back in Anger* and *Room at the Top*.[1] This is not, of course, an unusual conclusion and many of the films of this period are now quite commonly accepted as 'classics' of British film-making. Indeed, having been too young myself to view them on their first release, it was precisely this reputation (and that of *Saturday Night and Sunday Morning* in particular) which first led me to actively seek them out as a teenager. What attracted me to them then – and, to some extent, still does – was, as Robinson suggests, their commitment to addressing contemporary social realities and, perhaps more importantly, their corresponding commitment to a politically serious representation of working-class experiences. While this still strikes me as an important achievement, my response to these films has also altered. My intention in returning to them now, therefore, is not to simply reiterate the by now familiar acts of critical homage. What I would like to do, instead, is offer a form of critical reassessment and, in the process, open up to scrutiny precisely those critical judgments which led me to the films in the first place.

Not that the presentation of a different view of these films is, in itself, entirely unprecedented. Even at the time of the films' appearance there was already an influential group of critics ready to do battle with the commonly accepted view of a cinematic renaissance. The very first issue of *Movie* in 1962, for example, pronounced the British cinema 'as dead as it was before' and poured scorn on the idea of a film-making 'breakthrough'.[2] Peter Graham's polemical pamphlet, 'The Abortive Renaissance' (1963) was no less scathing, vigorously denouncing the 'badness' of 'good British films'. In both cases, the British cinema was found to fall short of the standards of both European art cinema and Hollywood, with neither the artistic presence of the one nor the directorial intelligence of the other. However, given their commitment to the virtues of authorial expression and *mise en scène*, it was inevitable that these critics should prove primarily occupied with issues of aesthetic, rather than social and political, value. While this was entirely consistent with their telling diagnosis of the artistically crippling effects of an over-emphasis on the 'social problem' in the British 'quality' picture, it did, nonetheless, leave largely uninvestigated just how such films then handled contemporary social realities and what interpretations of social reality they could then be seen to be encouraging. It was, after all, the importance of this

I

which advocates of a 'breakthrough' had stressed. It was precisely because of the success of these films in depicting hitherto under-represented social groups and social problems that it was claimed the British cinema had been rescued from its middle 1950s stupor and stagnation. But, how far was this, in fact, the case and just how 'successful' were the films in tackling the issues and problems they presented? Was their adoption of 'realism' quite so straightforward a virtue and what were the representations of class and sexuality which resulted? These are the sorts of question which the discussion which follows attempts to answer.

In order to do so, it also adopts a particular form of critical approach or perspective. What this consists of is not simply an analysis of the films themselves and the representations (of class and sexuality, for example) which they provided, but also an assessment of the significance of these representations in relation to the society of which they were a part. From this point of view, it is not only what films tell us about society which is important but also what an understanding of the society can then tell us about the films and the nature of their representations. This is, in fact, an important distinction. For example, the difficulty of such a well known book as Raymond Durgnat's *A Mirror for England* is that it simply assumes that conclusions about British society can be arrived at on the evidence of the films alone. Films, he suggests, can be understood as the 'reflections' of the society which makes them.[3] But, of course, films do more than just 'reflect'; they also actively explain and interpret the way in which the world is to be perceived and understood. Moreover, the views which a film, or films, may be suggesting do not necessarily correspond to those of society as a whole. In a society divided by class, sex and race, access to the means of communication is not equal. Some groups are better placed than others to apply and communicate their definitions of social reality and more advantaged in their ability to represent their views of society as the most 'natural' and 'normal'. So, what a film, or films, tells us about society cannot just be accepted as 'evidence', but must itself be explained and interpreted in terms of the groups and the viewpoints with which they are connected.

It is basically such an inquiry which the following discussion is providing. Chapter One provides an analysis of the economic, political and ideological relations characteristic of British society during the period 1956–63. Chapter Two presents a discussion of the film industry during the same period. The remaining chapters deal with the films themselves – not only the 'new wave' of working-class realism already mentioned, but also the social problem film, whose history was by and large concurrent, and which, like the 'new wave', was generally applauded for its determination to tackle such contemporary issues as juvenile delinquency, homosexuality and racial tension. In setting these analyses alongside each other – both of the films themselves and the social and economic context of their production and reception – the discussion sets out to consider not only how adequately such issues and problems were dealt with but also what perspectives and attitudes were adopted and to whose benefit they may be seen to have contributed. This then leads to the conclusion that the films, and the views of the world which

2

they promoted, may well have obscured as much as they enlightened, and obstructed as much as they initiated the potential for social change and reconstruction.

The discussion of the films which then follows is clearly not intended to highlight my own critical ingenuity nor to radically 're-write' these films according to deconstructionist protocols. The rather more modest ambition is to 'bring out' some of the ways in which these films appear to encourage particular ways of interpreting the world or assume and take for granted particular ideological attitudes and assumptions. This does not, of course, imply that my analyses are then without novelty. Indeed, there is ample evidence to suggest that my accounts of these films go against the grain of not only contemporary critical writing but also, in some cases, the enthusiastic responses of friends and colleagues who can still recall the initial impact of these films. My argument is not that my explanations of the films were consciously registered by contemporary audiences, as they clearly were not, but that the attitudes and assumptions which my discussion reveals were nonetheless implicit in the organisation of the films' material and, indeed, all the more ideologically powerful because of the way they were able to pass without notice. To take an example, while my analysis of the representations of women in the films of the 'new wave' is clearly indebted to recent feminist writing, this does not imply that the conclusions arrived at are only possible from a modern standpoint. These representations were, in a sense, always 'there'; that they should have passed without comment for such a long period is no more than a testimony to the degree to which they were accepted as both 'normal' and unproblematic and, thus, to the extent to which ideologies of gender had become effectively 'naturalised'.

This also implies that my discussion of the films, in the first instance, is analytic rather than evaluative, more attentive to questions of ideological attitude than cinematic 'quality' or 'merit'. But, as my opening remarks suggested, this does have a bearing on the way in which such films are valued. I do not, of course, suggest that an assessment of a film's ideological viewpoint should, in itself, provide a decisive criterion of judgment – there are, for example, quite legitimate reasons for the defence of the films of Sam Fuller and Sam Peckinpah irrespective of their often unsympathetic politics – but I would want to argue for its central importance. To take one of my own examples, a film such as *Petticoat Pirates* (see Chapter Seven) has been conventionally dismissed as trivial and of little cinematic interest. Yet, in its treatment of sex roles, it displays a number of qualities entirely absent from such an aggressively misogynistic, but critically celebrated film like *Look Back in Anger*. This does not automatically make *Petticoat Pirates* a 'better' film than *Look Back in Anger* or even an especially 'good' film in itself, but it does, at least for me, offer a complexity and value that is worth defending. While this may appear somewhat iconoclastic, it is precisely the sort of re-evaluation which this book may succeed in provoking.

Notes

1. David Robinson, 'United Kingdom' in Alan Lovell (ed.), *Art of the Cinema in Ten European Countries*, Strasbourg, Council for Cultural Co-operation of the Council of Europe, 1967, p.197.
2. V.F. Perkins, 'The British Cinema' in Ian Cameron (ed.), *Movie Reader*, London, November Books, 1972, p.7.
3. Raymond Durgnat, *A Mirror for England*, London, Faber and Faber, 1970.

4

1

British Society 1956–63

Almost at once, affluence came hurrying on the heels of penury. Suddenly, the shops were piled high with all sorts of goods. Boom was in the air.[1]

Ten years ago it was possible, and indeed usual, to look back on the 1950s as an age of prosperity and achievement . . . Today we are more likely to remember the whole period as an age of illusion.[2]

There can be little doubt that the key to understanding Britain in the 1950s resides in the idea of 'affluence', of a nation moving inexorably forward from post-war austerity and rationing to 'Macmillan's soap-flake Arcadia'[3] and purchase on the never-never. It was certainly in this confident, if now rather infamous, spirit that Prime Minister Harold Macmillan was able to proclaim in 1957 that 'most of our people have never had it so good. Go round the country, go to the industrial towns, and you will see a state of prosperity such as we have never had in my lifetime – nor indeed ever in the history of this country'.[4] To some extent, he was right. As Pinto-Duschinsky has argued, 'From 1951 to 1964 there was uninterrupted full employment, while productivity increased faster than in any other period of comparable length in the twentieth century'.[5] During these years, total production (measured at constant prices) increased by 40 per cent, average earnings (allowing for inflation) by 30 per cent, while personal consumption, measured in terms of ownership of cars and televisions, rose from $2\frac{1}{4}$ million to 8 million and 1 million to 13 million respectively.

Conservative pride, in this respect, derived from the fact that they were the government in power throughout this period, winning three elections in a row for the first time in the twentieth century. Having lost office in 1951, Labour had anticipated a retrenchment of traditional Toryism, as the new government reneged on the Attlee administration's commitment to welfare and full employment. In fact, the reverse was true. Following the principles of Rab Butler's Industrial Charter of 1947, the 'New Conservatism' stood by the welfare state and, with the exception of some de-nationalisation, upheld the necessity of state intervention in managing the economy. 'With a few modifications the Conservatives continued Labour's policy,' writes Andrew Gamble. 'So alike did the parties seem, especially in their economic policies, that it appeared indeed as though Mr Butskell had taken over the affairs of the nation.'[6]

'Butskellism', of course, was the term coined by *The Economist* to register the similarity in economic policy pursued by the Tory and Labour Chancellors and correctly identified the convergence which was beginning to emerge in the political arena. How this occurred can again be related to the question of affluence. For the Tories, the generals of the 'new affluence', their successful adaptation to and management of a mixed economy seemed to prove, without recourse to traditional moral claims of the superiority of the market and private ownership, their superior fitness to run a welfare capitalist system. Pragmatics supplanted ethics: 'Conservative freedom works'. In the process, it was also believed that the forward march of Labour had been successfully halted:

> The fantastic growth of the economy, the spectacular rise in the standard of living, the substantial redistribution of wealth, the generous development of social welfare and the admitted humanisation of private industry, have rendered obsolete the whole intellectual framework within which Socialist discussion used to be conducted.[7]

Or, as put more succinctly by Macmillan himself, 'the class war is over and we have won'.[8] It was a verdict that Labour itself seemed compelled to accept.

Their response, as David Coates suggests, was to move increasingly away from 'class perspectives and socialist rhetoric' towards a revisionism which shared much of the Tory diagnosis.[9] The context is clear: Labour were defeated in three successive elections with their share of the vote falling absolutely and proportionally on each occasion. Against this background, it was not surprising that by 1960 Abrams and Rose, in their influential analysis, could ask the question, 'Must Labour Lose?'[10] By a process of inversion, the reasons for Tory success became the causes of Labour decline. 'The changing character of labour, full employment, new housing, the new way of life based on the telly, the fridge, the car and the glossy magazines – all have had their effect on our political strength,' observed Labour leader Hugh Gaitskell.[11] In particular, the successes of Tory rule appeared to have negated the need for Labour's continuing commitment to public ownership of the economy, and it was at the 1959 party conference that Gaitskell led the attack to remove Clause 4 from the party constitution. As Crosland had argued, in his important revisionist work *The Future of Socialism*, Britain no longer corresponded to a 'classically capitalist society' and Labour's goals of full employment, welfare and abolition of poverty no longer depended on nationalisation but were perfectly compatible with a mixed economy.[12]

Such economic and social changes were also assumed to be undermining the traditional base of Labour support. 'The revisionists,' writes Coates, 'relied on the studies of voting behaviour to show that the old manual working class was a dwindling section of the labour force, that affluence was in any case mellowing the class dimensions and that the electoral fortunes of the Labour Party turned on its ability to woo the new and rapidly growing white collar, scientific and technical classes who were the key workers in this post-capitalist, scientifically based industrial system.'[13] This was a view, once again, shared with the opposition. Thus, the Right Progressives of the Tory Party, gathered round *Crossbow*, also argued that 'economic growth dissolved the old class structure and created new social groups, in particular affluent workers and the technical intelligentsia, whom a dynamic Toryism could attract'.[14] In such a context of political agreement, 'it became plausible to suppose that the consensus between the parties . . . reflected a consensus in the nation. In the spectrum of political opinion from right to left, the majority of the electors had moved towards the middle, the breeding ground of the floaters, leaving only minorities at the extremes . . . Success in the political market now seemed to depend on capturing the centre and winning the support of the floaters'.[15] As such, we can see how the 'key terms' of affluence, consensus and 'embourgeoisement' became gathered together 'into an all-embracing myth or explanation of post-war social change'.[16] The new post-war mix of Keynes, welfare and capitalism had 'delivered the goods', the prosperity and affluence of the 1950s 'boom period', and in the process secured a 'consensus' amongst political parties on the framework within which governments should now work. At the same time, affluence was dismantling old class barriers, 'embourgeoisifying' the old working class with rises in living standards and an accompanying conversion to 'consensual' middle-class values.[17]

Barely had the ink dried on such confident prognoses than the reality of Britain's economic difficulties became apparent with the balance of payments crisis in 1961 and subsequent imposition of a pay-pause, credit squeeze and higher taxation by Chancellor Selwyn Lloyd. The roots of this crisis, however, were not local but deep-seated. As Glyn and Sutcliffe put it: 'British capitalism faced increasing competition in world markets: it was continuously losing part of its share of world output and exports. Its level of investment and economic growth was low by international standards. This lack of competitiveness, combined with unwillingness to devalue the exchange rate, led to repeated crises in the balance of payments which were always answered by restrictions on home demand, further checking the rate of growth.'[18] Organically related to these problems was the Conservative Party's reluctance to acknowledge its changed role in a world economic and political system characterised by the decline of Empire and increasing American hegemony. Its attempt to maintain sterling as a world currency led to an artificially high exchange rate, inhibiting to domestic growth and vulnerable to runs on the pound, while its commitment to an international political and military role produced an expenditure on defence (7–10 per cent of GNP) higher than nearly any other nation except the USA and the USSR. As Shonfield has argued, such a heavy defence programme inhibited (non-military) industrial investment, restrained overseas demand and imposed an additional strain on the balance of payments (whose deficits often amounted to no more than a fraction of overall military expenditure).[19] In sum, although British economic growth had looked impressive in isolation, when compared with other industrial nations it looked decidedly poor (lagging well behind such European competitors as West Germany, France and Italy). As such, Britain's economic 'miracle' rested upon purely 'temporary and

We are the Lambeth Boys (1959)

fortuitous circumstances'[20] (such as the fall in world commodity prices) and lacked foundation in any policy of economic re-structuring or long-term investment (which once again lagged well behind its West European competitors). Moreover, such failures were exacerbated by the Tory administration's devotion to stop-go tactics of economic management and its policies of 'Bread and Circuses': what Pinto-Duschinsky describes as 'the sacrifice of policies for long-term well-being in favour of over-lenient measures and temporary palliatives bringing in immediate returns'.[21] Butler's purely expedient pre-election budget of 1955 provides the most notorious example.

What the rise in incomes and apparent abundance of consumer goods disguised then was the fragile and temporary base upon which such 'affluence' had been secured. Moreover, what it also disguised was the persistence of inequality in the enjoyment of 'affluence' and its continuing complicity with a structure of class division. As I have suggested, the assumption increasingly gaining credence in political rhetoric, with support from the academic community, was that capitalism was undergoing fundamental changes (indeed, no longer remaining capitalist at all), that inequalities in the distribution of income and wealth had been reduced and, as a consequence, that the old class divisions which such inequalities had maintained were in the process of being dissolved. However, as Westergaard and Resler point out, there was no particular novelty attached to the affluence of the 1950s: increasing incomes had also characterised the pre-war era with gross wages rising by an average of about $1\frac{3}{4}$ per cent from the early 1920s to 1938.[22] Moreover, such absolute increases did not in themselves imply any automatic decrease in relative inequalities. Indeed, once this question of distribution is examined a whole new light is shed upon the ideology of 'affluence'. Thus, despite some redistribution of income following the Second World War, the overall pattern detected by Westergaard and Resler is that of 'continuing inequality'. In 1961, 1 per cent of the adult population derived 10 per cent of total post-tax incomes (i.e. much the same as the poorest 30 per cent) while the richest 5 per cent enjoyed much the same income as that of the poorest 50 per cent.[23] Figures for the distribution of private wealth reveal a similar picture. According to estimates made by *The Economist* for 1959–60, 88 per cent of tax payers owned only 3·7 per cent of private wealth while the richest 7 per cent owned 84 per cent.[24] Moreover, these figures retain a remarkable consistency with the early 1950s.[25]

Despite the claims to the contrary, it is clear that economic inequalities had not been eroded. What is also clear is that their primary derivation also remained the same: the relations of capitalist production (with its structure of private ownership and associated control of the productive apparatus). While revisionist and post-capitalist commentators tinkered with slide-rules, what they missed was this *relational* character of social classes. Increases in income, shifts in occupational structure or changes in values (as emphasised by theses of 'embourgeoisement') only located movements within classes while the overall contours of class relations, constitutive of a capitalist mode of production, remained intact. Of course, occupational divisions and values are crucial to an understanding of how classes operate 'on the ground'. As Stuart Hall has observed, 'class in its singular, already unified form is really a political metaphor . . . "fracturing" and diversity is the real empirical experience of the class'.[26] Nonetheless, it remains the economic relation, the relation between capital and labour, which prescribes 'the parameters or outer boundaries of class structure.'[27]

In a sense, it was the ideological achievement of the period to focus on the local shifts and transformations while concealing the essential continuity of the 'outer boundaries'. 'Affluence assumed the proportions of a full-blown ideology precisely because it was required to cover over the gaps between real inequalities and the promised Utopia of equality-for-all and ever-rising consumption to come', write Clarke *et al.* 'By projecting this ideological scenario, the "affluence" myth aimed to give the working classes a stake in a future which had not yet arrived, and thus to bind and cement the class to the hegemonic order. Here the ideology of affluence reconstructed the "real relations" of post-war society into an "imaginary relation".'[28]

'Youth and the hazards of affluence'

> And then came the gay-time boom and all the spending money, and suddenly you oldos found that though we minors had no rights, we'd got the money power.[29]

If it was classes that were presumed to be disappearing there can be little doubt that it was 'youth', by contrast, who were making an appearance. As Hopkins puts it, 'Never had "Youth" – with the capital "Y" – been so earnestly discussed, so frequently surveyed, so extensively seen and heard.'[30] With its trail of Teddy Boys, Angry Young Men and *nouveau riche* pop stars it seemed to many that the 1950s was not only the 'age of affluence' but also the 'age of youth'. Not that this was purely coincidental, for what above all seemed to define the novelty of youth in this period was its access to the benefits of affluence and, as a consequence, the ability to map out for itself a distinctive cultural status. In this respect, what the 1950s discovered was not so much 'youth' as the 'teenager'. As a number of commentators have observed, 'youth' itself is something of a social invention, a cultural expression of social and historical circumstance rather than a biological fact. In particular, the expansion of compulsory education, decline of child labour and development of child welfare legislation in the nineteenth century created 'adolescence' (a term formalised in academic discourse by the writings of Stanley Hall) in which young people were forced into a period of extended dependence.[31] The idea of the 'teenager', however, dates from much later and was apparently coined in the 1940s by American market researchers who wished to describe young people with money to spend on consumer goods. It is this linking of youth with consumption which came to define the role of the teenager in the 1950s: 'The distinctive fact about teenagers' behaviour is economic: they spend a lot of money on clothes, records, concerts, make-up, magazines: all things that give immediate pleasure and little lasting use.'[32]

Indeed, this 'distinctive fact' assumed a peculiar prominence with the publication of *The Teenage Consumer* by Mark Abrams in 1959 with its revelations that real teenage earnings had increased by 50 per cent since 1938 (and possibly by 100 per cent in terms of real 'discretionary' spending) and that teenage spending now amounted to £900 million a year.[33] Although the significance of such figures might be queried (Abrams estimates that in 1959 teenage expenditure accounted for only 5 per cent of the total national consumer expenditure)[34] they undoubtedly fuelled the popular imagery of the incredibly affluent teenager devoted to an enormous expenditure on leisure:

> The *Sunday Graphic* in 1960 found a boy who could hang £127 worth of suits in his parents' back yard to be photographed, another who earned £5 a week and owned: five suits, two pairs of slacks, one pair of jeans, one casual jacket, five white and three coloured shirts, five pairs of shoes, twenty-five ties and an overcoat. A sixteen-year-old typist owned six dresses, seven straight skirts, two pleated ones, one overcoat and a mac, one Italian suit, one pair of boots, one of flat shoes and three of high heels. One eighteen-year-old drove a new car which he had bought for £800; many who earned something under £7 a week had motorbikes at £300. A hire purchase firm said they had 4,000 teenagers on their books and not a single bad debt.[35]

Central to the imagery of the 'affluent teenager' was the idea of a dissolution of old class barriers and the construction of a new collective identity based on teenage values. Abrams suggested that the collective habits of teenage consumption constituted a 'distinctive teenage spending for distinctive teenage ends in a distinctive teenage world'[36] while Laurie contrasted this new breed of teenager with the street-corner gangs of ten years before: 'The teenagers have come into nationwide contact with each other. They have formed a society of their own.'[37] Teenagers, indeed, represented the new 'class' whose very badge of identity was their rejection of traditional class boundaries:

> No one, not a soul, cares what your class is, or what your race is, or what your income is, or if you're boy, or girl, or bent, or versatile, or what you are – so long as you dig the scene . . . and have left all that crap behind you.[38]

It was in such terms, as Clarke *et al.* suggest, that 'youth' came to symbolise the most advanced point of social change: 'youth was the vanguard party – of the classless, post-protestant, consumer society to come'.[39] But, as these authors also suggest, this metaphor of youth as the vanguard of social change was also tinged with ambivalence: 'Social change was seen as generally beneficial ("you've never had it so good!"); but also as eroding the traditional landmarks and undermining the sacred order and institutions of traditional society'.[40] Youth, in particular, came to serve as a metaphor for the 'underside' of the 'affluent society': its slavish devotion to consumerism, allegiance to superficialities and absence of 'authentic' values.

11

'Today's high income receivers are without background, education and information necessary to the cultivation of stable tastes', observed one commentator. 'They are exposed in innumerable ways to commercial exploitation, and induced to pay high prices for the merely novel and ephemeral . . . Consequently people, and especially young people, become confused about their norms, values, tastes and standards.'[41]

In this respect, unease about affluence reflected a broader anxiety about the quality of life which new patterns of consumption and the explosion of mass communications (television, advertising, pop music) seemed to entail. Mass production, it was argued, eschewed the values of individual design and craftsmanship in favour of an imposed standardisation and phoney egalitarianism of taste; while the mass media (particularly television, with its subservience to ratings and advertisers) necessarily gravitated towards the popular and lowest common denominator.[42] Thus, the Pilkington Committee, set up to advise on the future of broadcasting in 1960, reported the 'dissatisfaction . . . that programme items were far too often devised with the object of seeking, at whatever cost in quality or variety, the largest possible audience: and that, to attain this object, the items nearly always appealed to a low level of public taste'.[43] Most influential, in this respect, was *The Uses of Literacy* by Richard Hoggart (subsequently a central contributor to the Pilkington Report). Although sharing the assumption of a cultural debasement consequent upon the emergence of a mass culture, Hoggart's point of contrast was not the 'high art' of more conservative critics but that of a traditional, but declining, working-class culture:

My argument is not that there was, in England one generation ago, an urban culture still very much 'of the people' and that now there is only a mass urban culture. It is rather that the appeals made by the mass publicists are for a great number of reasons made more insistently, effectively, and in a more comprehensive and centralised form today than they were earlier; that we are moving towards the creation of a mass culture; that the remnants of what was at least in parts an urban culture 'of the people' are being destroyed; and that the new mass culture is in some important ways less healthy than the often crude culture it is replacing . . . We are becoming culturally classless . . . No doubt many of the old barriers of class should be broken down. But at present the older, the more narrow but also more genuine class culture is being eroded in favour of the mass opinion, the mass recreational product and the generalised emotional response.[44]

As such, it was youth, and, in particular, 'the juke-box boys' who signified this cultural fall most clearly, spending 'their evening listening in harshly lighted milk-bars to the nickelodeons' and capitulating to the 'hollow-cosmos effect' of rock'n'roll. 'The hedonistic but passive barbarian who rides in a fifty horse power bus for threepence to see a five million dollar film for one and eight', he concludes, 'is not simply a social oddity: he is a portent'.[45]

This 'barbarianism' of youth, however, did not apparently stop at cultural

Some People (1962)

philistinism: for what also came to dominate the imagery of youth in this period was the association of the teenager with sexual immorality and violence, such that the terms teenager and delinquent were to be applied almost synonymously. Figures for crime amongst the 14–21 age group had been increasing from 1955 onwards while details of Teddy Boy violence (including the notorious *Rock Around the Clock* cinema riots of 1956) had fuelled an avid press interest. In 1958 teenage violence also interlinked with social anxiety about race and rapidly increasing immigration rates when a riot in Nottingham sparked off three nights of fighting between black and white youths in Notting Hill. Thus, by 1959, as one commentator observes, it was as if 'the collective adult mind had become neurotically imprinted with the idea of the menacing teenager.'[46]

As if to confirm his point, Butler's White Paper in January 1959 introduced a programme of prison-building for young offenders together with plans for the administration of 'a short, sharp shock' at new detention centres and Borstals. Flick-knives were outlawed by an Act of Parliament the same year while Tory Party conferences bayed for blood. In 1958 thirty motions on crime and punishment were submitted, while in 1960 ten of the resolutions on law and order explicitly advocated the return of corporal punishment. 'Corporal punishment must be brought back', argued one Mrs Tilney in 1958, 'otherwise we shall find ourselves in a society dominated by young toughs who violate our girls and frighten or savagely attack older people.'[47] In more subdued tones, the Albemarle Committee recommended increased funding for the Youth Service in 1960.

13

As with so many cases in the sociology of youth much of this 'moral panic' can be associated with media amplification. As Montgomery suggests, 'the wide coverage given to violence and thuggery by the press, film and television, gave the public an overdrawn, too lurid picture of the state of affairs'.[48] Although teenage convictions doubled during the 1950s its peak was still only twenty-one per thousand in 1958. Moreover, offences for violence still represented only a small proportion of these. As Montgomery once again points out, in London they accounted for only two convictions a day for under twenty-one-year-olds: 'figures which hardly justify the popular belief that there was a teenage crime-wave'.[49] In a similar spirit, Laurie has suggested that 'the popular image of the giddy sex-crazed teenager', as feared by Mrs Tilney, 'is rather out of touch with the facts'.[50] Drawing on the Central Council for Health Education survey on the sexual behaviour of young people, he points out that only a third of the boys between seventeen and nineteen and a sixth of the girls in the same age group had ever had sexual intercourse. Moreover, those that had, had usually only done so with a regular partner.[51] Even such a concerned observer as T.R. Fyvel was forced to admit in his study of Teddy Boys that sexual relationships were more usually characterised by 'insecurity' than any over-arching rapaciousness.[52]

As Stanley Cohen suggests, the designation of youth as a whole in terms of sex and violence – the ascription of a number of stereotypical traits to the whole adolescent age group – represents a common ideological man-oeuvre.[53] At the same time, it also constitutes a mirror-image of the affluent teenager mythology: for in both cases, the teenage group is rendered homogeneous, bound together in the communality of either habits of consumption or a perplexing proclivity for anti-social behaviour. On inspection, however, the reality proves more complex. As Abrams rather ambivalently acknowledged, his apparently 'distinctive teenage spending' was almost 'entirely working class', with 'typical teenage' commodities, such as magazines, being 'largely without appeal for middle-class boys and girls'.[54] In a sense, this was only to be expected in so far as the extended education characteristic of middle-class children tended to deprive them of the spending power enjoyed by many of their working-class peers. Moreover, many of the most visible forms of youth culture, such as the Teddy Boys, were quite clearly working-class in origin and practice. The 'teenage phenomenon' was not at all some manifestation of a new 'classless' youth but almost exclusively working-class.

As Murdock and McCron suggest, it is this stress on 'classlessness' which has consistently underpinned the study of youth but only at the expense of denying an accumulating body of evidence:

Theories of youth have been tied to the withering away of class primarily by the argument that the division between the generations has increas-ingly replaced class inequalities as the central axis of the social structure, and that this shift has been accentuated and confirmed by the emergence of a classless culture of youth, separated from, and opposed to, the dominant

14

adult culture. Variations of this argument have underpinned a great deal of both the popular and sociological commentary on youth, with the result that in much of the writing, class is seen as largely irrelevant and either evacuated altogether or treated as a residual category. At the same time, however, research on youth, including much of the work generated from within the 'youth culture' paradigm itself, has persistently produced evidence which points to the continuing centrality of class inequalities in structuring both the life styles and life chances of adolescents.[55]

In other words, far from transcending old class barriers the experience of the teenager was, and still is, in fact, both shaped and mediated by the structural constraints of a class-divided society.

In this respect, ideas about youth's mindless conformity to the values of mass culture and commitment to 'meaningless' violence assume a new significance. For example, Clarke *et al.* argue how the youth sub-culture may be seen as the means whereby sections of working-class youth negotiate their shared conditions of existence, 'resolving' at a symbolic level the problematic of a subordinate class experience (with its accompaniments of unemployment, educational disadvantage, dead-end jobs, low pay, and lack of skills).[56] Seen in this light, the working-class youth sub-culture represents less a group of passive consumers than creative stylists, appropriating and making use of commodities according to their own sub-cultural ends. As Hebdige observes, 'Far from being a casual response to "easy money" the extravagant sartorial display of the Ted required financial planning and was remarkably self-conscious – a going against the grain, as it were, of a life which in all other respects was, in all likelihood, relatively cheerless and poorly rewarded'.[57] By the same token, the attraction towards violence – apparently so inexplicable in an era of material well being – may well assume a rationality (if not necessarily a justification) once it is inter-related with a continuing structure of relative class disadvantage. As Stuart Hall suggests, the degree of violence which has characteristically been associated with traditional working-class communities 'has a perfectly rational source in the conditions of life and work in which working-class men, women and young people are obliged to live, and which is indeed implicit in their very position as a class with a more-or-less permanent subordinate position in society'.[58] Not that this should lead us to assume that all working-class teenagers were then violent, for, as the evidence suggests, the degree of teenage violence was still more apparent than real.

As such, the dominant representations of youth in the 1950s tend to tell us more about the social groups producing them than they do about teenagers themselves. Friedenberg has suggested that the attribution to teenagers of 'a capacity for violence and lust' serves the adult community 'as the occasion both for wish-fulfilment and for self-fulfilling prophecy'.[59] While both the double-edged condemnation of the culture's 'repressed' non-productive values and the implicit incitement to further acts of deviance through media exposure, as in the case of the cinema riots, provide evidence to support this, it is, perhaps, Stanley Cohen's notion of 'ideological exploitation' which is

15

the most appropriate. For Cohen, teenagers are not only economically 'exploited' through the commercial provision of goods but ideologically in the way they are used to further the social and political ends of the dominant culture. In particular, their construction as 'folk devils' is fundamentally a normative one – fashioning and confirming the contours of the consensus.[60] Moreover, the need to reconfirm normative boundaries through the use of 'folk devils' can itself be seen as the surface sign of more deep-seated troubles. 'Troubling times, when social anxiety is widespread but fails to find an organised public or political expression, give rise to the displacement of social anxiety on to convenient scapegoat groups', write Clarke *et al.* 'It is not surprising, then, that youth became the focus of this social anxiety, focusing, in displaced form, society's "quarrel with itself".'[61] In this respect, the 'problem of youth' really has its roots in the anxieties of the parent culture: its concerns with the social changes wrought by 'affluence', the advent of mass culture and, more particularly, the changing role of the family and proliferation of 'perverse sexualities'.

'Married women go out to work . . . yes, but should they?'

A popular perception of the 1950s is one of a period of domestic and sexual stalemate prior to the explosion of 'permissiveness' in the 1960s. As one writer puts it, it was the 'permissive society' of the 1960s which finally began to free male and female sexualities from 'the cloying stranglehold of marriage, family and domesticity which had characterised the 1950s'.[62] With the end of the Second World War, women abandoned their role in the labour force, the average age of marriage dropped and birth-rates increased with a 'boom' at the end of the 1940s. The social and domestic strains of wartime over, it seemed as if it was 'business as usual' and the traditional status of the home and the family was assured.

However, on a closer inspection the picture becomes more complex. Although the late 1940s had witnessed a baby boom, the tendency of the birth-rate was still downwards. Family size was decreasing and the bearing of children was being compressed into a shorter time scale. Taken together with the decrease in the average age of marriage and increase in female life-expectancy, the prominence of the role of motherhood was diminishing in relation to a woman's overall life-span and was increasing her availability for work. Thus, in spite of the 'return home' of women after the war this proved to be of only temporary significance. Shortages of labour, a Government-led export drive and the renewed rearmament precipitated by the Korean war soon led to a return to work by, mainly married, women in the post-1947 period. Thus, the number of women in employment rose from 6,620,000 in 1947 to 7,246,000 in 1951 and 7,650,000 in 1957. Between the two census periods of 1951 and 1961 the proportion of married women working outside the home likewise increased from 1 in 4 to 1 in 3.

Although such a seasoned commentator as Richard Titmuss felt justified in designating such changes as 'revolutionary',[63] they were not matched by corresponding changes in cultural attitude. In a society where 'the domestic sphere, the world of work, the welfare state are all organised *as if* women were continuing a traditional role',[64] the dominant ideological tendency was to play down the significance of women's role in the labour force. The reality of woman-as-worker might be acknowledged but only as a subsidiary role, one which remained subordinate to her traditional activities as a housewife and mother: 'working was something women sometimes "did", it did not define what they, essentially, "were" '.[65] In this respect, it became a prevalent misconception that women did not really need to go to work. It was either a way of 'getting out of the house' or, more pervasively, of making 'pin money', a mere supplement to an otherwise adequate household income.

In one way, such an ideology served a precise economic function. For if women's essential role was defined in relation to the family, to which paid employment remained secondary, so could they be expected to perform work which was the least skilled and worst paid (in 1958 women's average earnings represented 62 per cent of men's). As such, the bulk of working women were employed in the distributive trades, in the clothing and textile industries and the manufacture of electrical goods. As Myrdal and Klein observe, 'this had nothing to do with their innate abilities or . . . psychological characteristics . . . but with the fact that their fate is so closely linked with their role in the family.'[66]

But what was also being obscured at the same time was the vital contribution that women were then making to the economic achievements of the period. Not only had economic growth depended on the availability of female labour (as well as that of immigrants) but it was also women's work which underpinned the rises in household incomes and patterns of consumption characteristic of the 'affluent society'. Yet it was the corollary of the emphasis on woman's domestic role that her place at the point of production should be undermined and reinstated at the point of consumption. The dynamic underlying 'affluence' was less female labour than female consumption. It was the 'housewife' – with her new washing machine, vacuum cleaner and New Look fashionwear – to whom affluence was aimed and who was its prime beneficiary:

> Liberated at an early age from cradle-watching, spending not only the household's money but 'her own' (one third of wives, twice the 1939 proportion, having jobs), fashion's eager slave, the woman of the fifties possessed at once the time, the resources and the inclination to bring to perfection the new arts of continuous consumption. She was the essential pivot of the People's Capitalism, and its natural heroine.[67]

According to this formulation, then, women's work was not really work at all. For despite paid employment (on top of the conventional chores of housework) the new woman possessed time in abundance to perfect her art of continuous consumption. Neither was her income apparently a real wage but one separate from the household money and frittered away in a slave-like pursuit of the inessential (such as fashion). Of no consequence, then, that women's earnings might more probably be used on basics or that the new consumer durables themselves might not necessarily be items of leisure but rather the tools of domestic labour (a washing machine, for example).

Yet, despite such downplaying of women's role as worker it was also apparent that increasing female participation in the labour force was provoking anxiety in some quarters and, indeed, prompting a variety of stratagems, especially in the fields of psychology and social welfare, designed to return women to their 'proper place' in the home and family. A crucial influence, here, was the work of John Bowlby on the mother's role in the rearing of children. In his book *Child Care and the Growth of Love* (1953), Bowlby sought to establish the absolute centrality of mother-love to a child's mental health (as crucial as vitamins to physical health) and the adverse consequences of 'maternal deprivation'. Yet it was not so much the ideas in themselves (many of which were derivative and vulnerable to criticism) which seemed to matter but the extraordinary impact they were to have on both academic and popular thinking. 'Maternal deprivation was made the scapegoat for retarded development, anxiety and guilt feelings, promiscuity, instability and divorce – even for stunted growth', writes one commentator. 'It took the place in mid-twentieth century demonology that masturbation filled for the Victorians'.[68] In particular, it seemed to query the propriety of women in employment. 'The theme of latch-key children was taken up in the popular press,' writes Elizabeth Wilson, 'and neglectful working mothers, their values perverted by materialism and greed for more and more possessions, were blamed for juvenile delinquency'.[69] Thus, despite evidence from the Second World War that children in daytime nursery care (as opposed to the institutionalised children of Bowlby's study) revealed no substantial differences in mental behaviour from children cared for at home, it was the working mother who was singled out for opprobrium.[70] 'The mother of young children', writes Bowlby, 'is not free, or at least should not be free, to earn.'[71]

From here it was not difficult to link the prevalence of the working mother (and the concomitants of disturbed children and juvenile delinquency) to a more generalised anxiety about the breakdown of the family and moral standards. Increasing divorce rates (27,471 divorces in England and Wales and 2,200 in Scotland in 1954 compared with 4,735 and 637 respectively in 1937) led to the establishment of a *Royal Commission on Marriage and Divorce*, whose report in 1956 refused to countenance a liberalisation in divorce law for fear that divorce 'contagion' might spread. Indeed, such was the alarm registered by the commissioners that they concluded 'it may become necessary to consider whether the community as a whole would not be happier and more stable if it abolished divorce altogether'.[72] Central to their diagnosis of the problem was 'the social and economic emancipation of women'.[73]

Such worries gained momentum with the 'moral panics' of the late 1950s over homosexuality and prostitution and the subsequent report by the Wolfenden Committee in 1957. Although interpreted by many as heralding the new permissiveness of the 1960s by its emphasis on a 'private' realm of morality and consequent recommendation for the de-criminalisation of 'homosexual behaviour between consenting adults in private', the Wolfenden Report can more properly be 'read', as Stuart Hall suggests, 'against a moral climate directed not towards liberalisation but towards the tightening up of the legal regulation of moral conduct'.[74] As with the *Royal Commission on Marriage and Divorce*, the 'impression of a growth in homosexual practices' was located against a background of 'the general loosening of former moral standards' and 'emotional insecurity, community instability and weakening of the family, inherent in the social changes of our civilisation'.[75] Although the Report deplored the damage being caused to family life ('the basic unit of society') by male homosexuality, it did not consider this sufficient grounds for making homosexual behaviour a criminal offence (adultery, fornication and lesbianism, it is argued, cause equal harm). Thus, while the Report recommends the de-criminalisation of homosexuality it does so within a general framework of moral censure, a concern with the 'treatment' of homosexuality and an ideological privileging of marital heterosexuality. As Bland *et al.* conclude:

> Wolfenden's recommendations on homosexuality, while they opened up a privatised space in which adult male homosexuals could now operate without the threat of criminal sanction, in no sense advocated the abandonment of 'control' from that space. Power is no longer to be exercised through the operation of law, but what the Report recommends for homosexuality is the *diversification* of forms of control in the proliferation of new discourses for the regulation of male homosexuals. It explicitly marked out a 'course for treatment' for the homosexual which is distinct from that of the criminal model – henceforward, medicine, therapy, psychiatry and social research are to form alternative strategies for the exercise of power. The State abandons legal control of the homosexual, only to call into play a net of discourses which constitute a new form of intimate regulation of male homosexual practice in the private sphere.[76]

Such a 'double taxonomy' (greater freedom and leniency combined with stricter penalty and control) also characterised the Report's treatment of prostitution. 'The guiding principle of Wolfenden was the distinction between law and morality, and the individual's right to make his/her own moral choices without legal interference as long as harm is not inflicted on another. Privacy became the key note to this principle', writes Carol Smart. 'What this concept of privacy entailed for certain classes of prostitutes who needed to be publicly visible to meet their clients was, however, little more than a justification for an extension of policy control over them'.[77] As such, the Report was able to recommend increased penalties, including imprisonment, for street offences, increased powers of remand to the courts and the extension of the practice of referral of prostitutes to 'moral welfare workers'. Thus, while the Committee's recommendations on homosexuality had to wait until 1967 for legislative action, its more directly punitive proposals on prostitution were quickly incorporated into the *Street Offences Act* of 1959.

As has been occasionally noted, the concern of both Report and legislation in this respect seems less to be with a reduction in the actual incidence of prostitution (which, as Wolfenden partly anticipated, would merely re-structure in the form of agencies and call girl rackets) than with the removal of its visibility. A characteristic British hypocrisy perhaps, but what this emphasis also seemed to underline was the anxiety provoked by prostitution's flaunting of sexuality outside of marriage (with its all too evident reminders of marital failure and 'sexually frustrated' husbands). While prostitution may have provided a necessary safety-valve in the past, it now clashed with the tenets of the 'new sexual morality' and its emphasis on the importance of satisfying sexual relations within marriage. As Carol Smart suggests, this new morality no longer conformed to 'the repressive Victorian variety' but demanded, instead, a new 'sexual mother figure', whose 'sexuality was not excluded but used instrumentally to increase pair-bonding and provide stability for developing children'.[78] Once again, it was the re-stabilisation of the family and marriage, rather than any 'permissiveness', which represented the predominant concern of both Report and legislation.

However, these ideologies of welfare and legislative actions could not overcome entirely the continuing contradiction between woman as housewife and mother and woman as wage labourer (precisely the 'woman's two roles' so much discussed in the period) which the economic changes of the 1950s had increasingly set in motion. While many writers have attempted to argue the necessity of the family and women's domestic labour to the maintenance of capitalist relations of production through their reproduction (both biologically and ideologically) of labour power, there is at the same time a contrary tendency under capitalism towards the weakening of the family. As Barrett has argued, the logic of a capitalist mode of production in itself is 'sex-blind' and the articulation of the family-household structure with capitalism is a historically contingent relation and not a necessary one.[79] As such, ideologies of the family predate capitalism and cannot be entirely explained in terms of economic functions. Indeed, the irony of the 1950s is that it is precisely the logic of capital, the drive for economic expansion, which is pressing women into the labour force and loosening their exclusive identification with home and family (or relocating it in terms of a household-based model of consumption). As such, the ideologies governing women, as manifested in the state, display an unevenness, indeed a tension, with the increasing reality of women's economic position. If ideologies of family and motherhood appeared to gain the upper hand it was once again only an imaginary resolution bought at the expense of a denial of the realities increasingly being wrought by economic change.

Look back on anger
Just as the combination of welfare capitalism and Cold War ideology appeared to have produced a consensus in the political arena, so, in the arts, did it seem that it had also produced a conformist and contented intelligentsia. 'Who criticises Britain now in any fundamental sense except for a few Communists and a few Bevanite irreconcilables?' asked Edward Shils in 1955. 'There are complaints here and there and on many specific issues, but – in the main – scarcely anyone in Great Britain seems any longer to feel there is anything fundamentally wrong ... Never has an intellectual

class found its society and its culture so much to its satisfaction.'[80] Writing in the same year, Noel Annan appeared to confirm this viewpoint when he addressed himself to the 'paradox of an intelligentsia which appears to conform rather than rebel against the rest of society.'[81]

By the following year, however, the picture did not look quite so cosy. In the field of politics, Britain's military escapade in Suez and the Russian invasion of Hungary mocked the idea that there was no longer anything 'fundamentally wrong'. At the same time, the performance of John Osborne's *Look Back in Anger* at the Royal Court (8 May) and the publication of Colin Wilson's *The Outsider* (26 May) suggested the emergence of a group of writers who were far from satisfied and complacent. Although the two sets of events are not so closely interlinked as is sometimes imagined – the performance of Osborne's play predated the Suez crisis by several months – it was undoubtedly the coincidental eruption of the latter which was to ensure the prominence which the 'angry young man' phenomenon was to enjoy in the period that followed. In doing so, it was also to bind together all the key issues of the period: youth, class, affluence and the status of women.

The 'angry young man' label itself was much more of a label of convenience employed by the press than a term used by the writers themselves. Indeed, the work of many of the writers so designated extended back well before 1956 and more properly belongs to that of 'the Movement'. The term, 'the Movement', was first employed by *The Spectator* in October 1954 to refer to a group of poets and novelists whose work had first appeared on the BBC radio programmes 'New Soundings' (1952) and 'First Reading' (1953) and were subsequently published in two collections: *Poets of the 1950s* (1955) and *New Lines* (1956). Included in this group were Philip Larkin, John Wain (editor of 'First Reading') and Kingsley Amis, whose novels *Jill* (1946), *Hurry on Down* (1953) and *Lucky Jim* (1954) had undoubtedly registered a shift in the development of the English novel. Although this received some degree of recognition (most notably in Walter Allen's *New Statesman* review of *Lucky Jim* in 1954), it was really only in 1956 that such changes accrued a retrospective significance. 'The timing of Suez and Hungary was coincidental', writes Hewison, 'but their combined effect was to exacerbate disaffections and tensions. Some of these disaffections had been voiced in the novels of Amis and Wain, but there was nothing that gave them particular focus. What was needed was a myth, and in 1956 there appeared the myth of the Angry Young Man'.[82] What this myth did was not so much identify any real grouping as create one by fabricating together earlier writers such as Amis and Wain, and to some extent John Braine (whose first novel, *Room at the Top*, appeared in 1957 but who had prior connections with the Movement), the new ones such as Osborne, Wilson and then Stuart Holroyd (whose *Emergence from Chaos* was published in 1957) and the fictional characters themselves (in particular, Amis' Jim Dixon and Osborne's Jimmy Porter). A contrivance it may have been but one with a peculiarly potent cultural resonance.

As with their counterparts the 'teenagers', the explanation for the 'angry young man' also seemed to lie with the economic changes wrought by post-war Britain. Allsop, for example, explicitly linked the advent of a teenage market to the attention given to young writers: 'in a full employment economy, with a vast, monied juvenile market, youth is cultivated, flattered and pampered, and bestowed with a glamour it has never previously had'.[83] In particular, he argues that the attention given to Michael Hastings (whose first play *Don't Destroy Me* was performed in August 1956) derived less from his theatrical talents than the fact that he was a teenager. In a similar spirit, Lewis describes the 'angry young men' as 'the first pop stars of literature' while Wilson himself was to observe 'how extraordinary' it was that his fame 'should have corresponded with that of James Dean, Elvis Presley, Bill Haley and Lonnie Donegan'.[84]

But, more than their 'youth' it was also their status as both products and bearers of a new 'welfare' culture which commanded attention. As Feldman and Gartenberg put it, in their quasi-manifesto of the period:

> In origin they are sons of the lower middle and working classes who came of age with Socialism, had their bodies cared for by the government health programme, and their minds nourished through government scholarships in red brick universities (though, now and then, at Oxford). Prepared to seek their places in the new England that had been created by Parliamentary revolution, they found they had nowhere to go.[85]

Although characteristically hazy in detail (none of Osborne, Wilson or Braine, for example, had been to university, red brick or otherwise), such sentiments clearly summed up the popular perception of the 'angry young men'. Sons of Labour's post-war Brave New World and the 1944 Education Act, harbingers of the new 'classless' culture, their voice spoke the 'anger' of a generation for whom in the end nothing really seemed to have changed (e.g. Suez):

> They are angry because England is still riddled with class-consciousness, because the Establishment still rules, because the English upper and middle classes tend to be ignorant, insensitive philistines, because English films are ghastly, because the English theatre means *The Reluctant Debutante* and *Dry Rot*, because the Conservative government is ineffectual if not actually dangerous, because the English Elite, who should after all be educated, would rather read the *Tatler* than *The Spectator*, and because the attitude of the English towards such venerated traditions as Royalty, the Archbishop of Canterbury, the BBC etc. is unhealthy and in every way sickening.[86]

As with the 'myth' of affluence, so the reality behind the mythology of the angry young man is in many ways more complex. In particular, their anger was more selective, occasionally more unpleasant, and certainly more conservative than is generally acknowledged. If the adoption of right-wing views by many of the 'angries' in later years has bemused some, it may well be that the explanation lies not so much in some unaccountable change of heart as in the continuation of ideas which were already present in their work in the 1950s. Morrison, for example, has commented on how much of a priority is given in the work of the Movement to 'adjustment' and compromise: 'There is little sense that the social structure could be altered: the more common enquiry is whether individuals can succeed in "fitting in".'[87] Thus, Jim Dixon is happy to accept Gore-Urquart's offer of a London job at the end of *Lucky Jim* while Charles Lumley rejoices in the offer of a contract from Terence Frush at the end of *Hurry on Down*: 'Neutrality; he had found it. The running fight between himself and society had ended in a draw'.[88] As Allsop was to comment, 'Wain seems to be the first of the new dissentients to display signs of readiness to conform, to opt for orthodoxy after all.'[89]

Part of this political quietism can be traced to the post-war experience of Stalinism and a determination by the Movement writers not to ape the 'errors' of such politically committed intellectuals as Auden and Isherwood in the 1930s. As one commentator puts it, the 'correct approach' seemed to be less of taking a stand than taking 'a stand against having a political stand',[90] or as Movement poet Donald Davie explained in *Re the Thirties*, 'a neutral tone is nowadays preferred.'[91] For his part, Amis contemptuously denounced the 1930s generation, arguing how their 'solution of political writing and other activity' merely served 'as a kind of self-administered therapy for personal difficulties'. Apparently in sympathy with Jimmy Porter's complaint about the absence of 'good, brave causes', he went on to declare that 'when we shop around for an outlet, we find there is nothing in stock, no Spain, no Fascism, no mass unemployment' before concluding 'perhaps politics is a thing that only the unsophisticated can really go for'.[92] Drawing a parallel here with 'Butskellism', Morrison aptly sums up: 'To be

Look Back in Anger (1959)

politically astute in the 1950s, the Movement implied, was to be politically inactive'.[93]

Yet, if the 1930s represented the bogey, such writers were not entirely without a taste for the past. Bergonzi has noted, for example, how the cult of Edwardianism manifested itself during the 1950s not only in the style of Macmillan and the dress of the Teddy Boys but in the writing of the period as well: 'John Osborne offers a clear example of this . . . Colonel Redfern, the only sympathetic character in *Look Back in Anger*, exemplifies it, and so, at a lower social level, does Archie Rice in *The Entertainer*: both are anachronistic Edwardian survivals'.[94] Or as Allsop puts it, 'Jimmy's secret regret is that everything isn't the same, and his secret hero is Colonel Redfern'. In this he was apparently not alone. As Allsop goes on to explain, less in anger than regret, 'a great many men and women in my age group have an intense nostalgic longing for the security and the innocence that seems to have been present in Britain before the 1914 war'.[95]

What excited most anger, then, was less political issues than cultural ones. In particular, such writers seemed to share the concerns of contemporary critics with Britain's debasement by materialism and accompanying 'spiritual dry-rot'. 'Our civilisation is an appalling, stinking thing, materialistic, drifting, second rate', complained Colin Wilson.[96] Allsop, in his turn, drew on Hoggart (and his suggestion of 'shiny barbarism') for an explanation of his subjects' anger. This is borne out by the writing itself. What is striking is less any protest against social and economic inequalities than a contempt for superficiality: the class snobberies decried by Jim Dixon, the surface values pursued by Joe Lampton, the absence of authentic feeling despaired of by Jimmy Porter. In the writings of Colin Wilson and Stuart Holroyd this becomes a quite explicit call for a spiritual, as opposed to materialist, freedom. Wilson coined the term the 'outsider' (after Camus) to designate those artists and intellectuals who had transcended the limitations of the modern age through religious intensity or 'pure will' to achieve an authentic freedom of the imagination and understanding of human life. In *Emergence from Chaos*, Stuart Holroyd counterpointed the work of poets such as Yeats, Rilke, Rimbaud and Eliot to the alienated condition of modern man produced by materialism, egalitarianism, large institutions and machine technology. Both works shared with the others a sense of cultural decline but, with their demands for the political elevation of the 'outsider' and corresponding requirement for discipline of the masses, went much further in their political implications. It was certainly a chastened Kenneth Allsop who was to write in the wake of Bill Hopkins' *The Divine and the Decay*:

> A cult of fascism has grown among a generation who were babies when Europe's gas-chambers were going full blast. We seem to be on the edge of a new romantic tradition which is sanctifying the bully as hero. It is exceedingly strange, and profoundly disturbing, if the dissentience (the 'anger') in our present semi-socialised compromise welfare society is going to swing retrogressively to the discredited and hateful system of murder gangs and neurotic mysticism which perished in its own flames.[97]

While others in the 'angry' camp clearly had no time for such dubious flirtations, their criticisms of materialism and superficiality did nonetheless assume other, somewhat dubious, connotations. For just as the 'female consumer' had served more generally as a metaphor for the 'affluent society', so was it in their imagery of women that the angries were most successful in finding a target for their objections. 'What these writers really attack', writes D.E.Cooper, 'is effeminacy . . . the sum of those qualities which are supposed traditionally . . . to exude from the worst in women: pettiness, snobbery, flippancy, voluptuousness, superficiality, materialism'.[98] It is in the work of Osborne where this attack on women becomes most extreme. Commenting on the work of Tennessee Williams, for example, he notes how women 'all cry out for defilement' before cheerfully concluding that 'the female must come toppling down to where she should be – on her back'.[99] A similar coarseness of feeling and misogyny haunts the whole of *Look Back in Anger*. For had the critics been less spellbound by its surface rhetorical outpourings they could not have helped but notice that the real subject of the play was neither social injustice nor hypocrisy but the debasement and degradation of women:

> Perhaps, one day, you may want to come back. I shall wait for that day. I want to stand up in your tears, and splash about in them, and sing. I want to be there when you grovel. I want to be there, I want to watch it, I want the front seat. I want to see your face rubbed in the mud – that's all I can hope for. There's nothing else I want any longer.[100]

In this respect, the praise normally accorded such writers for their 'tough' and 'virile' presentation of character and accompanying mode of writing assumes a different complexion. For if the object of attack is effeminacy so the virtues of style and character are those of masculinity. To this extent, the Angry Young Man phenomenon was working over a more generalised cultural anxiety around the question of male identity. Hoch, for example, has suggested how an ethic of consumption, combined with a reduction of emphasis on production, narrows the range of activities yielding masculine status.[101] More specifically, the increasing involvement of women in the labour force and occupation of traditionally male roles deprives the male worker of his privileged status as head of the family and sole breadwinner.

In recognition of such trends, T.R.Fyvel saw fit to devote a separate section of his book, *The Insecure Offenders*, to a discussion of the 'decline in the status of the father'.[102] Even the Suez affair, to which the Angry Young Men were so much indebted for their subsequent prominence, was double-edged in its effects. On one level it was the last 'folie de grandeur' of a geriatric imperial order, at another, a symbolic castration – the final humiliation of a nation no longer in possession of its manhood. Osborne's nostalgic yearning for a settled Edwardian era, in this respect, was more than tinged with a reverence for its old imperialist virility. In an age haunted by homosexual scandal (such as the Lord Montagu/Pitt-Rivers affair) and the fear of its increase (cf. Wolfenden), there can be no doubting that the heroes of the angry decade were most virulently heterosexual. As Leslie A. Fiedler was to put it, the young British writer represented a new class in the process of overturning the old; one which rejected, in turn, its defining characteristics of upper class aloofness, liberal politics, avant-garde literary devices and a homosexual sensibility.[103]

But, if it is these writers to whom the label of 'anger' is most normally attached, they were not the sole bearers of 'dissent' in this period. The invasion of Hungary, for example, was to register a significant change in the organisation of the left. A call for withdrawal of Russian troops by *The Reasoner*, a small magazine published by Communist Party members E.P. Thompson and John Saville, was followed by disciplinary action and the two men's resignations (along with 7,000 others). In its wake, Thompson and Saville were to launch a second magazine, the *New Reasoner*, in January 1957, while the first issue of *Universities and Left Review*, published from Oxford, appeared shortly afterwards. In 1959 the two magazines merged as the *New Left Review* and, echoing the Left Book Club of the 1930s, encouraged the organisation of discussion groups. In line with its origins, the New Left signalled a discontent with both the 'barbarities of Stalinism' and debilitated politics of Labour's complicity with 'low pressure . . . Welfare Britain'.[104] Even here, the emphasis was primarily ethical. Like the Angry Young Men, it was as if the achievements of 'affluence' were conceded. It was the 'moral' temper of affluence which was now in question. As Perry Anderson was subsequently to observe in the same magazine:

> British capitalism, under great pressure, learnt to satisfy certain fundamental needs: it had achieved a marked reduction in primary poverty, a considerable stability of employment, an extensive welfare network. Yet it remained a potentially intolerable and suffocating system even, or precisely for, groups in the population which enjoyed a relatively high standard of living . . . As material deprivation to a certain degree receded, cultural loss and devastation became more and more evident and important. The chaos and desolation of the urban environment, the sterility and formalism of education, the saturation of space and matter with advertising, the atomisation of local life, the concentration of control of the means of communication and the degradation of their content, these were what became the distinctive preoccupations of the New Left.[105]

Undoubtedly important as many of these issues were, the emphasis on moral and cultural questions seemed to concede too much, accepting the economic gains of 'affluence' on its own terms. Politically, such an emphasis was likewise to cast them adrift from the mainstream of working-class politics.

Finally, there was one other major dissenting group to appear towards the end of the 1950s in the form of the Campaign for Nuclear Disarmament, with its initiation of campaigns of civil disobedience and marches to Aldermaston (beginning Easter 1958). Like the New Left, its support derived mainly from the middle classes and, despite generous media attention, it was ultimately to make few political gains. The Labour Party Conference of 1960 passed a motion in favour of unilateral disarmament, against the wishes of the majority of MPs and the National Executive, but only to revoke it the following year. Once again, there can be no doubting the central importance of the campaign in which CND were involved; yet it is also perhaps significant that as the 1950s came to a close the most visibly radical movement was one whose politics had largely left social and economic questions behind in favour of a primarily moral and ethical attitude embodied in a liberal tradition of dissent.

Migration to racism

> I've got a brand new passport. It says I'm a citizen of the UK and the Colonies. Nobody asked me to be, but there I am. Most of these boys have got exactly the same passport as I have – and it was *we* who thought up the laws that gave it to them. But when they turn up in the dear old mother country, and show us the damn thing, we throw it back again in their faces.[106]

By the way of a conclusion, something should also be said about the issue of 'race' during this period. Under the British Nationality Act of 1948, UK citizenship had been granted to all members of the Commonwealth who now had the right to enter and settle in Britain. During the years that followed there was a steady rise in the numbers choosing to exercise this right. In 1951 the total 'coloured' population of Commonwealth origin in Britain had totalled 74,500; by 1961, it had reached 336,600. By far the largest percentage had come from the West Indies: in 1951 the number of people of West Indian origin had totalled 15,300; ten years later, it had risen to 171,800.[107] The reason for these increases was simple: employment. The expansion of the British economy required new sources of labour and, along with married women, it was migrant labour that was called upon to meet the shortfall (and, thus, help lay the foundations of the new society of 'affluence'). In 1949 a Royal Commission on Population had suggested that some 140,000 migrants per year would be required to meet the British economy's demand for labour. Yet it rejected 'large-scale immigration' as 'both undesirable and impracticable'.[108] However, such was the need for labour that migration, though hardly 'large-scale', was destined to become a reality.[109] Indeed, it was actively encouraged by British firms and organisations, such as London Transport, who proceeded to launch recruiting campaigns in Barbados, Trinidad and Jamaica.

The migration to Britain which followed, however, was no journey to the Promised Land. Incoming workers were usually offered low-status and ill-rewarded jobs, well below their level of skills and experience; in many cases, they had to make do with overcrowded and insanitary housing conditions and were faced with hostility and prejudice, both inside and outside of work. Matters were not helped by the absence of Government policy in facing up to the demands that this new source of labour would present. Paul Foot explains the dismal record:

> There were no Government arrangements for meeting the immigrants and dispersing them to their destinations in Britain . . . As the wives and children of immigrants came over . . . no Government arrangements were

The Angry Silence (1960)

made for the teaching of English . . . Worst of all, no provision was made by the Government for accommodation. The exploiter's paradise which immigration created . . . was watched over benignly, even encouraged, by the Conservative Government. The 1957 Rent Act . . . with its provisions for 'creeping decontrol' laid the immigrants open to still more exploitation, squalor and resentment. There was no Government propaganda, much less legislation, against racial discrimination or incitement, and not until 1962 was any Government organisation formed to help cope with immigrant problems . . . When the ten years of neglect reaped their inevitable resentment, bitterness and racialism, the Conservative Party, in

Mr Hugh Gaitskell's words, 'yielded to the crudest clamour – Keep Them Out'. Far from trying to counter the difficulties of housing, education and assimilative work, they simply decided to 'turn off the tap'.[110]

A crucial factor in the Government's submission to the 'crudest clamour' was provided by the events of 1958, or more properly speaking, the reaction which then followed. For although they were commonly described as 'race riots' it is clear that the incidents in Nottingham and Notting Hill in August and September 1958 were largely provoked by whites and conformed to an already established pattern of attacks on black people and their property. It was primarily British-born residents who were arrested and, as Fryer points

Sapphire (1959)

29

out, the absence of black people on the streets did not prevent twenty-four people from being arrested in Nottingham in the course of an all-white 'race riot'.[111] And, although it was the 'Teddy Boy' who was made the prime scapegoat for the trouble, it is also clear that involvement in the incidents was by no means confined to gangs of youths and was often actively encouraged by such explicitly racist organisations as the Union Movement and the League of Empire Loyalists. The response to these incidents was effectively to blame the victims. Two Nottingham MPs immediately called for a curb on the entry of migrants and the introduction of deportation, while Parliament responded with a debate on immigration control in December.

Attitudes and demands which had previously been confined to groups outside Parliament or isolated individuals within (such as Cyril Osborne and Norman Pannell) now enjoyed a much wider hearing, were aired in the press and, slowly but surely, began to make their impact felt on the Government. The events of 1958 were appealed to as an illustration of Britain's growing 'colour problem'. Moreover, it was a 'problem' whose cause was identified in only one specific way, i.e. the 'colour problem' was the result of 'immigration', and not the conditions and attitudes which the migrants had faced. It was a 'problem' which was caused by 'them' and not, as the events of 1958 had suggested, a 'problem' which was caused by 'us'. The seeds of the future immigration policy had now been successfully sown.

The election of 1959 increased the number of Tory MPs sympathetic to immigration control, and new organisations, such as the Birmingham Immigration Control Association (formed in 1960), carried on the campaign outside of Parliament. With the rise in migration during the years 1960 and 1961, their calls grew ever more vociferous. In fact, there was something of a self-fulfilling logic in this. As Walvin observes, the debates about immigration during this period, and the arguments for control and, even, repatriation, in particular, inevitably 'served to compound the very forces they wished to restrict or stop'.[112] In fear of impending restrictions, the numbers of migrants entering Britain accelerated, especially amongst the relatives of those who were already in residence. The result, however, was the Commonwealth Immigrants Act of 1962. The entry of Commonwealth citizens was now restricted to those who had been issued with an employment voucher, students, and dependents of those already living in the country. The aim of the Act, however, was not the restriction of immigration per se. It did not apply, for example, to Irish citizens, although some 60–70,000 Irish were entering Britain each year and constituted the largest migrant group in Britain. Nor were there any changes introduced in the controls governing the entry of aliens, for whom there was no fixed ceiling.

This is not to say that groups like the Irish were not themselves the victims of British racism, for they often suffered the same disadvantages as other migrant populations (i.e. low-paid and unwanted jobs, poor housing, racial hostility). What distinguished them, however, was that they were white. Their exemption from the workings of the Act made it clear that it was only 'coloured' migration, rather than migration in general, which the Government was attempting to obstruct. This is confirmed by the use of employment as a criterion for entry. Prior to the panic migration of the early 1960s, the flow of Commonwealth migration had generally corresponded to the demand for labour. As Foot points out, 'some ninety-five per cent of the immigrants got jobs within a few weeks of arrival, and their contribution to the economy was undisputed'.[113] The use of employment vouchers could not be justified by any need to regulate the labour supply; indeed, one reason for leaving Irish migration uncontrolled was precisely because of a continuing need for cheap, migrant labour. Their use simply provided the means for keeping 'coloured' migrants out. The 1962 Act represented 'the decisive turning-point in British race relations' according to Ben-Tovim and Gabriel. It effectively confirmed 'the principle that black people are themselves a problem and the fewer we have of them the better' and gave an official seal of approval to the equation of 'blackness with second-class and undesirable immigrant'.[114] It made physical characteristics a criterion for the entry of British citizens into Britain. In the words of Miles and Phizacklea: 'British politics were racialised at the highest level; state racism became a reality'.[115]

Notes

1. Harry Hopkins, *The New Look,* London, Secker & Warburg, 1963, p.309.
2. Vernon Bogdanor and Robert Skidelsky (eds.), *The Age of Affluence: 1951–1964,* London, Macmillan, 1970, p.7.
3. Nicholas Tomalin, quoted in John Montgomery, *The Fifties,* London, Allen & Unwin, 1965.
4. Quoted in T.F. Lindsay and Michael Harrington, *The Conservative Party: 1918–1970,* London, Macmillan, 1974, p.202.
5. Pinto-Duschinsky, 'Bread and Circuses? The Conservatives in Office, 1951–64' in Bogdanor and Skidelsky, *Age of Affluence,* p.55.
6. Andrew Gamble, *The Conservative Nation,* London, Routledge & Kegan Paul, 1974, p.61.
7. Quintin Hogg, quoted in Gamble, *The Conservative Nation,* p.65.
8. Macmillan, quoted in Gamble, ibid. p.66.
9. David Coates, *The Labour Party and the Struggle for Socialism,* Cambridge, Cambridge University Press, 1975, p.76.
10. Mark Abrams and Richard Rose, *Must Labour Lose?,* Harmondsworth, Penguin, 1960.
11. Quoted in Stuart Hall et al., *Policing the Crisis: Mugging, the State and Law and Order,* London, Macmillan, 1980, p.230.
12. C.A.R. Crosland, *The Future of Socialism,* London, Jonathan Cape, 1956.
13. Coates, *The Labour Party and the Struggle for Socialism,* p.84.
14. Gamble, *The Conservative Nation,* pp.74–5.
15. Ibid, p.67.
16. John Clarke, Stuart Hall, Tony Jefferson and Brian Roberts, 'Sub-cultures, cultures and class: A theoretical overview' in *Resistance through Rituals,* Birmingham, Centre for Contemporary Cultural Studies, Summer 1975, p.21.
17. For a critique of the 'embourgeoisement' thesis see David Lockwood, 'The new working class' in *European Journal of Sociology,* vol.1, no.2, 1960. See also the subsequent research of John H. Goldthorpe, David Lockwood, Frank Bechhofer and Jennifer Platt, *The Affluent Worker,* vols. 1–3, Cambridge University Press, 1968–9.
18. Andrew Glyn and Bob Sutcliffe, *British Capitalism, Workers and the Profits Squeeze,* Harmondsworth, Penguin, 1972, p.38.
19. Andrew Shonfield, *British Economic Policy since the War,* Harmondsworth, Penguin, 1959, p.105.

20. Bogdanor and Skidelsky, *Age of Affluence*, p.8.
21. Pinto-Duschinsky, in Bogdanor and Skidelsky, *Age of Affluence*, p.59.
22. John Westergaard and Henrietta Resler, *Class in a Capitalist Society*, Harmondsworth, Penguin, 1977, p.34.
23. Ibid. p.43.
24. See R. Blackburn, 'The Unequal Society' in R. Blackburn and A. Cockburn (eds.), *The Incompatibles – Trade Union Militancy and the Consensus*, Harmondsworth, Penguin, 1967, pp.17–20.
25. See H. Frankel, *Capitalist Society and Modern Sociology*, London, Lawrence & Wishart, 1970, pp.77–8.
26. Stuart Hall, 'A Long Haul' in *Marxism Today*, November 1982, p.17.
27. Alan Hunt, 'Theory and Politics in the Identification of the Working Class' in Alan Hunt (ed.), *Class and Class Structure*, London, Lawrence & Wishart, 1977, p.104.
28. John Clarke *et al.*, *Resistance through Rituals*, p.37.
29. Colin MacInnes, *Absolute Beginners*, Harmondsworth, Penguin, 1964, p.43.
30. Harry Hopkins, *The New Look*, p.423.
31. See Frank Musgrove, *Youth and the Social Order*, London, Routledge & Kegan Paul, 1964, chapter 3. See also John Springhall, 'The origins of adolescence' in *Youth and Policy*, vol.2, no.3, Winter 1983/4.
32. Peter Laurie, *The Teenage Revolution*, London, Anthony Blond, 1965, p.9.
33. Mark Abrams, *The Teenage Consumer*, London, The London Press Exchange Limited, July 1959.
34. Mark Abrams, *Teenage Consumer Spending in 1959*, The London Press Exchange Limited, January 1961, pp.3–4.
35. Laurie, *Teenage Revolution*, pp.20–21.
36. Abrams, *Teenage Consumer*, p.10.
37. Laurie, *Teenage Revolution*, p.11.
38. MacInnes, *Absolute Beginners*, p.69.
39. Clarke *et al.*, *Resistance through Rituals*, p.71.
40. Ibid. p.71.
41. Bryan Wilson, 'The Trouble with Teenagers' in *The Youth Culture and the Universities*, London, Faber and Faber, 1970, pp.23–4, (orig. 1959).
42. For a close to contemporary discussion of the 'mass culture' debate, see James D. Halloran, *Control or Consent?*, London, Sheed & Ward, 1963, chapter 6.
43. *Report of the Committee on Broadcasting 1960*, HMSO, 1962, p.16.
44. Richard Hoggart, *The Uses of Literacy*, Harmondsworth, Penguin, 1959, pp.12, 284, 285. Hoggart's concern with the break-up of traditional working-class culture found a parallel in more conventional sociological studies, especially Michael Young and Peter Willmott, *Family and Kinship in East London*, London, Routledge & Kegan Paul, 1957.
45. Hoggart, *Uses of Literacy*, pp. 203, 204, 205. Hoggart's concern with the debasement of taste amongst the juke-box boys can clearly be linked to an accompanying hostility towards the 'Americanisation' of British culture. See also Dick Hebdige, 'Towards a Cartography of Taste' in *Block*, 4, 1981.
46. Laurie, *Teenage Revolution*, p.123.
47. Quoted in Gamble, *The Conservative Nation*, p.82.
48. Montgomery, *The Fifties*, p.173.
49. Ibid. p.174.
50. Laurie, *Teenage Revolution*, p.114.
51. See Michael Schofield, *The Sexual Behaviour of Young People*, Harlow, Longman, 1965.
52. T.R. Fyvel, *The Insecure Offenders*, Harmondsworth, Penguin, 1964.
53. Stanley Cohen, *Folk Devils and Moral Panics*, Oxford, Martin Robertson, 1980, p.58.
54. Abrams, *Teenage Consumer*, p.13 and Abrams, *Teenage Consumer Spending*, p.10.
55. Graham Murdock and Robin McCron, 'Youth and Class: The Career of a Confusion' in Geoff Mungham and Geoff Pearson (eds.), *Working Class Youth Culture*, London, Routledge & Kegan Paul, 1976, p.10.
56. Clarke *et al.*, *Resistance through Rituals*, pp.47–8.

57. Hebdige, *Block*, 4, 1981, p.53.
58. 'The Treatment of "Football Hooliganism" in the Press' in Roger Ingham *et al.*, *Football Hooliganism*, London, Inter-Action, 1978, pp. 29–30.
59. 'Adolescence as a Social Problem' in Howard Becker (ed.), *Social Problems: A Modern Approach*, New York, John Wiley and Son, 1966, p.38.
60. Cohen, *Folk Devils and Moral Panics*, p.139.
61. Clarke *et al.*, *Resistance through Rituals*, pp.71–2.
62. Tony Bennett, 'James Bond in the 1980s' in *Marxism Today*, June 1983, p.37.
63. Richard Titmuss, 'The Position of Women' in *Essays on the Welfare State*, Unwin, 1963, p.91.
64. Ann Showstack Sassoon, 'Dual Role: Women and Britain's Crisis' in *Marxism Today*, December 1982, p.6.
65. Stuart Hall, 'Reformism and the Legislation of Consent' in *Permissiveness and Control: The Fate of the Sixties Legislation*, National Deviancy Conference, London, Macmillan, 1980, p.23.
66. Alva Myrdal and Viola Klein, *Women's Two Roles: Home and Work*, London, Routledge & Kegan Paul, 1956, p.74. Veronica Beechey accounts for the disadvantaged role of women in the labour force in terms of the Marxist conception of the 'industrial reserve army' in 'Some Notes on Female Wage Labour in Capitalist Production' in *Capital and Class*, no.3, Autumn 1977.
67. Hopkins, *The New Look*, p.324.
68. Peter Lewis, *The Fifties*, London, Heinemann, 1978, p.45.
69. Elizabeth Wilson, *Women and the Welfare State*, London, Tavistock, 1977, p.64.
70. Myrdal and Klein, *Women's Two Roles*, pp.127–8.
71. John Bowlby, *Child Care and the Growth of Love*, Harmondsworth, Penguin, 1963, p.105.
72. *Royal Commission on Marriage and Divorce*, HMSO, 1956, p.11.
73. Ibid. p.9.
74. Hall, 'Reformism and the Legislation of Consent', p.8.
75. *Report of the Committee on Homosexual Practices and Prostitution*, HMSO, 1957, p.20. This 'weakening of the family' was also interlinked with juvenile delinquency by the *Report of the Committee on Children and Young Persons*, HMSO,1960.
76. Lucy Bland, Trisha McCabe and Frank Mort, 'Sexuality and Reproduction: Three Official Instances' in M. Barrett, P. Corrigan, Annette Kuhn and J. Wolff (eds.), *Ideology and Cultural Production*, London, Croom Helm, 1979, p.109.
77. 'Law and the Control of Women's Sexuality: The Case of the 1950s' in Bridget Hutter and Gillian Williams (eds.), *Controlling Women: The Normal and the Deviant*, London, Croom Helm, 1981, p.51.
78. Ibid. p.53.
79. Michele Barrett, *Women's Oppression Today*, London, Verso/New Left Books, 1980.
80. Edward Shils, 'The Intellectuals – Great Britain' in *Encounter*, vol. 4, no. 4, April 1955, p.6.
81. Noel Annan, 'The Intellectual Aristocracy' in J.H. Plumb (ed.), *Studies in Social History*, Harlow, Longman, 1955, p.285.
82. Robert Hewison, *In Anger: Culture in the Cold War 1945–60*, London, Weidenfeld & Nicolson, 1981, p.129.
83. Kenneth Allsop, *The Angry Decade*, London, Peter Owen, 1958, p.141.
84. Lewis, *The Fifties*, p.161 and Allsop, *The Angry Decade*, pp.177–8.
85. Gene Feldman and Max Gartenberg (eds.), Introduction, *Protest*, London, Quartet, 1973, p.6.
86. William Donaldson, quoted in Allsop, *The Angry Decade*, p.137.
87. Blake Morrison, *The Movement: English Poetry and Fiction of the 1950s*, Oxford, Oxford University Press, 1980, p.73.
88. John Wain, *Hurry On Down*, Harmondsworth, Penguin, 1960, p.250.
89. Allsop, *The Angry Decade*, p.75.
90. Dave Rimmer, 'Inside the New Outsiders' in *City Limits*, no. 11/12, 8–13 December, 1981, p.60. Although this article is in fact a spoof of an alleged 1980s Angry Young Man revival, its observations are often very much to the point.

91. Donald Davie, *Collected Poems 1950–70*, London, Routledge & Kegan Paul, 1972, p.27.
92. Kingsley Amis, quoted in Feldman and Gartenberg, *Protest*, p.271.
93. Morrison, *The Movement*, p.95.
94. Bernard Bergonzi, *The Situation of the Novel*, London, Macmillan, 1979, p.151.
95. Allsop, *The Angry Decade*, pp.117,26.
96. Colin Wilson, quoted in Allsop, *The Angry Decade*, p.172.
97. Allsop, *The Angry Decade*, pp.194–5.
98. D.E. Cooper, 'Looking Back on Anger' in Bogdanor and Skidelsky, *Age of Affluence*, p.257.
99. John Osborne, 'Sex and Failure' in Feldman and Gartenberg, *Protest*, p.282.
100. John Osborne, *Look Back in Anger*, London, Faber and Faber, 1969, pp.59–60.
101. Paul Hoch, *White Hero, Black Beast: Racism, Sexism and the Mask of Masculinity*, London, Pluto, 1979, p.98.
102. T.R. Fyvel, *The Insecure Offenders*, pp.130–1.
103. Leslie A. Fiedler, quoted in Allsop, *The Angry Decade*, p.18.
104. *Universities and Left Review*, vol.1, no.1, Spring 1957, p.1.
105. Perry Anderson, 'The Left in the Fifties' in *New Left Review*, no.29, 1965, p.15.
106. MacInnes, *Absolute Beginners*, p.198.
107. These figures are provided by James Walvin, *Passage to Britain*, Harmondsworth, Penguin, 1984, p.111.
108. *Royal Commission on Population*, Command 7695, HMSO, 1949, p.125.
109. According to 1961 Census statistics, the 'coloured' population still represented only 0.6 per cent of the total UK population of 52, 673,221.
110. Paul Foot, *Immigration and Race in British Politics*, Harmondsworth, Penguin, 1965, p.159. Hugh Gaitskell's remarks were made in the House of Commons, 16 November 1961.
111. Peter Fryer, *Staying Power*, London, Pluto, 1984, p.377.
112. Walvin, *Passage to Britain*, p.112.
113. Foot, *Immigration and Race in British Politics*, p.140.
114. Gideon Ben-Tovim and John Gabriel, 'The politics of race in Britain, 1962–79: A review of the major trends and of recent debates' in Charles Husband (ed.), *Race in Britain*, London, Hutchinson, 1982, pp.145–6.
115. Robert Miles and Annie Phizacklea, *White Man's Country*, London, Pluto, 1984, p.44.

2

The Film Industry

COMBINE POWER AND INDEPENDENT PRODUCTION

If the 1950s was taken to be a period of 'boom', one industry at least did not seem to be aware of it: the cinema. The evidence can be quickly presented: in 1951 cinema admissions were 1,365 million; by 1960 they were down to 501 million and still falling. Ironically, those very elements which in one light betokened affluence only spelt decline for the cinema. Rising incomes, increasing home-ownership and home-oriented consumption, the diversification of leisure facilities and increasing popularity of motoring all seemed to conspire to diminish the cinema's importance. Even the increase of women at work had its part to play: 'So many women go out to work in offices, shops and factories these days', complained one exhibitor, 'that I think it is one of the reasons why we have had a bit of a slump in cinemas, especially during the afternoon periods. A lot of them have their housework to do in the evening'.[1] Apparently in recognition of this, ABC decided to launch a new advertising slogan in 1958: 'Don't take your wife for granted – take her out to the "pictures".' But, of course, it was the increase in televisions which most dramatically summed up the trend away from the cinema. The televising of the Coronation in 1953, watched by twenty-five million, the advent of commercial television in 1955 and the extension of television reception to practically the whole of the country in 1958 and 1959 all spurred on the demand for television sets. Thus, while in 1951 the number of TV licences issued amounted to less than 764,000, by the end of the decade the figure had risen to almost 10½ million and was still increasing.[2]

Not surprisingly, then, one of the first campaigns mounted by the film industry to defend itself was directed towards its television competitor. Following a plan devised by Cecil Bernstein of Granada Theatres, the Film Industry Defence Organisation (FIDO) was established in 1958 to try and prevent the appearance of British films on TV.[3] By levying exhibitors, a defence fund was mounted to acquire the television rights to British films and co-ordinate boycotts by exhibitors of producers and distributors (both British and foreign) who sold such rights to the television companies. However, such a policy was to prove both expensive (in October 1961, FIDO announced that they had spent more than £1 million in acquiring the rights to 665 films) and difficult to implement. All-industry solidarity was broken in 1959 with the departure of the Kinematograph Renters Society (KRS), under pressure from its US members threatened by anti-trust legislation. Meanwhile, it had been revealed in 1958, shortly after the group's constitution, that the Associated British Picture Corporation (ABPC) had reached an agreement with ABC Television for the transmission of Ealing films, recently acquired through a take-over of Associated Talking Pictures Ltd. Although FIDO succeeded in preventing the extension of the agreement to other Ealing films, it still could not stop 60 of the 95 films concerned reaching television. Other such cases were to follow (in October 1959, for example, the Cinematograph Exhibitors Association General Council passed resolutions against David Selznick, John Woolf and Daniel Angel) and with funds becoming increasingly scarce (such that by 1962 FIDO was unable to make deals for more than a few films) it was clear that the FIDO line could not be maintained. Thus, in November 1962 the General Council of the CEA agreed to 'wipe the slate clean' and make further deals dependent on the effect television screenings would have on box-office takings. In September 1964, this was formalised into a five-year rule whereby boycotts would only operate in respect of films televised in the UK less than five years after their Board of Trade registration. The effect of this was a sudden release of films to TV and dramatic reductions in the prices paid. FIDO itself decided to call it a day in November, promising to sell back the rights it had purchased at the prices originally paid.

The other campaign mounted by the industry met with rather more success, albeit not immediately. In July 1955 the All Industry Tax Committee (AITC) was set up to campaign against the payment of Entertainments Duty, a tax on cinema admissions, originally imposed in 1916 as a contribution to the war effort, which by 1954 accounted for £35.9 million or 34.4 per cent of gross box-office takings.[4] Complaints about this tax were not new – the Plant Committee, for example, had complained of its 'quite excessive' rates in 1949 – but it was the decline in cinema attendances which were to cause them to be taken up with a renewed vigour.[5] Accordingly, the AITC was to petition the Chancellor for three years before the 1957 Budget brought some small relief by way of a reduction (of about 6 per cent) and a simplification of the scales. By this time, however, the sharp falls in attendance for 1957 (1,101 million to 915 million) had led the AITC to abandon their claims merely for tax relief and replace it with a demand for the abolition of the tax altogether. The Chancellor responded with more dramatic reductions in 1958 and 1959 before finally succumbing to pressure and abolishing the tax in April 1960.

Entertainments duty and the televising of films, however, only represented the more obvious of external targets. More important changes were to occur within the industry itself. The primary changes here were economic, as the industry attempted to rationalise and re-structure in the face of a declining income; but it was also to lead to changes in the nature of the film product itself as the industry adapted itself to the competition now provided by television. What success there was in the latter, however, remained crucially dependent on the changes being wrought by the first.

The framework within which economic reorganisation was to take place had basically been determined by the developments of the 1930s and 1940s when the film industry had evolved from small-scale entrepreneurial activity towards large-scale oligopoly through a process of horizontal and vertical integration. In this respect it was typical of British industry in general, whose response to the depression had been the maintenance of profits through the elimination of competition. The specific impetus, however, derived from the 1927 Cinematograph Films Act which had established for the first time quotas for the exhibition and distribution of British films by way of a response to the decline in British product on the cinema screen (in 1926 only 33 out of 749 films exhibited in British cinemas were British-made). The immediate effect of the legislation was the rise of the 'quota quickie'; the long-term effect was to speed up the integration of exhibition and renting interests with production. Thus, in January 1928 the formation of Associated British Cinemas Ltd as a holding company for the interests of John Maxwell integrated all three sectors of the industry and precipitated a programme of cinema acquisitions. By the end of 1929 the company's cinemas had increased in number from 29 to 88 and by 1933, when the Associated British Picture Corporation was formed as a new holding company, had reached a total of 147. Similarly, the formation of Gaumont-British Picture Corporation in 1927 consolidated the various interests of the Ostrer brothers. This company's cinemas increased from 21 to 187 in a year and then to 287 in 1929, through the acquisition of Provincial Cinematograph Theatres, the largest cinema circuit prior to 1927.

A further major force appeared in 1933 when Cinema Service changed its name to Odeon Theatres Ltd and under Oscar Deutsch embarked upon a policy of cinema building, increasing its total from 26 in 1933 to 144 in 1936. In 1938 Arthur Rank, who had interests in production and distribution, but not yet exhibition, joined the Odeon board and on the death of Deutsch in 1941 acquired control and became chairman. As he had already acquired Gaumont-British the same year, through his General Cinema Finance Corporation, Rank's ascendancy in the industry was now complete. Thus, by the end of the Second World War, two organisations effectively dominated all aspects of the British film industry. The Rank Organisation owned two of the largest cinema circuits (Odeon and Gaumont-British), the largest film distributor (General Film Distributors Ltd) and the lion's share of studio space (at Pinewood, Denham, Shepherd's Bush, Islington and Highbury). The Associated British Picture Corporation, on the other hand, owned the other large circuit, the second largest distributor as well as studio space of their own (at Elstree, Welwyn and Teddington).[6] On the face of it, then, it might appear as if it would be these two groups who had most to lose from the decline of attendances in the 1950s. In fact, the reverse was true: for far from weakening the combines the 1950s was to witness an intensification of their monopoly power.

A good example of this can be found in the case of cinema closures. The most straightforward response to falling admissions was the closure of uneconomic cinemas and the figures for the 1950s tell the story: 4,851 cinemas were open in 1951; by 1956 this had dropped to 4,391 and by 1960 to 3,034. However, the burden of such closures was not evenly spread. In the period 1956–60, for example, cinema closures overall amounted to 1,357. Of these, only 103 belonged to Rank and 55 to ABC. Thus, while the percentage drop overall was 30.9 per cent, the rates for Rank and ABC respectively were 19.7 per cent and 14.8 per cent. The net result of such a trend was that while Rank and ABC owned 20.3 per cent of cinemas in 1950 by 1960 they had increased this to 24.2 per cent and by 1962 to 26.7 per cent. If this is then converted into seating capacity the proportions rise even higher: thus by the end of 1962 Rank and ABC owned 41.5 per cent of seating compared with 33 per cent ten years before.[7] Moreover, what cinemas Rank and ABC did close were usually the oldest and most ill-placed while they still maintained their dominance in the most attractive areas, such as the key box-office area of London. Rationalisation by Rank also helped consolidate this monopoly. In October 1958 Rank announced the amalgamation of the Odeon and Gaumont circuits (hitherto prohibited by a Board of Trade ban imposed under the 1948 Cinematograph Films Act). The bulk of Rank cinemas (280) became part of one large and powerful Odeon circuit while the remainder (126) were to contribute to the 'National Circuit' designed for more 'specialised booking'. The weakness of the National Circuit in terms of box-office (in 1961, returning an average of about £35–40,000 compared with £85–95,000 for the Rank release and £75–85,000 for ABC) diminished its viability from the very start and by October 1961 it had ceased operation. Despite ideas for a 'third' circuit, the net result was that two circuits now dominated, where previously there had been three. A measure of Rank's success in re-organising its exhibition can be found in their box-office receipts. In the period 1956–60, gross box-office takings declined overall from £104 million to £63½ million. By contrast, Rank's profits from exhibition in the British Isles remained more or less constant: £2½ million in 1956, £2.3 million in 1960, and, indeed, £3.7 million for 1962.

In terms of exhibition, then, the pattern of the 1950s was the maintenance and, indeed, further concentration of power in the hands of the majors. The question of production, however, was more problematic. In January 1958 Rank announced redundancies at Pinewood and the postponement of some of its productions. By the end of the financial year, losses on production and distribution amounted to £1¼ million and were to be followed by further losses the following year. Such production problems were not entirely new. Rank's ambitious £9¼ million production programme, at the end of the 1940s in the wake of an American embargo, met with disaster when the offending 75 per cent import duty was lifted in 1949 and a flood of Hollywood product hit Britain just as Rank's films were beginning to emerge. By the end of 1949 Rank had accumulated losses of over £4½ million and production was severely curtailed. A similar hesitation continued to mark Rank's production programme throughout the 1950s but intensified from 1957 onwards under pressure from diminishing admissions. Thus, for the year ending 31 March 1958, Rank had produced 14 films. This fell to 12 the following year, 6 the next and to only 4 for the year ending March 1961. ABPC's output was similarly modest, producing only 2 films per year for the same period. Thus, for the year ending March 1961, only 6 out of 81 British films (over 6,500 feet) registered with the Board of Trade were either Rank or ABPC productions.[8]

In this respect, the declining interest in production was paralleled by an attempt to spread financial risks through a policy of diversification and accumulation of interests outside the cinema – often, indeed, in those very areas which most seemed to threaten the film industry. Thus, while television represented the film industry's main competitor, both the combines developed an early interest in commercial broadcasting. ABC Television Ltd was a wholly-owned subsidiary of the ABPC (and, as we've seen, the source of a conflict of interests in the case of film sales to TV) while Rank held substantial interests in Southern Television Ltd. Such diversification of interests extended to leisure provision more generally (bingo, dancing, bowling) and, particularly, in the case of Rank, to 'home entertainment' – TV sets, radios and records. As Lord Rank correctly observed in 1959: 'It will not be long before profits from non-cinema interests exceed those from cinema activities'.[9] A particularly striking example, in this respect, is the case of Rank Xerox Ltd, half owned by Rank and incorporated in 1956. A profit of £29,000 by 1962 had jumped dramatically to £8¼ million by 1965. In the same year, profits derived from film exhibition, distribution, production, studios and labs combined came to £4.4 million.

Film was still profitable but what is also clear from the figures is that it was distribution and exhibition, rather than production, which supplied the main revenues. Rather than engage in direct production themselves, the majors preferred to rent their studio space (itself decreasing) and devolve the responsibility for provision of circuit releases on to the independent producer:

A revolution is in progress in British studios . . . Britain's creative talents are copying Hollywood where the big stars have set up their own companies to make independent pictures for the studios which once employed them . . . The revolution has been forced on the industry by the box-office crisis. It suits the creative artists who want independence to choose their films and make them their way. In return they are willing to share the financial risk . . . It suits the big companies, who are cutting down production, sacking their starlets, but still need film for their cinema chains. By backing independent productions they get the films without studio overheads, and without bearing the full financial risk.[10]

A good example of this process at work can be found in the establishment of the Allied Film Makers group in November 1959. Bringing together Richard Attenborough, Bryan Forbes, Basil Dearden, Michael Relph, Jack Hawkins and Guy Green, the group was set up on the basis of the filmmakers' own investments plus financial guarantees from Rank and the National Provincial Bank. While Rank were also to provide the end 10 per cent of production finance, they were not to be directly involved in the development of projects. 'We shall be able to choose our own scripts and our own stars', commented Attenborough. 'We believe that we can give a shot in

39

the arm to the British film industry.'[11] *The League of Gentlemen* (suggested by some to be an apt title for the AFM group themselves) was chosen as the first production and its results appeared to vindicate the system: it was the sixth biggest box-office success (and fifth highest British film) for 1960. Subsequent titles included *Man in the Moon* (1960), *Victim* (1961), *Life for Ruth* (1962) and *Seance on a Wet Afternoon* (1964).

Similar in structure to Allied Film Makers, but lacking direct Rank involvement, was Bryanston, formed a few months earlier in April 1959. This too brought film producers and directors together in a co-operative enterprise, each again investing their own finance but this time with backing from Gerald and Kenneth Shipman (owners of Twickenham studios) and Lloyds Bank. British Lion were to handle the distribution and provide production facilities at Shepperton (with Rank getting a small look in through the provision of lab space at Denham). 'We are not an arty crafty experimental organisation', commented part-time chairman Michael Balcon, 'but we do want to tackle original and unusual subjects of international importance. We are now in a position whereby, working through a small selection panel, we can give a producer financial backing to make these subjects. And we welcome any outside producer who has an exciting project . . . we hope our venture will give a fresh impetus to production'.[12] In this respect, Bryanston's first two productions were less than inspired, drawing on Balcon's old stablemates at Ealing, Charles Crichton and Charles Frend, to direct *Battle of the Sexes* (1959) and *Cone of Silence* (1960) respectively. Nonetheless, by the time the company joined forces with Seven Arts in November 1961, in an attempt to gain a foothold in the American market, Bryanston had completed a further seven features including *Spare the Rod* (1961), and a number of supporting features including *The Big Day* (1960), *Linda* (1960) and *The Wind of Change* (1961).

Of these, undoubtedly the most significant – *The Entertainer* (1960), *Saturday Night and Sunday Morning* (1960), *A Taste of Honey* (1961) and, later, *Loneliness of the Long Distance Runner* (1962) – were brought to them by another independent company, Woodfall. Partly drawing on the ideas of Free Cinema (screenings of which took place at the National Film Theatre over the period 1956–59), this company had been formed by John Osborne and Tony Richardson, on the basis of Osborne's theatre royalties, to make a film version of *Look Back in Anger*. Of all the independents, it was Woodfall who were the most determined to initiate new types of film project and defend the principle of artistic control. 'It is absolutely vital to get into British films the same sort of impact and sense of life that what you can loosely call the Angry Young Man cult has had in the theatre and literary worlds', declared Tony Richardson.[13] 'The important thing about our company is that we insist on having artistic control', added producer Harry Saltzman. 'We want to make them honestly. In other words, we control the script, the cast, the shooting and the completion of the picture'.[14]

This expansion of the role of the independents can also be seen in relation to the activities of the National Film Finance Corporation. Established in October 1948 as a specialised bank to make loans in support of British film

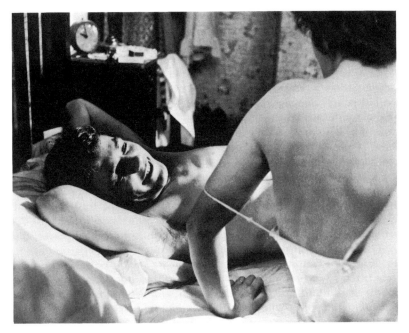

Saturday Night and Sunday Morning (1960)

production and distribution, the NFFC was originally designed as a temporary measure to help alleviate the crisis in British production. The extension of its life by the Cinematograph Film Production (Special Loans) Bill of 1949, and then the Cinematograph Films Act of 1957, quickly ensured the Corporation a more permanent and critical role in the raising of production finance. Thus, for the period 1950–61, the NFFC provided loans for 366 of the 730 British quota films released as first features on the three major circuits. In this respect, its rise to prominence reflected the declining interest of the majors in production and the consequent necessity for a financial structure more closely geared to the needs of the independents. Both Bryanston and Allied Film Makers, for example, relied upon the NFFC for part of their funding.

Taking stock of such developments, it was perhaps not surprising that *Kine Weekly* should see fit to celebrate 'a new pattern of production and distribution in which creative individuals have as much say as impersonal mammoth corporations'.[15] The figures, moreover, seemed to bear out their confidence: the *Motion Picture Herald*, for example, reported that 28 out of the 37 most popular British movies between 1958 and 1962 were independently produced.[16] In the cool light of analysis, however, a more cautious assessment is undoubtedly appropriate. For if independent producers were enjoying a new prominence it was, as I have argued, because it was in the interests of the majors for them to do so. Moreover, whatever new-found

41

freedoms they might claim it was clear that they were still heavily circumscribed by the realities of combine power. 'Without virtually limitless resources', commented Michael Balcon, 'the independent producer is a myth'.[17]

For what, above all, continued to restrict the independents' exercise of their 'freedom' was their subservience to a system of distribution and exhibition still dominated by Rank and ABPC. Central to the raising of production finance, for example, was the 'distributor's guarantee', on the basis of which a production company was able to negotiate a bank loan for about 70 per cent of the total. In this respect, the NFFC had little by way of countervailing power. Crippled by limited resources (about £6 million a year), and committed by law to making loans on 'a commercially successful basis', the Corporation was unable to provide the total costs of production. Instead, it had to make use of the existing system of bank loans and distribution guarantees, normally providing the 'end money' or final 20–25 per cent of a film's budget. Rather than challenging combine power, the NFFC effectively had to adapt itself to its structures. As PEP comments, 'because of the existing structure of the industry and the power of the main circuits there was only a limited number of distributors who could risk an unbroken series of guarantees . . . In fact, that left GFD and ABPC'.[18] A measure of the power which distributors wielded here can be found in the fees they charged for their services: usually about 25–30 per cent of the gross from which costs and services were deducted afterwards. As Kelly observes, this is a remarkably high percentage by the standards of other distributive trades, the more so when only one major circuit deal is conventionally involved and with very little risk attached.[19] As the NFFC discovered to its cost, the distributor rarely lost money on a film even when the film itself failed to make a profit and the 'end money' was written off. As the Corporation's Annual Report for 1959 explained, the NFFC loan was not normally guaranteed and thus depended for its recovery on the commercial results of the film. By contrast, 'a distributor may be inclined to give a front money guarantee for a film in which he does not necessarily have whole-hearted confidence; if the whole of the end money (and even part of the front money) is lost, the distributor may still secure benefits by way of extra product (which he needs to pay his overhead costs) and the profit element included in the commission charged for distributing, as distinct from financing, the film; he may also benefit from the use of his studios and his contract artists'.

But if the distribution guarantee was critical to the raising of production finance this in turn can be related to the access to the main circuits enjoyed by the two leading distributors (GFD and ABPC) through vertical integration. As the Monopolies Commission indicated, 'a booking with all or most of the cinemas of one of those circuits normally yields so much more than a booking with any other exhibitor, and so high a proportion (as much as 70 per cent) of a film's total earnings in Great Britain, that for most feature films what is known as a circuit booking or circuit deal (i.e. with ABC or Rank) is now regarded as essential. For several years now . . . distributors have

42

usually not released films for distribution at all unless they have obtained a circuit deal with one of the two remaining circuits'.[20] In this respect, a distribution guarantee from one of the majors was of enormous benefit – effectively guaranteeing access to the circuits and the chance to recoup production costs. The tribulations of British Lion, Britain's third largest distributor but without a circuit of its own, are a salutary reminder of this. In 1963, British Lion's managing director, David Kingsley, complained of the delays in the booking of British films: a total of 18 features and 13 second features in which they held a £2¼ million stake. As the company's Annual Report put it: 'a number of independent British-made films are having to wait an excessive time for a release date on one of the two major circuits. Some films completed early this year (1963) are unlikely to secure a showing until well into 1964'.[21] One of the most celebrated cases here was *The Leather Boys*. Delivered to British Lion on 22 March 1963, it had to wait eleven months before gaining a circuit release with ABPC, by which time £8,000 had been added in interest charges to the film's original cost of £107,000. Finally reviewing the film in 1964, Philip Oakes commented, 'There never was a clearer case for the shake-up of the circuits'.[22]

What becomes clear then is that while independent production might have been increasing, the independents' room for manoeuvre was severely compromised by the exercise of combine power which greatly restricted both the possibilities for raising finance and opportunities for securing exhibition. Going back to the companies discussed previously we can identify some of the problems which were involved. Take, for example, the case of Woodfall. Producer Harry Saltzman summed up his experiences as follows: 'If you want to be a producer in this country, you have to be subservient, obsequious, and listen to business people rather than creative talents as to who to cast, how to have it written and what to do with it . . . The National Film Finance Corporation certainly help, but when a producer comes to them he already has to have a distribution agreement. But the distribution company has already put him in chains . . . When we made *Look Back in Anger*, Tony Richardson directed. He has never directed a picture before . . . it was an incredible job to get him accepted by the distributors and financing groups'.[23] Indeed, the film might not have been financed at all had Richard Burton not developed an interest in the production: 'Burton owed Warners a film on a "play him or pay him" basis. If he did *Look Back in Anger* at least they'd get a picture out of their deal; if they didn't they'd still have to pay him $125,000'.[24] On this basis, Saltzman was able to extract a budget from Warners, but with no director's fee for Richardson and a deferment of payments to both him and Osborne. Although Warner's connections with ABPC had ensured a circuit release for *Look Back in Anger*, dissatisfaction with Warner's interference led to Woodfall's next project, *The Entertainer* (also after Osborne's play), being offerred to Bryanston. Bryanston put up 75 per cent of the budget with the NFFC and Walter Reade providing the rest (the latter in return for the American rights). But, although this guaranteed less interference in production, the film was still to be plagued by distribution problems. As Derek Hill explained at the time: 'Months ago

43

NO TREES IN THE STREET

a novel by
CHARLES HATTON

based on the screenplay by
TED WILLIS

CORGI BOOK 2/6

THE **BOOK** OF THE **FILM**

Spin-off: the film was directed by J. Lee Thompson in 1958

stories were circulating that every major circuit had rejected *The Entertainer*, that it would never be given any kind of general release, that it might not even be risked in the West End. When a scheduled première and press show were suddenly cancelled there was a smug glow over Wardour Street'.[25]

Re-editing and re-dubbing were undertaken in the weeks that followed, before an eventual première took place over three months later. Hitherto scheduled for a general release on the Rank circuit in May, it now had to content itself with a release on the National Circuit in October. Although Saltzman attempted to claim that the company was 'extremely commercial-minded' with an interest in 'commercial properties', the strain was clearly beginning to tell. Thus, in 1960 he attempted to interest the company in two comedies, one entitled *The Coffin and I*, starring Tony Hancock, Sid James and Terry-Thomas. 'I offered them to the boys (i.e. Osborne and Richardson) but they just wouldn't wear them.'[26] Fortuitously, the company hit lucky with their next production, *Saturday Night and Sunday Morning*, the third biggest box-office success of 1961 (and second most successful British film after the doubtfully categorised *Swiss Family Robinson*). But even here the raising of finance had not been easy. 'I had a terrible time trying to raise money for *Saturday Night and Sunday Morning*', reports Saltzman. 'Everyone laughed at the idea of a big budget for a film with unknown names. They told me to be realistic and think in terms of making the picture for about £40,000.'[27] Although Bryanston once again came to the rescue, the film's commercial release was far from assured. As Walker explains, 'when it was finished and shown to the bookers, not one would agree to show it in a cinema, much less a chain of cinemas . . . only the unexpected failure of a Warner Brothers film at their West End showcase cinema, plus the advantage of at least playing a British film and gaining quota credit before getting back to the money-making American product, gave Woodfall the chance to open *Saturday Night and Sunday Morning*, on an advertising budget that was one-third of the minimum of £5,000 then current in London's West End. It had to be supplemented, according to Saltzman, by a loan from a relative of his in North America'.[28] Much to the astonishment of the industry the film then proceeded to do phenomenal business, grossing £100,000 on the London circuit cinemas alone and easily outpacing the then current blockbuster, *Hercules Unchained*. Finance problems eased considerably as a result. After two and a half years of trying, Richardson was now able to go ahead with *A Taste of Honey*. In a portent of the future, Woodfall managed to secure 100 per cent financing from United Artists for *Tom Jones* and thus by-pass Bryanston from then on.

The loss of *Tom Jones* by Bryanston (partly because of its prior commitments to *Sammy Going South*) was to prove disastrously damaging to the company and its subsequent demise is eloquent of the independents' precarious status in the industry. It continued to support independent productions but found its liquidity at risk from the increasing availability of American finance (intensified after the success of *Tom Jones*) and failure to secure circuit releases through its distributor, British Lion. In 1963, for example, *A Place to Go* had to wait ten months for a release with ABPC while *Ladies Who Do* had to wait seven before being shown by Rank. 'Independent pictures were taking longer and longer to be released', complained Balcon. 'Our bank payments had to be made within eighteen months of the delivery of a film to the distributors and in the pile-up which developed at this time (1963–4) it was often taking that length of time for a film to be released. Those films which were eventually released although produced as first-feature films, were often forced to share the bill with another film. Two films for the price of one – and thus anticipated revenues in those cases were cut by 50 per cent. So there arose not only the danger of default in terms of bank payments but also the grim fact that our costs were being artificially increased by our having to pay interest on borrowed money for longer than had been anticipated.'[29] The result was inevitable. Ironically, the company whose origins in part derived from television's challenge to film now had to succumb to its competitor. In January 1965 the company was sold (partly for its back-catalogue of features) to the independent television company, Associated Rediffusion.

Allied Film Makers were to fare little better. Although Rank had some financial stake in the company, this was not guaranteeing circuit release as their experience with *Seance on a Wet Afternoon* demonstrated. By 1964 they were in severe debt and forced to cease production. Writing in his autobiography, Bryan Forbes revealed his sense of exultation on the group's formation: 'I had . . . the great good fortune to be involved with people I respected who were embarked with me to give life and substance to cherished dreams. For the first time in my career I had control of my own material. There was nobody to blame but myself if I failed'.[30] His comments to Alexander Walker, however, reveal a more reflective tone: 'The experience proved to me that films can be profitable but must be well handled; and that the distribution company can come successfully out of the deal well in advance of the actual film producers having anything to show for their efforts.'[31] Walker himself sums up the evidence:

> The total negative cost of the seven AFM films made for Rank was £1,042,157, the distributor's gross was £1,820,940 giving them a gross profit of £778,783. But the producers of the films had to carry a loss of £142,934. Moreover, after the cinemas had taken their cut, some 65 per cent overall, there was still a return of over 75 per cent on initial capital investment. Thus the distributors did well, the exhibitors did very well, and the producers did modestly and were forced to shut shop.[32]

Concluding their analysis of tendencies towards monopoly in ownership of the media, Murdock and Golding suggest that 'economic pressure means a curtailment of available choices and alternatives . . . it means more of the same'.[33] What I have been arguing here, however, suggests a rather more complex, and less uniform, process. What is generally under-emphasised in the Murdock and Golding analysis is the difficulty of standardisation in media output. In part, this results from the peculiar nature of the film product. Audiences do not buy copies of a film but pay to see a film, presumably in the expectation of entertainment and pleasure. Unlike other commodities, such as cars or record players, films cannot all be the same, conforming to a single model, but must display variation and difference if audiences are to be attracted back to the cinemas. As such, film production displays a kind of double movement. On the one hand, the drive of the

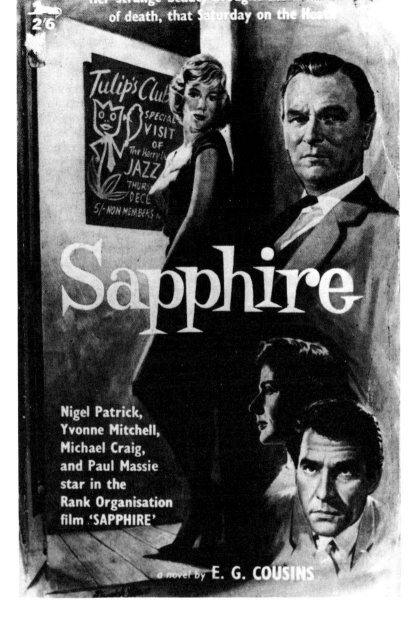

Her strange beauty brought the
of death, that Saturday on the Heath

Tulip's Club

SPECIAL
VISIT
OF
The Harry
JAZZ
THURS
DECE
5/- NON MEMBERS

Sapphire

Nigel Patrick,
Yvonne Mitchell,
Michael Craig,
and Paul Massie
star in the
Rank Organisation
film 'SAPPHIRE'

a novel by E. G. COUSINS

Selling pictures: the book of the film

47

industry is, as Murdock and Golding suggest, towards a regularisation, if not standardisation, of output through the repetition of the financially proven in terms of genres, cycles, sequels and the like.

On the other hand, new films cannot merely be duplicates but must show variation, something novel, if audience attention is to be maintained and their desire for pleasure fulfilled. Such a demand for novelty and variation becomes particularly acute in a period of crisis when set-backs in audience numbers require new initiatives and stratagems to counter them. In this respect, the role of the independents in the period under scrutiny became crucial. As I have suggested, two sets of conditions underpinned this. First, the changed economic situation of the cinema precipitated an internal reorganisation of the industry whereby the independent producer assumed a more prominent role in the initiation and development of film projects. Second, competition from television encouraged a concern with the production of films which might emphasise cinema's difference from television and help stave off decline. The general trend here, drawing primarily on American product, was towards the spectacular – the emphasis on colour and the large screen through the employment of CinemaScope, 3–D and the like.

What it also meant in the British context was the possibility of new contents: working-class realism, horror, more explicit sex. In respect of the latter, the increasing leniency demonstrated by censor John Trevelyan, on his arrival in office in 1958, probably gave Britain the advantage over their American counterparts who were yet to break free from the constrictions of the Hays code.[34] As such, it was the independent production companies who were increasingly well placed and most inclined to innovate. Woodfall provided the new working-class realism, Bryanston and AFM developed the 'social problem' film, Hammer offered horror, while the 'new comedy' of the *Carry On* films and the Boulting brothers emerged through independent companies as well.

But, of course, such developments still remained subject to the restraints of a system of distribution and exhibition dominated by the majors. As I have suggested, their response was initially conservative. Subsequently, it became more opportunistic. The weight of the system was, indeed, against change and balanced in favour of the tried and conventional. But in a period of decline it was proving increasingly difficult to gauge the market and be sure of what would sell – the unexpected success of a film like *Saturday Night and Sunday Morning* certainly helped prompt revisions of judgment. To deliberately misquote Althusser, in the last instance it was economic self-interest which was determinant. The strategy of the majors was thus to adapt and incorporate such innovations by making them their own. Thus, it was not long before even Rank had jumped on the social problem/realism bandwagon with productions of its own like *Flame in the Streets* (1961) and *The Wild and the Willing* (1962).

A good example of the mix of conservatism and adaptation can be found in the case of the x-certificated film. The 'x' certificate – for adults only – had been introduced by the British Board of Film Censors in May 1950 on the

Room at the Top (1959)

recommendation of the Wheare committee. Rank and ABPC experimented with one film each (*Detective Story* and *Murder Inc.*) but, fearful of the financial consequences, Rank announced they would not show 'x' films in future while ABPC would only exhibit those they considered 'outstanding'. Thus, between 1951 and 1957 Rank circuits exhibited only six (non-British) 'x' films. Rank appeared to continue its opposition into the 1960s. The 1960 Annual Report, for example, complained that the x-category film was being 'misused to the detriment of cinema entertainment' and they would continue to resist them. Rank chairman John Davis was still pursuing the theme in 1963 when he denounced those film producers who forgot that 'fundamentally a film production is intended to satisfy the demand for family entertainment'.[35] In this he seemed to have the support of the CEA General Council who likewise demanded 'the making for general release of films of family entertainment value' and 'the avoidance of themes and incidents which . . . were offensive to the reasonable taste and standards of those whose patronage was necessary to the health and future of the industry'.[36]

However, while the exhibitors and distributors continued to denounce the 'x' film, the figures were revealing a different pattern. Between 1958–61, for example, Rank circuits had exhibited 51 'x' features while ABPC, who had always had the advantage in this respect, screened 65.[37] *Films and Filming* pinpointed the discrepancy:

> We are surprised the producer associations are as polite to the CEA as they have been to date. Because the exhibitor mentality that wants to plunge the cinema back to pre-TV days is as out of touch with reality as the man who ordered the charge of the Light Brigade. There is no evidence that a good 'x' film does not make money: neither is there evidence that a bad 'U' film will.[38]

The explanation for the 'x' film's popularity, implicitly suggested by *Films and Filming's* reference to 'pre-TV days', once again seemed to lie with the rise in competition from cinema's small-screen opponent. For television was not only denying the cinema the family audience, so much beloved by Rank, but challenging its role as a provider of fictions. The 'x' film was thus a key weapon in differentiating cinema from TV, allowing representations unlikely to be seen in the home (e.g. horror and sex). Thus, when Jack Lee Thompson launched his well-publicised campaign against film censorship in 1958 one of the primary reasons cited was that of competition from the box.[39] And, once again, it was the independents who led the way in making the 'x' film acceptable while the majors trailed behind, only making peace with their moral objections once the economic benefits were clear. The successes of *Room at the Top* (the third most successful film of 1959) and *Saturday Night and Sunday Morning*, despite their 'x' certificates, were helpful in this respect. Needless to say, it was not long before Rank had an 'x' film of their very own – *The Wild and the Willing*.

Summing up, we might suggest that the organisation of the film industry represented a 'structure in dominance', in which the independents were accredited a 'relative autonomy'. But it was a *relative* one, subject to combine power in distribution and exhibition, and as such precariously founded. Once American capital became readily available (so that by 1967 American finance accounted for 75 per cent of British first features) the independents' economic base collapsed and companies like Bryanston and AFM went into decline. What, in effect, independence had implied was an increasing freedom to initiate projects and maintain control over methods of production; what it did not mean was an independence from the structure of combine control. The philosophy of Free Cinema had in fact already anticipated this. Although announcing its opposition to commercial cinema, and championing the cause of a 'personal' and 'poetic' cinema, it had no alternative base from which to develop its activities, except, ironically, commercial sponsorship or state funding (the British Film Institute Experimental Film Fund). Once such finance became unavailable, as with the withdrawal of funding by the Ford motor company, Free Cinema's survival was no longer viable.

As a final proviso, it should also be remembered that while innovations did occur it was still by and large against a backdrop of 'business as usual'. Despite their limited number of productions, Rank and ABPC were able to exploit their control over the circuits to ensure a maximum return. Six of the most profitable films for 1959–61, for example, were still Rank or ABPC productions. Writing in 1963, Penelope Houston suggested that the national cinema might most readily be summed up 'in a view of a boy and a girl wandering mournfully through the drizzle and mist of industrial Britain, looking for a place to live or a place to make love'.[40] How far this was the case for the average cinema-goer, however, is not at all clear. A year after *Room at the Top* it was *Doctor in Love* which topped the British box-office, with *Sink the Bismarck!* not far behind. Thus, while *A Kind of Loving*'s mournful couple proved sufficiently popular to make it the sixth most successful film of 1962, it was *The Guns of Navarone* which topped the group with Britain's No. 1 box-office attraction, Cliff Richard, not far behind with *The Young Ones*. All had not changed as utterly as some of the critics might have us believe.

Notes

1. A. Robert Gordon, Chairman of Sussex Cinematograph Exhibitors Association, reported in *Kinematograph Weekly*, 13 November 1958, p.7.
2. For an attempt to quantify the impact of television on cinema admissions, see John Spraos, *The Decline of the Cinema*, London, Allen & Unwin, 1962, Chapter 1.
3. Five trade organisations were involved: the British Film Producers Association (BFPA), the Association of Specialised Film Producers (ASFP), the Federation of British Film Makers, the Kinematograph Renters Society (KRS) and the Cinematograph Exhibitors Association (CEA).
4. Membership of the AITC was the same as FIDO but did not include the Federation of British Film Makers which was only founded in 1957 by a group of independent producers and directors (including the Boulting brothers, Frank Launder and Sidney Gilliat, and Michael Balcon).
5. *Distribution and Exhibition of Cinematograph Films* (Chairman: Arnold Plant), HMSO, 1949, p.27.
6. For a more detailed discussion of the industry during the 1930s and 1940s, see *The British Film Industry*, Political and Economic Planning (PEP), London, 1952. For an analysis of the impact of the 1927 Films Act, see Simon Hartog, 'State Protection of a Beleaguered Industry' in James Curran and Vincent Porter (eds.), *British Cinema History*, London, Weidenfeld & Nicolson, 1983.
7. These are calculations of my own, employing figures derived from P. Braithwaite, *The Cinema Industry 1950–70 and its Customers*, March 1970, and *The British Film Industry*, BFI Information Guide no.1, October 1980. Figures for seating capacity come from *Recommendations of the Cinematograph Films Council: Structure and Trading Practices of the Films Industry* (Chairman: S.C. Roberts), HMSO, 1964.

8. All figures derive from the *British Film Producers Association Annual Reports*, 1958–61. They do not include films in which Rank and ABPC had an indirect financial interest.
9. Lord Rank, quoted in Derek Hill, 'Where the Holy Spirit Leads', *Definition*, 3.
10. Edward Goring, *Daily Mail*, 5 November 1959.
11. Richard Attenborough, quoted in *Daily Mail*, 3 November 1959.
12. Michael Balcon, quoted in *Films and Filming*, June 1959, p.28.
13. 'The Man Behind the Angry Young Man' in *Films and Filming*, February 1959, p.9.
14. 'New Wave Hits British Films' in *Films and Filming*, April 1960, p.11.
15. Alexander Walker, *Hollywood England: The British Film Industry in the Sixties*, London, Michael Joseph, 1974, p.468.
16. Bernard Husra, 'Patterns of Power' in *Films and Filming*, April 1964, p.54.
17. 'The Money in Films' in *Films and Filming*, July 1963, p.9.
18. PEP, *The British Film Industry*, p.263.
19. Terence Kelly, *A Competitive Cinema*, London, The Institute of Economic Affairs, 1966, p.24.
20. *Films: A Report on the Supply of Films for Exhibition in Cinemas*, HMSO, 1966, p.12. Both Rank and ABPC were deemed guilty of monopoly, but the commission rejected the breaking-up of circuits or enforcement of competitive bidding as a solution.
21. *Survival or Extinction? A Policy for British Films*, London, ACTT, 1964.
22. Philip Oakes, *Sunday Telegraph*, 26 January 1964.
23. Harry Saltzman, quoted in *Films and Filming*, April 1960.
24. Harry Saltzman, quoted in Walker, *Hollywood England*, p.88.
25. Derek Hill, *Tribune*, 5 August 1960.
26. Harry Saltzman, quoted in *Evening Standard*, 28 November 1960.
27. Ibid.
28. Walker, *Hollywood England*, p.88.
29. Ibid, p.152.
30. Bryan Forbes, *Notes for a Life*, London, Everest Books, 1977, p.292.
31. Walker, *Hollywood England*, p.248.
32. Ibid.
33. 'Communications: The Continuing Crisis' in *New Society*, no.603, 25 April 1974, p.181.
34. For a discussion of Trevelyan's role here, see Guy Phelps, *Film Censorship*, London, Victor Gollancz, 1975.
35. Rank Annual Report, 1963, p.18.
36. CEA Annual Report, 1960, p.9.
37. Details of 'X' films distributed by the two circuits can be found in Neville March Hunnings, *Film Censors and the Law*, London, Allen & Unwin, 1967.
38. *Films and Filming*, July 1963, p.4.
39. See 'The Censor Needs a Change' in *Films and Filming*, June 1958, and *Kine Weekly*, 20 March 1958, p.3.
40. Penelope Houston, *The Contemporary Cinema: 1945–63*, Harmondsworth, Penguin, 1963, p.119.

3
Narrative and Realism

We cannot, as a consistent policy, play films which are unacceptable to the public as entertainment . . . I do feel that independent producers should take note of public demand and make films of entertainment value.[1]

If the economic organisation of the industry exerted pressures and constraints on the type of films which could be made, it did so not just in the specific ways discussed in the previous chapter, but also in a more general fashion. For films to be made within a commercial framework, they have to be seen as capable of generating a profit. Calculation of potential commercial success, however, is not simply a product of individual hunches and inspiration, but also of deeply ingrained notions of what kind of film is likely to appeal to audiences. While these may vary according to cinematic fashion, there remain, nonetheless, a set of underlying assumptions about what a film is and how it can 'entertain' and, thus, fulfil an audience's demands for both meaning and pleasure. Indeed, it is these assumptions which effectively underwrite the industry's requirement for a continuing audience by regularising what an audience can expect from a film and, in effect, 'promising' that their demands for a meaningful and pleasurable experience will be met. It is in this sense that Christian Metz argues that the 'cinematic institution is not just the cinema industry' but also 'another industry': 'the mental machinery . . . which spectators "accustomed to the cinema" have internalised historically and which has adapted them to the consumption of films'.[2]

One of the central expectations of spectators 'accustomed to the cinema' is that a film should, in some way or other, 'tell a story'. The conventions of the narrative guarantee that what an audience will see and hear will be interconnected and ultimately cohere into a meaningful whole while, as a number of critics have argued, their balancing of elements of novelty and repetition performs a critical function in the fulfilment of an audience's desire for pleasure. Moreover, as Richard Maltby suggests, this expectation of a 'story' is conventionally allied to that of 'realism', that an audience should be able to think of the story a film is telling them *as if* it were a 'real event':

That is not to say that they are intended to regard, say, the story of *The Wizard of Oz* as having actually taken place in front of a fortuitously-placed camera. But they are expected to operate a particular suspension of disbelief in which the mimesis of the photographic image reinforces the circumstantial and psychological 'realism' of the events those images contain, so that they can then presume upon those normative rules of spatial perception, human behaviour, and causality which govern their conduct in the world outside the cinema. Thus they may respond to the characters as if they were real people, and regard the story that is told through the characters as if it were unfolding before them without the mediation of cameras or narrative devices.[3]

Commercial cinema does, of course, rely on other expectations – those to do with stars and genres, for example – but it is these twin expectations of narrative and 'realism' which are, perhaps, the most fundamental in defining our sense of what constitutes a 'good' film and establishing the terms on which films are to be understood.

There is, of course, a vast literature on the subject of narrative and realism, in relation both to film and to the other arts, just as there is a wide diversity of issues raised by their analysis. My concern here, however, is fairly specific. My interest is not so much with these forms 'in themselves' as their inter-relationship with particular types of ideological 'content'. It is not just economic relations which exert pressures and set constraints upon film production but also these conventions. The conventions of narrative and realism are not simply neutral conductors of meaning but are already 'pre-stressed', encouraging the production of certain types of meaning while discouraging, or inhibiting, certain others. Thus, the ideas and attitudes expressed by the social problem film and the films of the British 'new wave' do not derive simply from the focus of their subject-matter but also from their deployment of certain types of conventions (in accordance with what an audience 'accustomed to the cinema' expects) which, then, inevitably structure and constrain the way in which that subject-matter can be presented in the first place. This is not, of course, a matter of strict and absolute determination. A diverse range of meanings can still be found within the parameters of narrative and realism. There are, however, general tendencies implicit in the logic of these conventions, especially as developed by the mainstream, commercial American and British film. What these are may be suggested by an initial consideration of some general, or 'model', characteristics.

Narrative

A definition of narrative, independent of any particular contents, is suggested by Tzvetan Todorov:

> The minimal complete plot consists in the passage from one equilibrium to another. An 'ideal' narrative begins with a stable situation which is disturbed by some power or force. There results a state of disequilibrium; by the action of a force directed in the opposite direction, the equilibrium is re-established; the second equilibrium is similar to the first, but the two are never identical.[4]

Thus, in the case of the detective story or film, a crime is committed (the disequilibrium), requiring a force directed in the opposite direction (the investigation), resulting in a new equilibrium (the capture of the culprit). Implicit in this requirement of a new equilibrium is the idea of a narrative 'solution'. As Seymour Chatman suggests, there is always a sense, in the traditional narrative, of 'problem-solving', of 'things being worked out in some way'.[5] To this extent, there is a presumption, built into the very structure of conventional narrative, that 'problems' can be overcome, can, indeed, be resolved. It is for this reason that Thomas Elsaesser has suggested a link between an ideology of 'affirmation' and the characteristic conventions of narrativity. As he explains, there is 'a kind of *a priori* optimism located in the very structure of the narrative . . . whatever the problem one can do something about it.'[6]

Inevitably, this has effects for the way in which both the social problem film and the films of the 'new wave' are able to deal with their subject-matter. Both loosely conform to the Todorov model. In the social problem film, it is characteristically a crime or 'deviant' action which represents the 'force' which initiates the plot; in the films of the 'new wave', it is more usually a socially or sexually transgressive desire. In both cases, it is in the nature of the conventions of narrative that these 'problems' be overcome. In this very presumption of a solution, so an atttitude toward the initial 'problem' is already taken. Thus, in the case of the social problem film, the articulation of the film's 'social problem' into the problem-solving structure of narrative necessarily implies that it too is capable of resolution. Russell Campbell, for example, has observed how the American 'social consciousness' movie may portray negative aspects of American society but only in so far as it then proceeds to assert 'the possibility . . . of corrective action' and celebrate 'the system for being flexible and susceptible to amelioration'.[7]

Such an ideological manoeuvre is, however, no accident but, more or less, a consequence of the conventions which have been adopted. For narrative form, of its nature, requires corrective action ('a force directed in the opposite direction') and amelioration ('the second equilibrium'), although this 'amelioration' need not, in itself, depend on the 'corrective action' of social reform. It may also result, as in the case of many British films, from the 'corrective action' of legal constraint and punishment. Either way, it is this need for some sort of narrative resolution which tends to encourage the adoption of socially conservative endings. An alternative account of social problems – say, poverty or juvenile delinquency – might, in fact, stress their intractability, their inability to be resolved, at least within the confines of the present social order. The solution to the problem of poverty, for example, would not be achieved by a tinkering with living standards but would depend on a transformation of the social structure whose constitutive principle is that of inequality. By contrast, the stress on resolution in the social problem film tends to imply the opposite – that these problems can indeed be overcome in the absence of wholesale change.

This is, however, a tendency rather than a strictly inevitable consequence of the problem-solving structure of narrative. It is possible, for example, to imagine a narrative in which revolution or radical social change *is* offered as a resolution. What makes this unlikely is not this convention alone but its combination with other characteristics of mainstream narrative cinema. The movement from disequilibrium to a new equilibrium is not, of course, random but patterned in terms of a chain of events which is not simply linear but also causal. One thing does not just happen after another but is *caused* or made to happen. For mainstream narrative cinema, it is typically individual characters who function as the agents of this causality. As Bordwell and Thompson suggest, 'natural causes (floods, earthquakes) or societal causes (institutions, wars, economic depression) may serve as catalysts or preconditions for the action, but the narrative invariably centres on personal, psychological causes: decisions, choices, and traits of character'.[8]

Thus, in the case of the British films under discussion, it is conventionally the actions or ambitions of an individual which precipitate the plot; the counter-actions of other individuals which provide the 'corrective action' and, thus, the establishment of a new equilibrium. Two main consequences stem from this stress on the individual as agent of causality. One, the 'making of things happen' is seen to derive from the aims and actions of individuals rather than social groups or collectives (or if the group does undertake an action it is usually under the wing of a clearly distinguished individual leader). Second, the origins and explanation of actions and events are seen to result primarily from the features of individual psychology rather than more general social, economic and political relations. It is for this reason that Russell Campbell complains that the social consciousness film concentrates on 'private, personal dramas' at the expense of 'political and social dimensions'.[9] Once again, this is not simply fortuitous, for individualisation, a stress on 'private, personal dramas', is already implicit in the conventions of mainstream narrative.

It is also this stress on the individual which helps confirm the ideology of containment characteristic of the narrative drive towards resolution. For the social problem film does not really deal with social problems in their social aspects at all (i.e. as problems of the social structure) so much as problems of the individual (i.e. his or her personal qualities or attributes). Thus, the responsibility for juvenile delinquency, for example, is attributed to the individual inadequacies of the delinquent (cf. *The Blue Lamp*, *Violent Playground*) rather than to the inadequacies of the social system itself. The social problem is a problem *for* society, rather than *of* it. And, obviously, if the causes of problems are located in the individual, then, *prima facie*, there is no necessity for a reconstruction of the social order. As a result, the endings characteristic of the social problem film tend to oscillate between one or other of two types, stressing, alternatively, the re-establishment of social order or the achievement of social integration. The latter is generally preferred by the more liberal, social-democratic form of problem film-making, emphasising a capacity for social absorption; the former is more hard-hat and conservative, underscoring the demand for punishment and discipline. Both successfully fulfil the requirement for a narrative resolution; but in neither is the social system itself put into question.

A similar set of issues are raised by the films of the 'new wave'. For despite their determination to represent the working class there is a sense in which the individualising conventions of classic narrativity render this problematic. Class is presented as primarily an individual, rather than collective, experience, a moral, rather than socially and economically structured, condition. As with the social problem film, the stress is on the inter-personal drama rather than the play of social and political forces. Inevitably, this has consequences for the types of resolution the films are then able to offer. Implicit in the structure of the narrative, its movement from one equilibrium to another, its relations of cause and effect, is a requirement for change. But, in so far as the narrative is based upon individual agency, it is characteristic that the endings of such films should rely on individual, rather than social and political, change. As a result, the resolutions characteristic of the working-class films tend to conform to one or other of two main types: the central character either 'opts out' of society or else adapts and adjusts to its demands. Alternative solutions, collective struggle or social upheaval are, in effect, excluded by the conventions upon which the films rely.

Realism
The stress on resolution and the role of the individual does not derive from the conventions of classic narrativity alone, however, but also from those conventions which are characteristic of the fictional film's particular brand of realism. A note of caution is appropriate here. There is probably no critical term with a more unruly and confusing lineage than that of realism. Such has been the diversity of art-works to which it has been applied, or for which it has been claimed, that its continuing use-value as either a descriptive or explanatory concept would often seem to be in question. Amidst this plurality of uses, one consistent implication does appear to survive: that the distinctive characteristic of realism resides in the ambition to, in some way or other, approximate reality, to show 'things as they really are'.[10] While this may be in agreement with a commonsense understanding of the term, it does not, in itself, resolve the critical difficulties. Part of the problem here derives from the very definition of reality itself. As Terry Lovell indicates, one of the main reasons for the diversity in application of the term has been the variation in accounts of the 'real' upon which they have been predicated.[11] What has counted as a valid or satisfactory approximation to reality has depended on the epistemology of the real which has been assumed in the first place.[12] The other part of the difficulty which then arises is that, even with agreement upon what constitutes reality, the sense in which an art-work may be said to approximate reality, or reveal things as they are, still remains problematic. No work can ever simply reveal reality. Realism, no less than any other type of art, depends on conventions, conventions which, in this case, have successfully achieved the status of being accepted as 'realistic'. It is this 'conventionality' of realism which also makes its usage so vulnerable to change. For as the conventions change (either in reaction to previously established conventions or in accordance with new perceptions of what constitutes reality) so too does our sense of what then constitutes realism.

The Angry Silence (1960)

This is quite clearly so of the cinema. Films which were accepted as 'realistic' by one generation often appear 'false' or 'dated' to the next. Thus, the working-class films of the British 'new wave', which initially appeared so striking in their 'realism', now appear 'melodramatic' and 'even hysterical' to at least one modern critic.[13] Indeed, even before the cycle of 'new wave' films came to an end, contemporary reviewers were already claiming that its 'realism' had become 'exhausted'.[14] As Thomas Elsaesser suggests, these films quite rapidly demonstrated a 'fundamental point' about 'realism': 'that it is purely conventional and therefore infinitely "corruptible" through repetition'.[15] If the British social problem and 'new wave' films are still to be regarded as 'realistic', then, it is clearly not in any absolute sense but only on the basis of the specific conventions which they employed and the relationship of these to those other conventions which the films saw themselves as superseding. As Raymond Williams suggests, it is usually a 'revolt' against previous conventions which characterises a 'break towards realism' in the arts.[16] He also distinguishes two types of 'revolt': on the one hand, an 'injection of new content' (new people, new problems, new ideas) but within a basically 'orthodox form'; on the other, an 'invention of new forms' which undermine 'habitual' versions of 'dramatic reality' and thus communicate new, and more fundamental, 'underlying realities'.[17] This is a distinction of relevance to an understanding of the British films. For, primarily, their 'break towards realism' was characterised by an 'injection of new content': new characters (the working-class, juvenile delinquents), new settings (the factory, the housing estate) and new problems (race, homosexuality). Although this was accompanied by a certain degree of stylistic novelty (location shooting, for example), it did not, in any major sense, entail the 'invention of new dramatic forms'. Both groups of film continued to depend on the conventions of narrative (albeit in slightly modified forms) and, indeed, the 'version of dramatic reality' made 'habitual' by the fiction film. The quarrel with earlier films was not so much with *how* they 'revealed reality' as with *what* they 'revealed'. To this extent, what both the new and the old films shared was a common epistemology: that it is basically through observation that the world is to be 'revealed' and understood (rather than, say, through a penetration of these appearances to the 'underlying realities' below).

It is for this reason that Colin MacCabe argues that, for all its local variations, the form of 'classic realism' remains substantially the same for not only the nineteenth-century novel but also the standard fictional output of film and television.[18] What he suggests remains a constant in all of these is not their 'content', but their formal organisation, their hierarchy of discourses, which is itself 'defined in terms of an empirical notion of truth'. This, he suggests, is to be understood in terms of the characteristic form of narration of the 'classic realist' text. MacCabe notes, for example, how the shift from first person narration to a form of impersonal narration in the nineteenth century novel results in a form of apparently anonymous enunciation whereby the 'truth' of what we read is guaranteed by the narrative itself rather than the voice of the author. This point is pursued in relation to the fiction film:

> [In the nineteenth-century realist novel] . . . the narrative prose achieves its position of dominance because it is in the position of knowledge and this function of knowledge is taken up in the cinema by the narration of events. Through the knowledge we gain from the narrative we can split the discourses of the various characters from their situation and compare what is said in these discourses with what has been revealed to us through narration. The camera shows us what happens – it tells the truth against which we can measure the discourses.[19]

What is specific to the 'classic realist' film, rather than the novel, is this articulation of narrative and vision. Like the novel, the 'classic realist' film is apparently 'author-less': the events of the narrative do not appear to proceed from anywhere in particular but simply unfold. But, unlike the novel, it is on the basis of what we see, what the camera shows, that the 'truth' of events is 'revealed'. It is in this sense that MacCabe identified the epistemology underlying 'classic realism' as 'empirical': for the knowledge which the 'classic realist' film delivers is founded, fundamentally, on sight: 'the unquestioned nature of the narrative discourse entails that the only problem that reality poses is to go and look and see what Things there are'.[20] His definition of 'realism', in this respect, does not depend on the 'mimetic accuracy', or, more properly, the 'diegetic plausibility', of what is shown, only on this dependency on the visible.[21] *The Sound of Music* (to take one of MacCabe's examples) is by this token as much an example of 'classic realism' as *Saturday Night and Sunday Morning*. It is also in this sense that it may be argued that, for all their novelty (particularly of subject-matter), the social problem film and those of the 'new wave' still remained attached to the basic conventions of 'realism', the 'habitual' versions of 'dramatic reality', made familiar by the mainstream fiction film.

The effect of this basic continuity in form, however, was a restriction on the type of knowledge of social 'realities' which these films could then provide. Knowledge of social and political relations, for example, does not derive from any simple observation of what is visible but also from an understanding of what is, in effect, invisible. It is partly for this reason that MacCabe complains that 'classic realism' is 'fundamentally inimical to the production of political knowledge'.[22] Christine Gledhill sums up the argument: cinematic 'realism' is dependent upon an 'ideological' proposition that 'reality equals what we can see, that perception equals cognition'. As a result, 'those material socio-economic forces which, though not immediately perceptible in phenomenal appearances, are responsible for their production' are, in effect, denied.[23] To take an example, it is possible to show how the poor live on the screen. It is rather more difficult, if not impossible, while remaining within the conventions of 'realism' to demonstrate how such poverty is the effect of a particular economic system or socially structured pattern of inequality. The mechanics of capitalism or distribution of wealth are not 'Things' which can be seen, except in their effects (e.g. disparate life-styles). As a result, the characteristic understanding of events provided by 'realism' will, of necessity, tend towards the personal, rather than the socio-political. In the case of *Days of Hope*, for example, it was an adoption of the form of realism which effectively militated against an explication of the social and economic forces leading to the collapse of the General Strike. The film's formal logic (with its dependency on the visible and hence the inter-personal) inevitably led towards conspiracy theory, the attribution of the strike's failure to the betrayal of trade union leaders. As Colin MacCabe explains:

In *Days of Hope* institutions have no reality over and above their ability to produce individuals who are betrayers. Instead of an analysis of the Labour Party or the TUC we are treated to the sight of the perfidy of a Wedgewood or a Thomas . . . There is . . . no possibility of an explanation of the structure and history of those institutions which would make the behaviour of a Thomas or a Wedgewood possible.[24]

It is also in this sense that the suppression of 'social and political dimensions' and corresponding concentration on 'private, personal dramas', already indicated as a characteristic of the social problem film and the working-class 'realism' of the 'new wave', does not derive from the individualising conventions of narrative alone but also from this emphasis on sight and dependency upon an epistemology of the visible.

MacCabe's observations do not apply solely to the kind of knowledge which 'classic realism' can deliver, however, but also to its form. The 'truth' provided by the narrative discourse, he argues, also guarantees a position to the spectator from which 'the material is dominated' and 'everything becomes obvious'.[25] It is in this sense, he goes on to argue, 'the classic realist text cannot deal with the real as contradictory'. It may expose contradictions but these are nonetheless contradictions which have already been resolved. What 'classic realism' cannot do is produce 'a contradiction which remains unresolved and is thus left for the reader (i.e. spectator) to resolve and act out'.[26] It is for this reason that the attitude of the social problem film so often appears to be comforting rather than disturbing. It exposes a social problem but only in a way in which it has been 'resolved' and the spectator is assured of his/her 'mastery' of it. The problem does not remain problematic and therefore up to the spectator to 'resolve and act out'. Inevitably, this has the effect of bolstering the films' tendencies towards socially conservative 'solutions'. It is not just the 'content' of the film which reassures an audience that the problem is 'under control' but also the way in which it is presented whereby the problem is now, in effect, put 'under the control' of the spectator.

There are, of course, problem films which adopt more liberal or reformist 'solutions' but even here the capacity to initiate social change, of the kind they would like, remains limited. *Victim*, for example, reveals the injustice of the law against homosexuals. But while the spectator is confirmed in a position from which he/she knows the law to be wrong they are, at the same time, denied any perspective for change. The film remains allied (in MacCabe's terms) to a social-democratic notion of progress: that the production of knowledge of injustices is sufficient in itself for wrongs to be somehow righted.[27]

Tensions in the text
The discussion so far has depended upon a relative degree of abstraction. It has avoided dwelling on the detail of individual films in favour of a consideration of more general, or ideal-typical, tendencies. In practice, the workings of individual films are more complex. Individual narratives, for example, are usually less neat and tidy than the general model suggests. The

movement from one equilibrium to another, in this respect, is never simply achieved but has to be worked through and worked for. In the process, there is always the possibility that the problem, force or threat which has set the plot in motion may defy or outrun the movement towards a resolution. As Stephen Neale suggests, 'a definitive equilibrium, a condition of total plenitude, is always an impossibility'.[28] This is often taken to be the case in 'film noir', for example. As Sylvia Harvey argues, the 'acts of transgression' (the causes of disequilibrium) committed by the film's female characters, and the vitality with which they are endowed, often produce 'an excess of meaning which cannot finally be contained . . . narrative resolutions cannot recuperate their subversive significance'.[29] Or, as Annette Kuhn puts it, there is 'an excess of narrative disruption over resolution'.[30] In the same way, the 'acts of transgression' characteristic of the social problem film and those of the 'new wave' may also prove too 'excessive' to be contained by the logic of repression implicit in the film's resolutions. The exhibition of active female sexuality in films like *I Believe in You*, *Cage of Gold* and *That Kind of Girl*, and of active male sexuality in a film like *Saturday Night and Sunday Morning*, to some extent remains defiant of the 'solutions' which the films are attempting to impose.

A sign of this 'stress' can often be detected in the endings themselves. The ending may itself appear 'excessive' or 'overloaded', as if in indication of the difficulty it is having in tying up all the narrative elements (e.g. *The Gentle Gunman*, *Spare the Rod*), or it may be inadequately integrated into the film's chain of causality, so that it appears either 'imposed' or peremptory (e.g. *Flame in the Streets*, *Beat Girl*). This is often the case in those films which adopt a sort of 'double ending': both the resolution proper and a concluding coda or epilogue which 'functions to represent the final stability achieved by the narrative'.[31] Here, the resolution may be adequately motivated by what has preceded but not the epilogue. Thus, in the case of *Violent Playground*, the action is brought to a successful resolution with the capture of Johnny; it is with the epilogue (and its reappearance of the black boy) that an apparent gap or deficiency in narrative motivation occurs which, in effect, 'jars' with what has gone before.

Such deficiencies in motivation do not apply to endings alone.[32] Specific events or actions within the narrative, for example, may also lack a proper integration and thus create an 'excess of meaning' which survives beyond the final resolution. As Maltby suggests, each scene in a conventional narrative film normally 'advances the plot by confirming the knowledge the audience have derived from previous scenes, and adding further information to it'.[33] It is also possible for scenes not to function in this way. In *Wind of Change*, for example, the scene between the white woman and the black youth is effectively 'redundant' in terms of the narrative's development. Not only does it fail to confirm the knowledge derived from previous scenes and then add to it, but the knowledge which it does provide actually runs counter to the knowledge which the other scenes have suggested. Because it is left 'outside of' the narrative's chain of causality, its significance remains 'unexplained', and still 'troublesome', by the time of the narrative's close.

Room at the Top (1959)

The same scene also provides an example of the way what we see can, on occasion, complicate rather than simply resolve our understanding of narrative events. As MacCabe's formulations make clear, it is what we see, rather than what we hear, which is privileged in the 'realist' film. And yet there is also a tendency, especially in the social problem film, to rely heavily on dialogue as a means of communicating the way in which a problem is to be understood. This is partly a consequence of the form itself: for if the film is to prove capable of expressing an attitude which can be generalised beyond the particularity of the story then this will, almost of necessity, fall on the shoulders of the dialogue. It is, indeed, this use of dialogue as a means of introducing more general themes and issues that so often ruptures the conviction of the 'realist illusion', especially if it appears not to grow 'naturally' out of the particular dramatic situation in which it is spoken. Colin's speeches in *Loneliness of the Long Distance Runner*, for example, were often criticised on precisely this basis. But, if the legitimacy of what we hear is dependent upon confirmation from what we see, then tensions can arise in the social problem film if this is not the case. This refers not just to the simple undercutting of what a character says by what is shown (e.g. the undermining of the mine-owner's speech by the image of troops at bayonet practice in *Days of Hope*) but to a more general 'unevenness' across a film as a whole. In the case of *Sapphire*, for example, the tension between what we are told about racial prejudice in the dialogue and what we actually see is not confined to a specific scene, nor explicitly marked as a discrepancy, but results from a more widespread failure of the conventions employed to substantiate the 'message' which the dialogue is attempting to offer. As a result, the 'solution' to the problem which the film provides is rendered only partly 'satisfactory'.

This question of vision is also raised, though in a different way, by the films of the 'new wave'. The 'motivation' of narrative elements in a film does not only refer to actions and events but also to how these actions and events are shown. The choice of an angle, camera position or movement, for example, will generally have a reason in terms of how what is shown is to be understood. A characteristic of many of the 'new wave' films, by contrast, is not only an inclusion of scenes or actions which are, strictly speaking, redundant but also an adoption of stylistic procedures which are themselves 'unwarranted'. Their use is, in effect, 'surplus' to the demands of the narrative. This is, of course, the case with other films but what is also striking is their degree of noticeability. As a result, they not only distract from the narrative but also undermine its 'anonymous enunciation' by rendering visible the authorship of the images. In this way, the knowledge provided by the films is, to some extent, qualified, for it also begins to raise the question of the position from which this knowledge is produced.

Conclusion

These are, of course, all points dealt with more fully in the discussion of individual films. The point to note is that although the conventions of narrative and realism can, indeed, be seen to exert pressures and constraints on the way in which the films are able to deal with their subject-matter, they do not necessarily do so in any simple and straightforward fashion. There is still a possibility of tensions and moments of excess or unease. My interest in such tensions, however, is limited. Kristin Thompson, for example, employs the idea of 'excess' as a means of encouraging the spectator to break free of conventional perceptual constraints and thus enjoy a new form of critical 'play'.[34] While this is a valid enough enterprise, in its own terms, it does seem content, as a *Screen* editorial suggests, with 'a celebration of the aesthetically aware individual spectator' as an end in itself.[35] What it ignores is the context of a film's production and reception and, thus, the inter-relationship between such textual 'excess' and the 'ideological effects' which any particular film may be seen to be producing. By contrast, the emphasis here *is* on these relations: the way in which such tensions and excess may also be seen to have a bearing on the ideological meanings (and, of course, tensions in meaning) which any particular film provides.

Notes

1. Rank Chairman John Davis, at the Dorchester Hotel, 12 December 1963, quoted by Husra in *Films and Filming*, April 1964, p.51.
2. Christian Metz, 'The Imaginary Signifier', *Screen*, vol.16, no.2, Summer 1975, pp.18–19.
3. Richard Maltby, *Harmless Entertainment: Hollywood and the Ideology of Consensus*, London, Scarecrow Press, 1983, p.187.
4. Tzvetan Todorov, *The Poetics of Prose*, Oxford, Basil Blackwell, 1977, p.111.
5. Seymour Chatman, *Story and Discourse: Narrative Structure in Fiction and Film*, Cornell, Cornell University Press, 1980, p.48.
6. Thomas Elsaesser, 'The Pathos of Failure: American Films in the 70s' in *Monogram*, October 1975, p.14.
7. Russell Campbell, 'The Ideology of the Social Consciousness Movie: Three Films by Darryl F. Zanuck', in *Quarterly Review of Film Studies*, vol. 3, no.1, Winter 1978, p.60.
8. David Bordwell and Kristin Thompson, *Film Art*, London, Addison-Wesley, 1980, p.58.
9. Campbell, 'The Ideology of the Social Consciousness Movie', p.57.
10. Raymond Williams, quoted in Terry Lovell, *Pictures of Reality: Aesthetics, Politics and Pleasure*, London, British Film Institute, 1980, p.65.
11. Lovell, *Pictures of Reality*, p.65.
12. It is for this reason that even modernists such as Brecht and Joyce have been conceived of as realists. See, for example, Damian Grant, *Realism*, London, Methuen, 1970, Chapter 1.
13. Robert Phillip Kolker, *The Altering Eye*, New York, Oxford University Press, 1983, p.90.
14. See review by Patrick Gibbs in *Daily Telegraph*, 9 February 1963.
15. Thomas Elsaesser, 'Between Style and Ideology' in *Monogram*, no.3, 1972, p.5.
16. 'Recent English Drama' in Boris Ford (ed.), *The Pelican Guide to English Literature 7: The Modern Age*, Harmondsworth, Penguin, 1970.
17. Ibid, p.497–9.
18. Colin MacCabe, 'Realism and the Cinema: Notes on some Brechtian Theses' in *Screen*, vol. 15, no.2, Summer 1974.
19. Ibid, p.10.
20. Ibid, p.12.
21. As Maltby suggests, the primary aesthetic end of mainstream narrative cinema is 'that of convincing the audience that the story being told is a plausible fiction (and) is, in that sense, real'. See Maltby, *Harmless Entertainment*, p.205.
22. Colin MacCabe, 'Days of Hope and the Politics of the past' in Claire Johnston (ed.), *History–Production–Memory*, Edinburgh '77 Magazine, no.2, Edinburgh Festival 1977, p.17.
23. Christine Gledhill, 'Recent Developments in Feminist Criticism' in *Quarterly Review* of *Film Studies*, vol.3, no.4, 1978, p.464.
24. MacCabe, 'Memory, Phantasy, Identity', p.16.
25. MacCabe, 'Days of Hope – A Response to Colin McArthur' in *Screen*, vol.17, no.1, Spring 1976, p.100. See also MacCabe, 'Realism and the Cinema', p.16.
26. MacCabe, 'A Response to Colin McArthur', p.100.
27. MacCabe, 'Realism and the Cinema', p.16.

28. Stephen Neale, *Genre*, London, British Film Institute, 1980, p.20.
29. 'Woman's Place: The Absent Family of Film Noir' in E. Ann Kaplan (ed.), *Women in Film Noir*, London, British Film Institute, 1978, p.33.
30. Annette Kuhn, *Women's Pictures*, London, Routledge & Kegan Paul, 1982, p.35.
31. David Bordwell, 'Happily Ever After, Part Two' in *The Velvet Light Trap*, no.19, 1982, p.4.
32. The term 'motivation' derives from Boris Tomashevsky, 'Thematics' in Lee T. Lemon and Marion J. Reis, *Russian Formalist Criticism: Four Essays*, Lincoln, University of Nebraska Press, 1965, pp.78–87.
33. Maltby, *Harmless Entertainment*, p.195.
34. 'The Concept of Cinématic Excess' in *Cine-Tracts*, vol.1, no.2, Summer 1977.
35. *Screen*, vol.17, no.2, Summer 1976, p.7.

4

The Social Problem Film

I

One of the most striking characteristics of the British cinema towards the end of the 1950s was its increasing concern to deal with contemporary social issues. Although individual examples of such films appeared earlier, it was in the period 1956–63 that this type of film became most prominent and topics such as juvenile delinquency, prostitution, homosexuality and race became standard preoccupations. The problem of youth was well ahead in this respect, giving rise to such titles as *The Blue Lamp* (1950), *I Believe in You* (1952), *Cosh Boy* (1953), *My Teenage Daughter* (1956), *It's Great to be Young* (1956), *Violent Playground* (1957), *The Young and the Guilty* (1958), *Too Young to Love* (1959), *Serious Charge* (1959), *No Trees in the Street* (1959), *Beat Girl* (1959), *Linda* (1960), *So Evil So Young* (1960), *Spare the Rod* (1961), *Some People* (1962), *Term of Trial* (1962), *The Boys* (1962), *The Wild and the Willing* (1962), *The Leather Boys* (1963), *That Kind of Girl* (1963), *The Yellow Teddybears* (1963), *The Party's Over* (1963) and *A Place to Go* (1963). The Teddy Boy also assumed a prominent role in movies such as *The Angry Silence* (1960) and *Flame in the Streets* (1961), while pop stars were employed to fill roles, not only in the expected musical vehicles, but in more serious social dramas as well. Cliff Richard appeared in *Serious Charge* (1959) and *Expresso Bongo* (1959), Adam Faith starred in *Beat Girl* (1959) and *Never Let Go* (1960), while Frankie Vaughan took part in *These Dangerous Years* (1957). The topic of race provided subject-matter for films such as *Sapphire* (1959), *Flame in the Streets* (1961) and *Wind of Change* (1961); while the subject of prostitution prompted *The Flesh is Weak* (1957), *Passport to Shame* (1959) and *The World Ten Times Over* (1963). Homosexuality was dealt with by *Oscar Wilde* (1960), *The Trials of Oscar Wilde* (1960), *Victim* (1961) and *The Pleasure Girls* (1963); while capital punishment, women in prison, artificial insemination, impotence, child molestation and rape also made an appearance in *Yield to the Night* (1956), *The Weak and the Wicked* (1953), *A Question of Adultery* (1958), *During One Night* (1961), *The Mark* (1961) and *Don't Talk to Strange Men* (1962). Although such a bare listing undoubtedly under-emphasises the variations in style and tone between films, what justifies their common grouping is their concern to raise topical social issues within a commercial cinematic form. They are, in effect, all examples of the British 'social problem' film and it is through them that many of the dominant ideological assumptions and attitudes of the period can be revealed.

Although it would be possible to discuss these films in a more direct relationship to the ideological themes already identified in Chapter One (e.g. affluence, classlessness, cultural degradation), I have opted, in the first instance, to focus on the work of two of the leading personalities associated with the problem film: the director, Basil Dearden, and writer, Ted Willis. It is *not* my intention, however, to offer a conventional auteurist analysis. As Stephen Neale suggests, 'no artist . . . is free . . . all forms of signification and meaning entail pressure (and) no subject is transcendent of such pressure or in control of its various modalities'.[1] Accordingly, my argument is not that Dearden and Willis can be identified as the conscious creators, or originators, of the meanings which I discuss but that the sources of these meanings are effectively 'overdetermined', deriving as much from the 'pressures' of the general ideological climate and the specific effectivities of the aesthetic conventions employed as the film-makers' own conscious 'intentions'.

Indeed, it is precisely because of these (generally unnoticed) pressures that the meanings which such films produce so often diverge from, even undercut, the intentions (in so far as we know them) that the film-makers actually profess. The reason for organising the discussion around the work of Dearden and Willis, then, is primarily heuristic. A focus on their work provides a relatively straightforward route through a diversity of material and also facilitates the drawing of connections across different films, not all of which, strictly speaking, can be counted as 'social problem' pictures. The conclusion of the discussion, however, does identify more directly the broader patterns of ideological meanings of which these films also constitute a part.

Of all the film-makers involved in the social problem film of the 1950s and 1960s, there can be little doubt that the largest and most consistent body of work belongs to director Basil Dearden and producer Michael Relph. Between 1947 and 1963 their films addressed practically all the main social problems characteristic of the era: anti-German feeling (*Frieda*), Ireland (*The Gentle Gunman*), youth (*The Blue Lamp, I Believe in You, Violent Playground, A Place to Go*), race (*Sapphire*), homosexuality (*Victim*), religious fundamentalism (*Life for Ruth*) and brainwashing (*The Mind Benders*). It was a type of cinema, moreover, which appeared to epitomise the 'best' of British film-making in the 1950s. *Sapphire*, for example, was voted the 'Best British Film' of 1959 by the British Film Academy. What appeared to distinguish such films, and win them critical reward (such as the BFA award) was their apparent determination not just to provide 'mere entertainment', but to confront 'real situations' and 'important' social issues and, in so doing, to make a positive contribution to the 'good' of society. A spokesman for Rank, the distributors of *Sapphire*, explained his belief in the cinema's 'tremendous influence' and the value of the film in promoting understanding of 'the problem of race'.[2] Michael Relph himself argued that, because the cinema was 'genuinely a mass medium', so it must also display 'social and educative responsibilities as well as artistic ones'.[3]

To this extent, the work of Dearden represents a continuity with the ideas of documentary developed by John Grierson in the 1930s. As Grierson himself pointed out, 'it is worth recalling that the British documentary group began not so much in affection for film *per se* as in affection for national education . . . if I am to be counted as the founder and leader of the movement, its origins certainly lay in sociological rather than aesthetic ideas'.[4] However, while Grierson assumed this emphasis on education and propaganda for democracy implied a privileged role for documentary, there was no particular reason why such functions should not also be performed by the fiction film. The mediating influence between documentary and the social problem film, in this respect, was provided by Ealing, whose wartime production programme not only drew upon documentary personnel (such as Alberto Cavalcanti and Harry Watt) but assimilated documentary ideas (a commitment to 'ordinary' people, damped-down narratives, location shooting) into its fictional dramas. It was in such a context that Dearden began his career as a film director (with *The Bells Go Down* in 1943) and it was also for Ealing that he directed the first of his social problem pictures (beginning with *Frieda* in 1947).

Central to Ealing's wartime mix of social purpose and fictional realism was the idea of a national community, pulling together to win the war. As Charles Barr suggests, it was also an idea which was to continue to preoccupy Ealing once the war had been won: first, as the 'daydream of a benevolent community' to be found in the post-war comedies and, then, as the 'backward-looking community, with no dynamism' of the late 1950s.[5] Although Dearden's work is distinct from much of this general tendency, in so far as it does not normally employ comedy, it does nonetheless display the same recurrent concern with community, and with wartime Britain as the pivotal expression of such a unity. Both *The Ship that Died of Shame* (1955) and *The League of Gentlemen* (1960) revolve around the problem of post-war experience and the inability of peacetime society to provide the excitement and solidarity represented by the war. As Norman Hyde (Jack Hawkins) puts it in *The League of Gentlemen*: 'I served my country well . . . and was suitably rewarded . . . by being made redundant'. In both films, ex-servicemen come together to engage in para-military activities. The trio in *The Ship that Died of Shame* retrieve their old ship to engage in smuggling while the gang in *The League of Gentlemen* plan and execute a bank robbery with military precision. But because both enterprises are illegal their attempts to reconstruct wartime community are necessarily doomed to failure and futility. The values may retain their potency but the methods are no longer appropriate.

As a result, the post-war films of Dearden are less concerned with a literal reconstruction of wartime community than with the exploration of the conditions necessary to the construction of a new community or consensus appropriate to peacetime. To this extent, the concern of Dearden's films with social problems can be understood. For it is precisely such problems (for example, youth and race) which threaten social stability and undermine the community or consensus of post-war Britain. The logic of the Dearden social problem movie is then towards an integration, or an assimilation, of troubling elements through an appeal to 'good sense' and reason. In practice, such an assimilation tends to be more problematic. For at the heart of the social problem in Dearden's films lies an excess of sex and violence, which constantly belies the programme of rational control and containment. As Barr has suggested: 'Poverty of desire comes to form an inevitable accompaniment to – no, it is deeper than that: constituent of – the notions of social responsibility and community which the British cinema, in the war years and after, so assiduously reflects and promotes'.[6] Such hesitation is appropriate: for in the Dearden films repression is not just coincidentally linked with social community but presumed by it, the price to be paid for its achievement. As such, the films' apparent liberalism, their programmes of 'rational' assimilation, tend to be undercut by the conservatism of their sexual repression. The opening title of *The Mind Benders* informs us that the film was suggested by experiments, being carried out in certain American universities, on 'the reduction of sensation'. The 'experiments' performed by the Dearden social problem films might be said to have a similar effect.

A useful starting-point, in this respect, is provided by *The Blue Lamp* (1950), the first of four Dearden films to tackle the problem of juvenile delinquency. The novelty and contemporaneity of the delinquent phenomenon is firmly established by the film's opening which in quasi-documentary style (anonymous voice-over, non-narrative information, a montage of newspaper headlines), locates the particularity of the story's events against a general background of violent crime and juvenile unrest. A new breed of 'restless and ill-adjusted youngsters', produced by the family breakdowns of war and lacking 'the code, experience and self-discipline of the professional thief', now exist as 'a class apart'. Standing outside of the established social order, they represent the new threat to the post-war settlement and a dramatic cypher for the struggle between order and chaos, the old and the new, reason and unreason. What is at stake here is underlined by the duality structured into the film's representation of youth. On the one hand, the film offers 'natural' progression, the son's inheritance of the father's role, the renewal of the old by the young. George Dixon (Jack Warner) directs an enquirer to Paddington station at the film's beginning; Andy Mitchell (James Hanley), his 'adopted' son, does the same at the film's close. On the other hand, there is the 'restless and ill-adjusted' Riley (Dirk Bogarde), who opposes this order, rejecting the old and killing the Dixon father-figure outside a cinema (below an ironic advertisement for 'Granny Get Your Gun'). Thus, while Mitchell's progression is linked to his absorption into the community (the family, the police, the final chase), Riley remains set apart, both in life-style (an isolated bed-sit) and absence of psychological or social purpose.

The indices of his threat, however, are clear enough: an ever-escalating violence and sexual menace. For the film, these appear to go hand in hand, linked by the phallic power of the gun. Riley uses it to threaten Diana (Peggy Evans) and explains its 'excitement' before taking her into his arms. In reimposing order, the film is thus rejecting not only Riley's violence but his sexuality as well. As Barr suggests, Diana's 'salvation' implies a rejection of both, a renunciation of her surrender to each of the impulses.[7] And, if this is true of Diana, so is it also of the community which rallies round to destroy Riley. For both the key forms of community celebrated by the film are, in effect, drained of sexuality. The family is represented by the elderly Dixon couple whose surrogate 'son' is immaculately conceived via 'adoption'. The police, on the other hand, are predominantly male with female characters assigned to narratively marginal or subservient roles (the most conspicuous female presence in the police canteen being that of the serving lady!). The model of community represented by the police is clearly an extension of the all-male group characteristic of the wartime films (e.g. *The Bells Go Down*), but running alongside it seems to lurk a suspicion of women and the threat they might pose to male camaraderie.

Both *The Ship that Died of Shame* and *The League of Gentlemen* are conspicuous in their absence of female characters. The death of Bill Randall's (George Baker) fiancée in *The Ship that Died of Shame* is almost a prerequisite for the action to really begin, while Lexy's (Richard Attenborough) desertion of the all-male group for a night in female company is rewarded with a fine in *The League of Gentlemen*. Similarly, the job of the police force in *The Blue Lamp* is not only to fight crime but regulate sexual deviance as well. The dramatic details employed to sketch in the typical work of the police force consistently imply this: the young girl who can't repeat what was said to her by a man, the young boy who is asked if he's come to give himself up for bigamy, the young couple cuddling in a shop doorway, interrupted by the beam of a police torch and forced to move on. In an analogous manner, the illegitimate liaison of Jordan (Norman Shelley) is 'punished' by the robbery of his jewellery shop. As Barr once again indicates, the film's plot corresponds exactly to the Todorov model: 'order shown, disrupted, restored'.[8] The restoration of that order, however, would appear to have its price: the reduction of sensation.

This fear of the socially disruptive potential of sexual desire is also in evidence in Dearden's next film, *Cage of Gold* (1950). Although not a social problem film itself, it is nonetheless worth examining for an explication of the attitudes and assumptions which come to form the bedrock of nearly all the social problem films that follow. As Annette Kuhn has suggested, it is a recurrent concern of mainstream cinema, particularly American, to recuperate woman to a 'proper place'. 'Woman' commonly constitutes the 'troubling' that sets the plot in motion, with resolution dependent on either the punishment of the 'woman' for her transgressions or her acceptance of home and marriage (her 'proper place').[9] *Cage of Gold* is similar. Like *It Always Rains on Sunday* and *Brief Encounter* before it, the film focuses upon a female character whose sexual desires pose a threat to conventional domestic order. As such, it is the logic of the plot to work out both the destructive consequences of such desires and the construction of a new stability in which the woman will accept her proper place. Formally, the film represents something of a hybrid: one which might most accurately be designated 'noir melodrama'. Like melodrama, the focus of the film is primarily domestic,

71

concerned with home and family; in structure and style, however, it is more characteristically 'noir'. As in 'noir', the plot is initiated by a chance encounter which leads first to passion and then destruction culminating in a nightmare shoot-out with the woman brandishing the gun. As in 'noir', the plot is convoluted and organised around repetition. Also as in 'noir', the style makes a pronounced use of chiaroscuro effects, imbalanced compositions and heavily angular shots.

The crucial difference from 'film noir', however, lies in terms of characterisation. Whereas 'noir' is conventionally organised in terms of a madonna/whore, virgin/femme fatale duality, in *Cage of Gold* this division is expressed in relation to the male characters. These are, however, the structural correlatives of the female duality, what Paul Hoch has distinguished as the division between the 'playboy' and the 'puritan'. As he explains, 'For the past three thousand years the manly idol of the leading social classes has oscillated between these two basic roles: on the one hand, a sort of hard-working, hard fighting "puritan" hero who adheres to a production ethic of duty before pleasure; on the other, a more aristocratic "playboy" who lives according to an ethic of leisure and sensual indulgence.'[10] Thus, just as the male hero of 'film noir' faces a choice between the exciting sensuality of the femme fatale and the respectable niceness of 'the girl next door', so Judith (Jean Simmons) faces a similar choice of male characters in *Cage of Gold*. Alan (James Donald) represents the 'puritan', the doctor who gives up his prosperous West End practice in favour of his father's in Battersea, and thus renews tradition after the fashion of Mitchell in *The Blue Lamp*. By contrast, Bill (David Farrar) is a 'Champagne Charlie', a 'playboy' dedicated to sensual indulgence and leisure. Like the hero of *The Ship that Died of Shame*, post-war society has rendered him redundant and he has turned to smuggling. His similarity with the 'noir' femme fatale is striking. His allure is predominantly sexual but used to deceitful, criminal and acquisitive ends. He has a disdain for work and, despite his smuggling activities, is effectively kept by his mistress (in the 'cage of gold' of the film's title).

While it is the femme fatale's portrait in *Laura* and *Woman in the Window* which seems to inspire male fantasies, so is it Bill's portrait in *Cage of Gold* which becomes the locus of desire, as the camera moves in on the bare canvas to begin a semi-subjective sequence of romantic passion (similar to the revelations of dark visions through the mirror in *Dead of Night*). Like the 'postman' to whom he refers, Bill rings twice, haunting (almost literally in so far as he had been presumed dead) marital and familial security. One shot sums this up eloquently. The camera follows Bill into the Palette club but halts in front of the table where Judith and Alan are sitting, while Bill takes a table behind. Judith and Alan occupy the foreground, facing each other across the table; but the pull of the eye is irresistibly towards Bill behind them, centre frame and facing the camera directly, a potentially troubling presence who refuses to go away.

It is Bill's appearance, then, that triggers off the narrative and his disposal which is necessary for the plot to be resolved. As in 'noir', giving in to

Cage of Gold (1950)

passion must prove destructive; but, unlike 'noir' where such destruction normally takes its toll of both characters (*Out of the Past*, *Double Indemnity*), *Cage of Gold* wishes to save its heroine. How this is achieved is of interest. Facing blackmail and the upset of her second marriage, Judith agrees to meet Bill at his lodgings, where she ends up drawing a gun . . . However, the film withholds an actual shot of the killing and, in a sort of visual rhyme, cuts from the camera moving in on the gun barrel to the camera pulling out from a car hooter, being pressed in agitation by Alan. Two shots later, we return to Judith, now seen fleeing down the stairs from Bill's rooms. Alan confronts her before proceeding up the stairs to discover Bill dead.

In Barthesian terminology, this constitutes a 'snare': 'a kind of evasion of the truth' characteristic of the hermeneutic code of narrative.[11] For although the organisation of shots clearly implicates Judith as the killer, it is only towards the end of the film that the identity of the real murderer is revealed as Bill's mistress, Madeleine (Madeleine Lebeau). Clearly, the film wants to have its cake and eat it. Judith is, in effect, morally culpable, requiring punishment, if not for murder, then for her sexual excess. But, in a manner characteristic of the social problem films, the movie wishes to allow for reform, the possibility of rehabilitation. By use of the 'snare', the film is able to 'double' its ending. The logic of the drama is destruction; by withholding a shot of the actual killing, it is able to retrieve the heroine for home and marriage. The corollary of salvation is then projection, the externalisation of violence in the form of the 'Other': the foreigner and night club owner, outside of home, marriage and public service.

But, as the idea of projection implies, such an externalisation is no more than the outward sign of a repression that is within; and it is the reality of such repression that the film finds hard to disavow. As in 'film noir', the acts of transgression possess a vitality which the return to normality can't quite suppress, or, as Barr suggests, 'in this film the woman is at least *there*, with a spiritual and sensual existence which – simply by being represented – splits the film apart'.[12] Thus, while the short sequence of Judith and Bill's courtship is marked as 'subjective' (the camera's forward movement into the canvas, the dissolves and abstracted compositions) and thus as somehow invalid, it is retrospectively acknowledged to have taken place, and thus as giving expression to a libidinal energy which has been otherwise repressed and, indeed, is due to be repressed again. Instead of sensuality, the film offers family, conceived as a kind of service. Just as Alan's life is one of doctoring, so Judith's lot (in a sort of expiation for her sins) becomes the nursing of her invalid father-in-law. Appropriately, Judith's appearance becomes more restrained and severe, stripped of its earlier glamour. Like the Dixons in *The Blue Lamp*, their marriage is asexual with no child of its own, only Judith's son by Bill, an extinguishment of passion underlined by Bill's fusing the Christmas tree lights shortly before the child's party.

This also gives a significance to the apparently inconsequential joke which begins and ends the movie. Alan's father is first introduced twiddling the knobs of his son's wireless and complaining about the 'comics and crooners' he seems unable to escape. As the film closes, the same character is again at work with the wireless. Confronted with yet another 'crooner', he quickly turns to the more proportioned sounds of the Third Programme, before sitting back in contentment. At one level, a sign of Ealing's characteristic and increasingly pronounced opposition to commercialism, as opposed to public service, at another, it also suggests a fear of the sensuality that popular culture, and music and dancing in particular, seem to represent. In both other Ealing films (*It Always Rains on Sunday*, *Dance Hall*) and Dearden's own (*Pool of London*, *I Believe in You*, *Violent Playground*, *Sapphire*), the world of music and dance is associated with sexual desire and social or family disruption. For Dearden, music and dancing is inextricably bound up with the primal and dionysiac, consistently upsetting rational order and control. It is thus no accident that Judith's 'descent' into libidinal fantasy should begin with a close-up of beating drums; the restoration of order, with classical music on the Third Programme!

I Believe in You is the second of Dearden's youth movies and presents something of a fusion between *The Blue Lamp* and *Cage of Gold*. Like *The Blue Lamp*, there is an emphasis on the renewal of tradition, with 'novice' Henry Phipps (Cecil Parker) taking over from father-figure Dove (George Relph) in his position in the probation service. There are, however, slight differences in emphasis. Phipps is an upper-class character who himself is changed in the course of the film (thus anticipating *Violent Playground*). Like so many of Dearden's characters, post-war society had made him redundant: 'The Colonial Office finding itself so short of colonies had made a lot of cuts. I was one of them.' But, unlike *Cage of Gold*, *The Ship that Died of Shame* and

74

The League of Gentlemen, he does not turn to crime but to public service. In the process, he must lose something of his class hauteur, no longer 'planning for people' but 'with them'. For, although Dearden's films may be 'establishmentarian', they also manifest a certain disillusionment with the 'old gang' and their responsibility for the war.[13] As Barr points out, the only other character, apart from Riley, who is excluded from *The Blue Lamp*'s community is the upper-class lady in the sports car, warned by Mitchell to 'drive more carefully in the future'.[14] Accordingly, Phipps' entry into the film's community is accompanied by a certain amount of humiliation: he sacrifices taxis for public transport, extends his knowledge of London beyond Knightsbridge and finally ends up dirty and bedraggled under a lorry with Hooker (Harry Fowler). The community which Phipps thus enters, however, represents a considerable degeneration from *The Blue Lamp*, providing little more than a gallery of Ealing 'eccentrics', whose harmless crankery seems to account for the bulk of the probation service's work.

In contrast to these primarily elderly eccentrics, there are, however, the more problematic cases of youth. Elaborating on the 'war baby' thesis presented by *The Blue Lamp*'s voice-over, *I Believe in You* begins to flirt with environmentalism, emphasising, in particular, the background of broken homes (in Hooker's case, caused by the loss of a father during the war) from which its juvenile delinquents emerge. However, such an emphasis only goes so far, undercut, in the end, by 'the widespread British inability to take psychology, sociology and, indeed, anything but knockdown fundamentalist notions of responsibility seriously'.[15] Two main strategies work to enforce this. First, by 'balancing' the youths from disadvantaged backgrounds with the upper-class Hon. Ursula (Ursula Howells), whose wartime loss of a lover has led to persistent drunkenness, the film effectively disavows the significance of class. While class background may appear to be a determinant, its influence is cancelled out by the variety of social backgrounds from which the probation service's clients are drawn. Second, this is reinforced by structuring a contrast within each class to bring out the morally redeeming value of choice. Thus, the Hon. Ursula is matched with Matty (Celia Johnson) whose husband was likewise killed in the war but who has turned to service not deviance.

Similarly, with the working-class youths, Ray Durgnat has complained that the film only 'skims the surface' because 'its portrayal of the reform of normal, misled but basically nice people leaves out . . . those delinquents who are nasty or neurotic or both'.[16] In fact, he is wrong. For just as Mitchell was counterposed to Riley in *The Blue Lamp*, so *I Believe in You* contrasts its 'basically nice' and reformable characters to the 'nasty' and irreformable youths who escape the net of benign authority. 'Each society possesses . . . a set of images of who constitutes the typical deviant', comments Stanley Cohen. 'Is he an innocent lad being led astray, or is he a psychopathic thug?'[17] In Dearden's films he tends to be both and it is precisely such a duality which lies at the heart of their treatment of youth (and, in turn, effectively undermines the sociological accounts of their behaviour).

I Believe in You (1952)

As in *The Blue Lamp*, the representation of the problem of youth is as much in sexual as criminal terms. Phipps' first encounter with Norma (Joan Collins), for example, is when she seeks refuge in his flat and promises to 'do anything' in return. Norma, indeed, represents something of a scaled-down version of Judith in *Cage of Gold*, rich in sensuality (Durgnat argues that her 'sullen, electric presence . . . dominates the whole film') but torn between its expression or suppression.[18] As with Judith, this dilemma is concretised in terms of competing male types: Hooker's 'innocent' but 'led astray' delinquent or Jordie's (Laurence Harvey) menacing 'psychopath'. Like Bill in *Cage of Gold*, Jordie's threat is first contained (he's sent to prison) but then re-emerges, disrupting the whole process of reform which has been taking place in his absence. How this occurs is significant. For what Jordie incites in Norma is not crime but her sensuality, once again expressed in terms of pop music and dancing. Stylistically, Harvey's re-appearance initiates a submergence into a 'noir' world at odds with the evenly lit and balanced compositions of the rest of the film. Marking a similar descent as the drums in *Cage of Gold*, the film dissolves into a close-up of a juke-box followed by a low-angle close-up of Norma, swaying from side to side. The camera proceeds to move down her body, capturing the way she fingers her glass, before coming to rest on her foot, moving as if by compulsion. Music is a snare, a fatal incitement to surrender to bodily impulses. What then follows is a desperate struggle between rational control and dionysiac descent. The pace of the editing intensifies with a rapid inter-cutting of shots of Norma's face, her foot, the juke-box, dancing couples and Jordie coming towards her. At first she submits but then resists, pulling away and abandoning her partner. The final image is of Jordie in sinister close-up, shot half in light and half in shadow, in a signification of dementia so characteristic of many of Dearden's films (cf. *The Gentle Gunman*, *Life for Ruth* and *The Mind Benders*).

Like Judith in *Cage of Gold*, Norma's 'salvation' is dependent on self-denial. As she puts it to Hooker the next day, 'I don't want a good time'. By once again running criminality and sexuality together, the logic of the film's conclusion is inescapable: the 'cure' for delinquency and the price of rehabilitation into the community is once again a suppression of sexuality, a reduction of sensation.

The film's stratagem then is not just reform *à la* Durgnat but also active repression. Just as Bill had to be expelled from the community in *Cage of Gold* and Riley in *The Blue Lamp*, so now the threat represented by Jordie must be 'destroyed'. How this is legitimated within the film's basically reformist brief is characteristic of Dearden's work as a whole. It represents what might be called the 'escalation' effect, whereby one act of deviance is seen to lead inevitably to evermore threatening forms of crime. Just as our culture imagines smoking a joint to lead inexorably to the heroin needle, so in Dearden's films there is a spiral of delinquency inevitably culminating in gun-toting. Thus, just as Riley's use of a gun justified his suppression in *The Blue Lamp*, so Jordie, whose threat up till now has primarily been sexual, calls retribution upon himself once he too turns to guns. Once Jordie is safely removed, the film's resolution in terms of Hooker and Norma's prospective marriage can enjoy a free passage.

Although *I Believe in You* finds its natural successor in *Violent Playground*, the summation of Dearden's interest in juvenile delinquents, his next film, *The Gentle Gunman* (1952) also provides some intriguing points of comparison. Although it deals with the problem of Ireland, and in particular the IRA campaign begun in London during the Second World War, Ray Durgnat found its appearance so perplexing that he assumed it must really be about juvenile delinquency.[19] Characteristic English parochialism although this undoubtedly is, to be fair to Durgnat the attitudes expressed in the movie do display a remarkable homology with those of the juvenile delinquent movies. Dearden had already given some attention to the Irish in *The Halfway House* (1944). There they had been berated for being insufficiently belligerent and were called upon to revoke their neutrality. Ironically, the complaint of *The Gentle Gunman* is now the reverse. The Irish have become far too violent and, like the delinquents in *The Blue Lamp* and *I Believe in You*, are acting entirely contrary to the canons of reason.

Once again, the link between violence and sexuality is explicit. Unlike Diana in *The Blue Lamp*, who ultimately turns her back on Riley's violence, her counterpart in *The Gentle Gunman*, Maureen (Elizabeth Sellars), functions as an incitement to violence, a femme fatale in thrall to blood-sacrifice. For her, sexuality is clearly signalled as a reward for violent endeavour and she quickly transfers her affections to Matt (Dirk Bogarde) once his elder

The Blue Lamp (1950)

brother, Terence (John Mills), the 'gentle gunman' of the film's title, abandons his commitment to violent nationalism. As in *The Blue Lamp*, possession of the gun assumes explicitly phallic connotations as Maureen's admiring (if stylistically demented gaze) is intercut with Matt, taking aim and having bullets poured into his cupped hands.

As such, the film's rejection of violence necessarily requires a rejection of Maureen, and the sexuality which she has to offer. This is emphasised by a closing scene, when in an almost tableau-like shot we see Matt and Terence distributed compositionally in the rear and foreground of the frame, with Maureen placed between them. Matt moves forward, hesitates for a moment beside Maureen, then carries on, taking off with Terence. The following shot leaves Maureen alone and isolated. It is the logical implication of the two brothers' abandonment of violence; but as a narrative, and by implication ideological, conclusion, it appears curiously strained. Not only does it refuse the conventional happy ending of boy getting girl (cf. *I Believe in You*) but in the way that it does so suggests an anxiety about heterosexuality *per se*. In the absence of any other young female characters in the film, the rejection of Maureen becomes tantamount to a rejection of female sexuality *per se*. It is the restoration of male camaraderie which closes off the narrative and in a way, moreover, that is ambivalently homosexual, especially given the Bogarde persona. That this is, indeed, a problematic resolution is suggested by the imagery of the film itself. Matt and Terence depart along a bare and deserted road, away from the only community they know and towards a destination which remains obscure. It is, moreover, the same spot from which Johnny (James Kemeny) had earlier departed to meet his death in the North and, as such, it prompts associations with fatalism.

As its title suggests, this problem of violence recurs in Dearden's next film to deal with juvenile delinquency, *Violent Playground* (1958). Inspired by the Liverpool Juvenile Officers Scheme (LJO) – 'an important and successful development outside the field covered by the probation service' – the organising principle of the film is once again reform.[20] But, as with *I Believe in You*, the film displays a distinct uneasiness about how far the process of reform can go. Indeed, in the case of the film's central character, Johnny (David McCallum), the scheme proves a failure and once more the ostensive liberalism of the reform position gives way to a logic of punishment and repression.

To a large extent, this is structured by the film's choice of conventions, in this case those of the criminal investigation, which effectively circumscribes the film's discourse on the prevention of juvenile delinquency within the confines of crime detection and solution. Thus, while CID man Truman (Stanley Baker) is taken off the case which initiates the film (an arson attack) it is through his transfer to juvenile liaison, by bringing him into contact with Johnny, that the crime can be solved. In this way, the focus on prevention does not so much displace the process of law enforcement as temporarily suspend it. The ideology of reform represented by the work of juvenile liaison must ultimately surrender to the requirements of the law and order position, of bringing to justice, implicit in the investigation format.

How this works out in detail can be seen in relation to the film's two main characters, Truman and Johnny. Like Phipps in *I Believe in You*, Truman is changed in the course of his experiences as a juvenile liaison officer. He is a bachelor, scathing of psychology and a firm believer in discipline (or 'walloping them'). As he himself puts it: 'I don't even like kids. I'm clumsy. I'm tactless. I'm brutal'. His transfer to juvenile liaison thus sets in motion a process of humanisation. Through his contact with the Murphy family, he begins to understand the problems imposed by bad housing and broken families while his contact with the school headmaster, Heaven (Clifford Evans), and the work of the youth club develops an appreciation of the virtues of a liberal educational philosophy (particularly in its effects on the two Murphy youngsters). Thus, by the halfway stage of the film his attitudes have undergone a dramatic reversal. He admits to no longer thinking like a policeman, takes exception to a colleague's reminder of his earlier disciplinarian prescriptions and successfully inverts the complaint of being 'a bachelor' by using it as a reprimand against an angry stallholder, the victim of juvenile theft. Meanwhile, his own bachelor status is at risk through a developing romantic interest in Kathy (Anne Heywood).

In this respect, the film's movement is logical and accumulative, with the experiences undergone by Truman marking a re-emphasis on prevention rather than punishment. But it is a re-emphasis of only limited scope. For what haunts and ultimately undermines this rational march forward is the

79

position occupied by Johnny. Catherine Belsey has noted how the process of 'scientificity', of explicit rational deduction, in the Sherlock Holmes novels is 'haunted by shadowy, mysterious and often silent women' who elude and ultimately subvert the detective's project.[21] The role of Johnny is similar. By virtue of his associations with violence and 'irrationalism', his presence is consistently marked as a threat, deflecting, eluding and ultimately undermining the project of reform which the film seeks to endorse.

The nature of his threat is once again clear. Introduced with his back to the camera, he stands opposed to the reason the film is concerned to promote. Dressed in the garb of Teddy Boys, he and his friends aimlessly throw stones, and then laundry-packages, to the accompaniment of a pop music soundtrack. This association with 'mindless violence' and a degraded pop culture is made concrete by the diversionary role he then performs in distracting from Truman's successes with his younger brother and sister: first, by his assumption of the film's attention on their arrival at the flats and, second, by his interruption of the conversation between Kathy and Truman once inside the flat. Kathy, Johnny's elder sister, is educating Truman in the wiles of young Mary (Brona Boland). Just as she is asking him whether he is now 'beginning to understand', Johnny appears in the rear of the frame, unbalancing the composition's symmetry in a fashion similar to Bill in *Cage of Gold*. As before, a cut to Johnny diverts attention towards him, as he now assumes compositional prominence his position dictates camera movement. In so doing, Truman's acquisition of 'understanding' is brought to a halt: 'It's no use talking now', announces Kathy. Once outside, he finds himself confronted by a gang of menacing youths, appearing as if from nowhere as the camera pulls back. Although he is allowed to pass (by virtue of an instruction from Johnny), the scene concludes with Truman alone and isolated in the frame, made small by the shot's high angle. The subsequent fade-out seems to mark, in turn, the darkness beginning to engulf his aspirations.

The most decisive setback to Truman's ambitions also occurs in the flat. At first, it would appear that Truman is making some headway with Johnny, when their discussion at the sports field suggests the beginning of a mutual understanding. To this extent, Johnny's characterisation is less that of the purely 'psychopathic' roles of the earlier films than the inner torment made fashionable by the American films of Montgomery Clift and James Dean (to whom McCallum was rather opportunistically compared by a contemporary critic in the press). The ensuing scene, however, reverts to traditional type. Returning from the sportsfield, Johnny invites Truman up to the flat where they discover his friends engaged in a frenzied dance. A dancer is seen from the joint point-of-view of the two men. A cut back to Johnny and Truman suggests another point-of-view shot of the dancing to follow; in fact, the film now cuts obtrusively to the rear of Johnny's head, overcast by a dark line of shadow. The men's joint point-of-view is dramatically fissured and with it Truman's ambitions collapse.

As with *I Believe in You*, such a collapse is marked by a surrender to music and dance. Johnny throws down his jacket, turns up the wireless and joins the frenzy of dancers. The main beneficiaries of reform, the twins, are meanwhile revealed imprisoned behind a clutter of table and chairs pushed aside to make way for the dancing. As Jonathan Simmons suggests, 'It is the rock music which changes Johnny from a reasonably mixed-up kid into a savage, dancing to the tribal beat, all his animal instincts let loose from the thin veneer of civilisation'.[22] Inevitably, the stage is now set for a full-scale eruption of the dangers the music has released: Johnny returns to arson and ends up waving a gun (significantly kept in a guitar case).

With this escalation of violence the film's logic of reform begins to crumble and the demands of authority begin to take over. As Truman explains to Kathy, 'You can feel too sorry for Johnny'. Accordingly, Truman informs the CID of his suspicions about Johnny and receives a kind of absolution from the local priest who promises to tell Kathy that 'you had

Violent Playground (1958)

to do your duty'. Back at the police station, the Chief Inspector (George Cooper) reinstates a law and order position, assuming a compositional prominence that temporarily removes Truman from frame: 'Haven't we had enough of these crazy mixed-up kids who go around bullying and ganging up on people, beating up old ladies . . . I'm a policeman. I've got respect for the law. I know it isn't fashionable. But let's spare a thought for the old lady. Not just for the old lady but you and yours. If these children want to try living outside the law then they can pay the price at the court. I'm tired of tough-guy fever . . . sick and tired of it.' But perhaps most strikingly of all, Heaven, who had previously denied the existence of juvenile delinquents ('they're only juvenile') and shown contempt for the 'rules and regulations' embodied in the fire-door, must now also change his mind and explain to the twins 'a rule's a rule'. The only place left for Johnny then is inside the police van. 'Deviants must not only be labelled', writes Stan Cohen. 'They must be involved in some sort of ceremony of public degradation'.[23] So it is now for Johnny. 'It's right that he should go in a black van', comments Truman. 'It's right that people should see him go in there. It's right that Patrick should see him go in there if only to stop him going the same way.' Johnny cannot be saved and, as the black van draws into a crowded street, must serve as an exemplary sacrifice for the good of the community.

As a result, the film is torn between voluntarism and determinism in its account of delinquent behaviour. As with *I Believe in You*, the final thrust of the movie is to defy environmentalism by emphasising the cultural heterogeneity of its youngsters who are English, Irish, Chinese and Jamaican. Thus, Truman is able to inform Johnny 'you are what you want to be'. Even in the film's own terms, this is clearly not the case. Johnny, for example, attempts to enter the Grand Hotel (with its Rolls Royce clientele) but is, of course, debarred by virtue of age and class. But rather than focus on the real disadvantages suffered by Johnny, the film opts for psychopathy instead. Johnny cannot assume full moral responsibility, not because of environmental circumstances, but because of the compulsiveness of his own psychosis (rooted in a childhood experience of fire-fighting). As such, he is fated by forces which belie rational control. In this respect, the film's appeal to religion is more than coincidental. The innocent/psychopath duality of delinquent demonology is now effectively supplanted by the good versus evil manicheism of a Christian theology. Truman reveals his parents to have been shepherds. Kathy kisses the palm of his hand and makes her way inside the church.

The film does seem partly aware of the damage now caused to its overall perspective as it adds a further ending effectively designed to reconfirm the propriety of its reform position. In doing so, however, it merely underlines the repression which lies beneath its notion of reform. What this ending does is reintroduce the young black boy, first seen at the film's beginning, when he had ignored the reprimands of Truman concerning the way he walked: 'Kids don't walk no more, they jive'. His subsequent reappearance, calling to Truman and then taking his hand, is clearly intended to be read as a sign of Truman's success. But, apart from its obvious contrivance, this reconciliation is hardly on equal terms. For Truman has moved no nearer an understanding of the boy's own culture and vitality. The boy, now walking 'properly', has merely submitted to Truman's terms.

Such a scene remains relatively incidental to the film overall. With *Sapphire* (1959) the 'problem' of blacks takes centre stage. Dearden had previously addressed himself to racial prejudice in *Pool of London* (1950). As with so many liberal films the concern to represent blacks positively had led to an over-compensation. Johnny (Earl Cameron) represents the model 'coon' – polite, deferential and reflective, trusting to a point where he becomes unwittingly involved in crime. As such, Johnny represents no 'threat' and this is underlined by the film's treatment of sexuality. Johnny pursues a rather antiseptic relationship with 'nice girl' Pat (Susan Shaw) before decently deciding it won't work because of the colour divide. By contrast, his white seaman colleague, Dan (Bonar Colleano), assumes the 'playboy' mantle, seducing the equally decent Sally (Renee Asherson). As with the other movies, deviant sexuality is inter-linked with criminality and thus the cause of justice to moral virtue. Accordingly, Dan returns to London not only to clear Johnny but to be worthy of Sally, seen smiling as she overhears the news. With *Sapphire*, however, the representation of blacks becomes considerably more complex than *Pool of London*'s simple idealisation (though there is an echo of it in the film's portrayal of Dr Robbins). Moreover, what is kept at bay in the former film – black sexuality – now becomes a dominant, not to say disturbing, preoccupation.

Like *The Blue Lamp* and *Violent Playground*, *Sapphire* draws on topical subject-matter (rising immigration, the Notting Hill riots) and frames its social concern within an investigation structure. While this structure provides the veneer of 'entertainment' felt necessary to hold an audience's attention, it also embodies a number of the film's values. For the principle of rational deduction upon which the classic detective formula is based in turn embodies the spirit of rationalism which the film wishes to apply to the problem of racial prejudice. In this respect, the end of the detective is not just that of crime-solution but a moral mission as well. Cawelti has suggested that such a missionary aspect to detection derives from the 'hard-boiled' detective novel, as represented by the work of Hammett and Chandler.[24] But whereas this is seen to result from a greater personal and emotional involvement with the criminals on the part of the detective, in *Sapphire* the detective remains aloof from his suspects in a manner more akin to the classic detective story. As such, the detective is not changed in the course of his investigation (cf. *Violent Playground*) but begins from a moral position which it is then his task to enjoin upon others.

Two effects become apparent. First, the moral position upon which the investigation is predicated is that of the detective, in turn, white, middle-class and heterosexual. Second, the moral authority which the detective represents no longer derives from a network of community values, as in *The Blue Lamp* – the Superintendent remains an outsider, travelling by car, even to speak to the local bobby on the beat – but solely from his superior rationality. In this respect, the tension between inquiry and action, fundamental to the detective story, is balanced in favour of inquiry and, in particular, discussion between characters. The aesthetic emphasis of the film is thus the conventional shot/reverse-shot structure with its focus on reasoned discussion. It also sums up for the film what is, at root, the cause of racism: racial prejudice. This does not imply any socially institutionalised form of oppression, only an attitude of mind amenable to change through argument and reason.

This disavowal of the social dimension and accompanying focus on individual attitudes is reinforced by the heterogeneity of characters with whom Supt. Hazard (Nigel Patrick) becomes involved. Such variety establishes the class differences within both black and white communities and emphasises the reciprocity in racial prejudice of blacks towards whites. Thus, the black community includes the wealthy son of an African bishop and barrister, Paul Slade (Gordon Heath), the respectable black professional Dr Robbins (Earl Cameron) and the semi-criminal elements associated with the Tulips club and with Horace (Robert Adams). Moreover, as Slade makes quite clear, racial prejudice works both ways. His father would not have allowed him to marry Sapphire, because 'she was part white'. But what, above all, clinches this removal of social and economic division is the film's ultimate reliance on an ideology of nature.

This is not made explicit but crucially underpins the logic of the investigation. The film begins with Sapphire's body falling to the ground; the reverse shot which would allow us to identify the murderer is, however, refused. This, then, is the enigma posed by the film's beginning: who is the killer and what were his/her motives? In effect, the answer to both questions depends on a third: what is the identity of the girl who has been killed? The victim is revealed to have been a half-caste and the implications of this revelation structure the whole direction of the inquiry. Like *Violent Playground*, the progress of the film is apparently linear and accumulative. The temporal sequence of the film is very simple, consisting almost entirely of scenes and sequences (in Metz's technical definitions). Complications, such as Metz's 'alternating syntagma', only occur in the absence of the detective.[25] Also, like *Violent Playground*, this rational progress is undermined by the eruption of an energy which once again defies rational control, shifting the balance away from inquiry onto action. Why this occurs can, in turn, be related to Sapphire's identity as part-black. Following Sapphire's murder, Hazard and Inspector Learoyd (Michael Craig) inspect the girl's clothes. 'Nice, simple things', comments Hazard. As he picks up a bright red underskirt, Learoyd replies, 'Are they? Don't quite go together, do they?'

In a sense, the clothes compound the enigma: the plain brown skirt on the one hand, the bright red petticoat on the other. As Sapphire's identity as a half-caste has yet to be established, this discovery is marked as a significant clue. Stylistically, the petticoat provides an explosion of colour, dominating the frame as the camera moves in, and striking a contrast to the otherwise drab, and predominantly brown, environment. The connotation is of 'colour' in a broader sense, the colour of its part-black owner. Moreover, the association is also sexual, the bright-red underwear suggesting a 'reality' at

Sapphire (1959)

odds with the plainness of the skirt above.

This is reinforced by a second scene. The two detectives visit Sapphire's room to find the bottom drawer of her chest locked. To the accompaniment of appropriately dramatic music, the drawer is opened to reveal yet more fancy and colourful clothing as well as a half-torn photograph. Once again, this discovery marks an eruption of colour into an otherwise muted setting while Hazard's fetishistic fascination with a nightdress underlines its significance. At the level of dialogue, the film seeks to disclaim such an interpretation. Reflecting on the meaning of the 'red taffeta under a tweed skirt', Learoyd offers the explanation 'that's the black under the white alright'. Hazard tells him to 'come off it'; but what we see, rather than what we are told, seems to support Learoyd rather than Hazard. The logic of the film's *mise-en-scène*, exploiting the novelty of Eastman colour, is that the coloured characters should add colour in a more general sense. As Dearden explained: 'My idea is to throw all this [the sombre winter backgrounds] into contrast with the sudden splashes of colour introduced by the coloured people themselves. The things they wear, the things they carry, their whole personality.'[26] This elision of skin colour with personality is significant. For it is precisely the effect of the film to expand the connotations of colour to the 'colour' of music and dancing, sexuality and violence. Moreover, it is such an attachment of secondary associations to the use of colour which ultimately undermines the film's ostensive rationalism and forces a retreat into notions of nature.

This becomes clear in one pivotal sequence. As has been suggested, the resolution of the crime which precipitates the film's plot is in turn dependent on a solution to the question of Sapphire's identity. Hence the importance of the clues implying Sapphire's 'other side' (the clothes and torn photograph) and leading to the sites of her 'other life' (the International Club, Tulips). The explanation for these is then provided by the revelation of Sapphire's life as a half-caste, passing herself off as white and thus attempting to hide her 'blackness'. The argument of the film, made at the level of dialogue, is that 'you can't tell' the difference between white and half-caste. Saying so, as Sapphire's doctor argues, is as 'silly' as identifying a policeman 'by the size of his feet'. Once again, what we are told is subverted by what we actually see (the empirical notion of truth upon which the film relies). Pam Cook has employed the term 'pregnant moment' to denote those moments in film when the ostensive ideological project of a film is undermined.[27] The scene occurring at Tulips provides a similar example.

The two detectives have entered the black club, Tulips, in an effort to identify Sapphire's dancing partner, the missing half of the torn photograph. The club-owner, Mr Tulips, claims to have no knowledge of Sapphire and, as he returns the photo to Hazard, observes Learoyd's outward gaze. Cutting to Learoyd's point-of-view we see an apparently white woman dancing in 'ecstatic abandon' (as the E.R. Cousins novel of the film puts it).[28] 'That's a lilyskin', comments Tulips as we cut back to the three men. A further point-of-view shot now reveals the woman to be dancing with a black man, Johnny Hotfeet. Returning to the three men, Tulips continues his comments, 'Your chick was a lilyskin, wasn't she . . . you can always tell . . . once they hear the beat of the bongo'. At precisely this moment, bongoes can be heard on the soundtrack, and the camera moves down and forward, past the three men, onto another apparently white woman behind them, as she begins to tap her feet. Learoyd observes the rapturous expression on her face before another eyeline match initiates a rapid montage sequence of twenty shots, all loosely conforming to the point-of-view of the three men. Cutting between the 'lilyskin' dancer, her partner Johnny Hotfeet, a black woman dancer, Johnny Fingers, the 'white' woman behind the men and the bongoes, the sequence concludes with direct intercutting between low-angle shots of the 'lilyskin's' pants and thighs, revealed below her twirling skirt, and close-ups of the bongoes.

Sapphire (1959)

Formally, the scene confirms British cinema's taste for sub-Eisensteinian and 'crudely emotive' editing techniques, noted by Dyer.[29] Like the similar scene in *I Believe in You*, it marks a 'descent' into music and dancing, once again associated with sexuality, with the low-angle shots below the girl's skirt referring back to Sapphire's red taffeta underskirt. Like the scene between Truman and Johnny in *Violent Playground*, the Superintendent is provoked into confrontation with forces apparently at odds with his project of rational control. Up to this point, it has been his position that you 'can't tell a lilyskin'. With this scene, it would appear that you can. For once the 'beat of the bongoes' begins, the 'white' women do indeed 'give themselves away', as Tulips suggests. As if to emphasise the point, the last six shots of the scene directly intercut shots of 'white' women dancing with close-ups of the bongoes. Significantly, when we cut out of the scene it is to shots of Tulips and Learoyd, not Hazard. It has been Learoyd's position throughout the film (and the apparent sign of his bigotry) that you can always tell. The cutback to him, rather than Hazard, thus seems to underline the displacement of Hazard's position that has occurred and temporarily constructs an identification with Learoyd rather than the 'rational' Superintendent.

Such a setback would seem to be confirmed by the scene which follows. As Johnny Fiddle (Harry Baird) flees the club, what had previously been a sedate enquiry transforms into a frenzied chase through the dark, wet streets of the city (once again, reminiscent of 'noir' in its choice of compositions and

87

lighting). Johnny's attempts to find a hiding place foreground the themes of sex and violence, once again running together the ideas of sexuality and criminality. He is evicted from the white, working-class café, Joe's: 'We got copper trouble too . . . but we ain't got your sort of woman trouble. So get out and stay out.' Continuing his flight, he is then set upon by a group of Teddy Boys. Although undoubtedly taking its cue from the Notting Hill riots, taken in context this explosion of violence stands entirely at odds with the reason the film is seeking to espouse. That such 'meaningless violence' should be the climax to the 'ecstatic abandon' of Tulips is, in the film's terms, hardly coincidental.

It is this association of blacks with sexuality, moreoever, that finally allows the murder to be solved. Contrary to most expectations set up by the movie, the killer turns out to be the sister of Sapphire's white fiancé. As Dyer has pointed out, the 'unfulfilled woman' (unmarried and/or childless) is a frequent culprit in the social problem pictures of the period (*Lost, Serious Charge, Victim*) and Mildred (Yvonne Mitchell) can be seen to conform to this category.[30] Although married, and with children, she is nonetheless the victim of a joyless marriage to a seaman who 'doesn't seem to get much leave . . . or doesn't want it'. In this respect, Mildred's relapse into hysteria makes sense. Hysteria was, of course, a recurring preoccupation of Freud's, conventionally identified with women and understood as the symptomatic transcription of repressed sexual desires.[31] At the same time, as Hoch suggests, the sexual mythologies surrounding blacks may themselves be understood as the externalised embodiment of internally repressed desires.[32] In effect, Mildred's hysteria is the complement to the explosion of black sexuality at Tulips, just as her act of murder had been provoked by Sapphire, pregnant and 'swinging her legs' before her. In a way, this is the irony at the heart of the movie. For the locus of violence is not in fact the blacks but the respectable white middle-class family home. The real danger is not the threat without but the sexual repression that's within.

It is, indeed, a troubling irony in so far as the film itself endorses an ideology of blacks as 'naturally' more vital, more rhythmic and more sexual (the implication of what we see at Tulips). So it is ultimately through an appeal to 'nature', to 'natural' racial difference, that the film attempts to resolve its attitude to racial prejudice. As has been argued, the solution to Sapphire's identity, and hence the crime, is the discovery of her 'real' nature-bound self, that is apparently white but 'really' black. Like Douglas Sirk's American film of the same year, *Imitation of Life*, the root of the half-caste's problem is passing themselves off as something they're not. In Sirk's film, the answer is to abandon the circle of deceit, or 'imitation of life', in favour of an acceptance of black identity.[33] But while Sirk views this as a progressive position, presaging the upsurge of the black civil rights movement, it nonetheless traps black people into an ideology of nature, an 'essentialism' in which nature becomes destiny. While Sapphire does not have *Imitation of Life*'s appeal to black solidarity, it does in a similar way confine its blacks, as 'essentially' different (rhythmic, sexual) and determined by nature ('lily-whites' really can't escape the beat of the bongo).

It is from this position that the film's attitude to racism is finally resolved. For if blacks could be accepted 'for what they are' then there would be no need to pass themselves off as white. In this respect, Mildred's twins occupy an interesting role. They are, in effect, 'freaks of nature' whose oddity does not then lead to social ostracism. If cultural attitudes were not overlaid on the natural fact of blackness then, similarly, there would be no problem. As Supt. Hazard explains, 'Given the right atmosphere you can organise riots against anyone: Jews, Catholics, Negroes, Irish, even policemen with big feet'. The flaw of the film, however, is that its ascription of natural qualities is not natural at all, but the projection of its own culture's values, values which form part of the problem and not a solution to it.

A similar tension in the treatment of blacks can also be found in *Wind of Change* which, although not directed by Dearden, is nonetheless worth considering alongside *Sapphire*, because of the similarity in attitude. Drawing on the famous Macmillan speech of 1960 for its title, *Wind of Change* deals with its problem of race within the context of Teddy Boy violence. Self-consciously set around Notting Hill, and employing the conventional iconography of coffee bars and jiving, its main focus of attention is Frank (Johnny Briggs), a discontented and racially prejudiced Teddy Boy. Unlike *Sapphire*, where the Teddy Boy amounts to little more than a malevolent 'folk devil', *Wind of Change* does attempt to provide a context for its character, particularly his family background. As with *I Believe in You*, the responsibility for Frank's delinquency seems to lie with 'the decline in status of the father'. Frank's father (Donald Pleasence) is timid and weak, evading his parental duties through a devotion to pet rabbits. The solution to Frank's behaviour is thus a re-assertion of paternal control. To do so, legal and parental authority become fused, with the 'symbolic father', represented by the police sergeant, assuming the role only imperfectly incarnate in the real father. Thus Sergeant Parker (Glyn Houston) is revealed to be a father himself and enters the family home to make his arrest of Frank. The arrest, however, is seen only in silhouette; our attention is focused on the real father outside, as he attends to one of his (black!) rabbits. In the process, the authority of the father is likewise imposed upon the mother, who had sought to help Frank escape; the 'symbolic', in effect, triumphing over the 'imaginary' pre-oedipal bond between mother and son.

The manifestation of Frank's deviance, however, is his deep-rooted hatred of blacks. Although the *Monthly Film Bulletin* found this 'unreasoning' and 'inexplicable' it is clear from the film's evidence that such hatred derives from sexual rivalry.[34] The first indication of Frank's prejudice, for example, occurs when a black boy begins to laugh and 'shake' with a white girl, previously seen talking to Frank, in the coffee bar. The accompanying pop music soundtrack makes the black boy's danger clear: 'My baby's going to give me what I want tonight'. Having so 'threatened' their white women, the black boy is confronted and chased down an alley. 'The black man must be "kept down",' writes Paul Hoch, 'not to protect the white goddess, but because on the subconscious level his liberation would signify the eruption of the sexuality confined in the racist's own unconsciousness.'[35] Thus, Frank

89

himself does not have a girlfriend; indeed, according to his father, he hasn't been seen with a girl for 'I don't know how long'. As with Mildred's murder of Sapphire, so Frank's violence towards blacks would also seem to have its source in his own internally repressed desires.

The intention of the film, in this respect, is clearly to signal such violence as 'imaginary' by undermining conventional stereotypes of blacks. Frank's sister has a black boyfriend who apparently shows no interest in the cinema, dancing or expresso bars; as yet he has not even attempted to touch her. By contrast, it is the white youth, Frank, who is devoted to leisure, has no job nor indicates a desire to have one. One curious scene, however, seems to undercut this general intention. Pursuing the black boy down an alley, Frank and his gang are interrupted by the appearance of a young white woman in a car. The boys disperse while the black youth remains. He helps the white woman open her garage door and is invited in for 'coffee'. In strict narrative terms, the scene is 'redundant': we see neither of the characters again and their encounter has no effect on subsequent events. Its effect, emphasised by the screen time allocated to it and the employment of near-silence, would seem solely to indicate the attraction of white women to black men and thus to some extent 'objectify' the fears which Frank's behaviour has been based upon. As with *Sapphire* and *Flame in the Streets* (where an equally redundant scene reveals a black couple in bed inviting a white girl to join them) the testimony of what we see ends up reproducing the stereotypes which it is the liberal intent of the films to dismiss. Thus, while *Wind of Change* seeks to make its protagonists' hatred 'irrational', by the logic of what it shows, it reinstates the very mythology which it wishes to undermine.

The real companion piece to *Sapphire*, however, is not *Wind of Change*, but Dearden's *Victim* (1961). Sharing the same scriptwriters (John McCormack and Janet Green), *Victim* also feeds off a topical subject (the Wolfenden Report) and 'sugars the pill' of its social concern by integrating its social debate into a criminal investigation structure. However, this employment of an investigation format has one major difference. Compared with *Sapphire*, the police in *Victim* play a much less pronounced role with much of the detective work being undertaken by a private individual, Farr (Dirk Bogarde). As such, the division between detection and personal involvement assumed by *Sapphire* dissolves. For the interest of Farr in crime solution is at the same time entwined with a personal interest in ending the persecution of gays. In this respect, *Sapphire*'s imposition of rational–legal authority from the outside is impossible and the attitude towards both law enforcement and sexual normality is accordingly more complex. For Farr is both inside the law (both as lawyer and agent of justice) and outside (as potential homosexual and opponent of its justice). At the same time, he is both within marriage and outside it (prey to his homosexual inclinations). By locating such an ambivalent character at its centre (upholding both law and marriage but at the same time threatening them), the film's attempt to harness the detective story's principle of rational deduction to an understanding of a social problem once again becomes problematic.

As with *Sapphire*, part of the film's difficulty can be associated with the attitude taken towards 'nature'. Although the film's main concern is to appeal for legal reform, as the means to ending unnecessary blackmail, it does so in a context which identifies gays not only as victims of crime but victims of nature itself. As Fulbrook (Anthony Nicholls) explains, 'the invert is part of nature'. Admittedly, as the film's title suggests, this nature is something of an affliction, the 'dirty trick' complained of by Henry (Charles Lloyd Pack), but it is nature nonetheless. The tension that results has been identified by Richard Dyer.[36] To be true to one's nature, as the ideology of *Sapphire* had proposed, is to flirt with abnormality and sickness: to repress one's homosexuality, on the other hand, is, of necessity, to be acting 'unnaturally'.

This contradiction might have gone unnoticed, as Dyer suggests, had this ideology of nature not also been invoked in relation to Farr's marriage. For what the film also implicitly suggests is how the existence of homosexuality is putting at risk the 'natural' form of the family and, in particular, the 'natural' expectation of motherhood. What characterises the Farr marriage is its absence of children and, although not explicitly addressed as a topic, is consistently alluded to by a repetitive use of images of children. Thus, in absence of a family of her own, Laura (Sylvia Syms) works part-time in a school for handicapped children. It is here that she reads the newspaper story reporting the death of Jack Barrett (Peter McEnery), her husband's 'lover'. The film then cuts dramatically to a shot of a child now savagely crossing out a drawing of a woman, as if to underline the cancelling out of motherhood represented by the revelation. A similar intrusion of children occurs when Farr reveals to his wife that he intends to go to the police (and by implication ruin his career). Laura is left alone in a deserted classroom, but only briefly. Almost immediately, a group of noisy children burst into the room, as if mocking the futility and sterility of her marriage. As if to emphasise the point, the culprit behind the blackmail is subsequently revealed to be a spinster, whose lack of 'normal' feminine fulfilment in motherhood and marriage has mutated into neurotic venom against gays.

To this extent, the film conforms to the parameters established by Wolfenden, fearing the consequences of homosexuality for family life and refusing to endorse it morally but, in so far as it is an 'affliction', counselling treatment rather than punishment. The slightly earlier *Trials of Oscar Wilde* (1960) adopts a similar attitude. Oscar Wilde's (Peter Finch) 'friendship' – as with *Victim* the film is evasive on detail – with Lord Alfred Douglas (John Fraser) consistently distracts from his family life; and while there is nowhere a sign of endorsement for Wilde's sexual preferences (forced into ending his relationship with Douglas by the film's close), the film does nonetheless query the propriety of legal persecution by appealing to our sympathy for his 'ailment'. 'What I can't understand is how a man of Wilde's taste and breeding can come to associate with such people', comments one character. Sir Edward Clarke (Nigel Patrick) provides the film's preferred explanation: 'To understand that – you'd have to understand the nature of Wilde's perversion. And I'm a lawyer not a doctor. To me it's loathsome, degenerate and unnatural . . . yet I feel sorry for him. It's a terrible thing . . . when a man of Wilde's talents and genius is slowly crucified by a lot of blackmailers and common criminals.'

Yet, just as this film probably gives an attractiveness to Wilde's socialising, entirely missing from his constricted home life (Yvonne Mitchell is particularly unsympathetic as his wife), so the problem for *Victim* is that, by appealing to nature in its defence of homosexuals, it does at the same time threaten the legitimacy of the heterosexual marriage it is seeking to uphold. For, while the film seeks to maintain the superiority of normal marriage (witness the narratively redundant but ideologically charged bedroom scene between Frank and Sylvia) and closes off its narrative with the Farrs' marriage intact and Barrett's photo burning safely in the grate, it does so only precariously and in a fashion that has put into question the 'naturalness' of their relationship (sterile and repressive). Indeed, what is noticeable about nearly all of Dearden's films is the absence of happy and successful young marriages. Marriages are either deeply troubled (*The Halfway House, Frieda, Cage of Gold, Life for Ruth, The Mind Benders*) or families are in disarray (*I Believe in You, The Gentle Gunman, Violent Playground, Sapphire*). It may of course be the case that this is the point: marriage and home are under threat and it is precisely the work of the films to secure the conditions under which they can prosper. Yet, in the absence of any such evidence, there is more than a strain of anxiety about the very viability of the family at all.

What, of course, makes this absence in *Victim* most pronounced is the film's concentration on the tight-knit world inhabited by its homosexuals, a world which by its nature is debarred to heterosexual couples. But the corollary of this is that, within the terms of the film, it is homosexuality which would appear to be normal, if only by sheer prevalence. In this respect, there is an interesting contrast with *Sapphire*. As has been suggested, the implicit perspective adopted was that 'you can tell': the lilyskin will indeed give herself away when confronted by 'the beat of the bongo'. In *Victim*, however, 'you can't tell', you can never be sure who's gay and who's not. Indeed, much of the play of the film revolves around the uncertainty of sexual identity and, by implication, of what's normal. First, much of the film is concerned with delaying the identification of homosexuality (as with Barrett and Farr) or surprising us with revelations of homosexuality in characters of whom we didn't suspect it (as with Lord Fulbrook). Second, this element of surprise is reinforced by the emphasis the film gives to class divisions (after the fashion of *Sapphire*) in its treatment of the gay community. Gays are identified as existing in all walks of life (from Lord to wage clerk) and one of the components of the film's strategy of surprise is the revelation of homosexuality in otherwise normal and socially well-adjusted characters. Despite verbal addresses to the contrary, the gay community is to this extent 'normalised'. Far from being socially isolated it conforms exactly to the 'normal' parameters of class and cultural division in British society.

Looking at it another way, in so far as homosexuality is rendered normal, so at the same time our conventional sense of normality becomes troubled. For if the film surprises us with revelations of homosexuality, so it also induces us to suspect homosexuality where there is none. This is most noticeable in the treatment of the undercover policeman. His attempts at picking up Eddie suggest he is just another Checkers regular; it is only later that his real identity as a policeman is revealed. Similarly, the behaviour and appearance of the Checkers barman tends to suggest homosexuality; again, it is only later that he expresses his disgust of gays to Madge. In effect, the uncertainty the film proposes with respect to sexual identities comes home to roost as a kind of worry about heterosexuality itself, that lurking behind normal heterosexuality there may indeed be a repressed homosexuality not so very far behind (which is, of course, precisely the problem faced by Farr). According to Freud, paranoia 'invariably arises from an attempt to subdue unduly powerful homosexual tendencies'.[37] In so far as the film's play with our expectations creates a kind of paranoia about sexual identity, so it also assumes a similar content.

What would seem to confirm this anxiety is the compulsion which other Dearden films give to male group relationships, as opposed to marital ones (cf. *The Blue Lamp*, *The Gentle Gunman*). This would seem particularly true of *The League of Gentlemen*. Here, Hyde (Jack Hawkins), is separated from his wife, Rupert (Terence Alexander) is the victim of infidelities, Porthill (Bryan Forbes) is kept by an older woman, Race (Nigel Patrick) is involved in a temporary affair, while Weaver (Norman Bird) is suffocated by a noisy wife and elderly father-in-law. By contrast, it is the all-male group which proves most positive and compelling and for which they all gladly abandon their domestic pasts. In the case of Hyde and Race this relationship becomes

Victim (1961)

93

almost explicitly homosexual. Race follows Hyde home ('I'm not very good at it, you see, I'm usually the one who's followed'). Hyde invites him in whereupon he dons an apron and helps him out with the dishes ('Mummy thought the world of me'). Race apologises for his use of the term 'old darling' ('One gets into terrible habits at the YMCA'). Hyde then invites him to stay for dinner ('All my men loved me'), to stay the night and even 'move in'. The combination of dialogue, acting and staging make it hard to resist the implication of a seduction; even the dissolve from the fridge on the line 'All my men loved me' to a post-dinner scene of smoking quite clearly invokes the cinema's conventional vocabulary for dealing with love-making.

In this respect, *The League of Gentlemen* provides a kind of shadow to *Victim*'s failure to institute an image of marital normality, pushing to the fore the satisfactions of male camaraderie (and, by implication, homoeroticism) conventionally absent from normal domestic routine. Although homosexuality has few positive connotations in *Victim* (its emphasis on the threat of blackmail reducing most of the gay characters to frightened passivity), its all-pervasiveness, combined with the accentuated fragility of its treatment of marriage, does in a sense put into crisis the very ideology which it is seeking to uphold.[38]

If *Victim* and *Sapphire* have the effect of producing an 'internal criticism' which is, to a large extent, unintended, Dearden's two later movies, *Life for Ruth* (1962) and *The Mind Benders* (1962) present a more self-conscious interrogation of the earlier confidence in rational-legal authority. If the earlier films can be seen as dramas of social control, reducing sensation to fit the social order, *Life for Ruth* and *The Mind Benders* seek to test the limits of this position by exposing authority to extreme cases: those of religious fundamentalism and scientific experiment on humans. In both cases, the resolution of the problem requires a tempering of authority in the interests of individual human need. The problem, however, is posed from different ends. With *Life for Ruth* it is an excessive individualism which threatens to undermine the rational order: in *The Mind Benders* it is the destruction of individuality altogether, at the hands of rationalism (in the form of science) gone wild, which poses the danger.

The problem faced by *Life for Ruth* is a fundamentalist religious belief that prevents John Harris (Michael Craig) from allowing his daughter the blood transfusion which would save her life. As with *Violent Playground*, what the film fears is extremity, in turn associated with irrationalism. 'Religion is a tricky business . . . Everybody feels. Nobody thinks', as one police officer comments. However, unlike *Violent Playground*, the film finds itself unable to impose a submission to reason through force because of the counter-claims of individual conscience and freedom of religious belief represented by Harris. Accordingly, the film adopts a kind of double ending, similar to *Cage of Gold*, which effectively 'punishes' Harris but leaves the way open for reform. Harris is taken to court but acquitted. In the process, he is forced to take stock of collective opinion, confront himself and finally accept his individual responsibility for his child's death. The state is thus rescued from an imposition of force by the individual's acceptance and internalisation of

5

The Social Problem Film

II

The other central figure in the development of the social problem film during the 1950s was undoubtedly scriptwriter Ted Willis. Although a large part of his work was for television (such that by 1961 he could be described as 'the country's No.1 television playwright'), his activities straddled the theatre, cinema and television and often involved adaptations from one form to another.[1] *Woman in a Dressing Gown*, *The Young and the Guilty* and *Flame in the Streets* were all adapted for the cinema screen from television plays, while *No Trees in the Street* was adapted for film from the theatre. The process also went the other way: Willis' creation of Sergeant Dixon (first seen in *The Blue Lamp*) provided the basis for television's long-running series, *Dixon of Dock Green*. It was the demands of writing for television, and, in particular, the example of American TV writers like Paddy Chayefsky and Rod Serling, which were to impose themselves heavily on Willis' aesthetic ideas. Reviewing Chayefsky's *Marty* and *The Mother*, he enthused: 'They both deal with the mundane, the ordinary and the untheatrical. The main characters are typical rather than exceptional: the situations are easily identifiable by the audience; and the relationships are as common as people . . . I am just now becoming aware of this area, this marvellous world of the ordinary.'[2] As a result, Willis' own work attempted to capture 'good, honest, fumbling people caught up in tiny tragedies', with his social problems firmly anchored to the domestic, rather than the public and directly political.[3]

The clearest expression of this credo is to be found in *Woman in a Dressing Gown*, described by Willis himself as an attempt to capture 'a group of human beings in the grip of a recognisable situation, and their ordinary human reactions to that situation'.[4] The resulting drama is constructed according to the classic pattern: domestic order is threatened by marital infidelity but re-established by the close, the threat now overcome. This structure and theme had led more than one critic to compare the film to *Brief Encounter*. Edward Goring, for example, dubbed it 'the *Brief Encounter* of the LCC tenants'.[5] The parallel, however, masks one critical distinction. In the former film, it is the wife who finds herself tempted by the prospect of a romantic escape from domestic constriction and the anodyne sexuality of her complacent husband. In *Woman in a Dressing Gown*, it is the husband who yearns for escape, while it is the wife who is the source of his problems and locus of his discontents. To this extent, the problem is not really external (the 'other woman') but

97

internal: Amy's failure to be a 'good' wife. Amy (Yvonne Mitchell) is loud, devoted to pop music on the radio and domestically ill-equipped (burning the toast and bringing her husband breakfast in bed too late). By contrast, Jim's mistress, Georgie (Sylvia Syms), is young and attractive, efficient and orderly, available and willing to marry him. In so far as the film's dénouement requires Jim (Anthony Quayle) to make a choice between the two women, so the parallel with *Brief Encounter* does obtain. Just as Celia Johnson relinquishes her desires and returns to domestic security, so George now opts for Amy. 'It's no good, Georgie', Jim explains, 'I'm no good at fighting . . . leaving her just now, she seemed so helpless. Perhaps she's what she is because I am what I am . . . I can't do it, Georgie. I've got to go back . . . It's been too long between Amy and me.' If this was all there was to the movie, little would remain to be said: a dour little morality play, counselling compromise and acceptance, and beset by a condescension so characteristic of writers who self-consciously attempt to write about 'ordinary people' and their 'ordinary lives'.

What adds interest to the film, however, is the peculiarity of the style adopted in telling the story. In Willis' prescription for the TV director, style should be as self-effacing as possible: 'The director will serve the script faithfully, avoiding tricks and devices which draw attention to his own contribution; his work, when completed, will be so unobtrusive that it can (and very often will) pass unnoticed'.[6] Jack Lee Thompson's adaptation could hardly be more different. As Derek Hill complained at the time, 'The director has adopted a style which acts as a barrier between subject and audience. Instead of letting us have the play neat, he makes the script an excuse for a non-stop series of camera tricks. We seldom get a straight, honest look at what is going on – we're too busy gliding up and down the larder shelves, through the banister rails, in and out of the bookcase'.[7] For Hill, such devices depth-charged whatever claims the film may have made for 'realism'. This may be so, but it nonetheless misses the interest then generated by this very dissonance between subject-matter and style, and the complex spectator-position then produced by this 'barrier between subject and audience'. To this extent, the film shares more than a passing resemblance to the work of Douglas Sirk, whose stylistic subversion of melodramatic content has generated a wealth of critical commentary. As Paul Willemen suggests, the Sirkian style operates upon a dialectic of involvement and alienation, of drawing an audience into identification with characters while maintaining a critical distance.[8] One formal strategy much favoured by Sirk, in this respect, is also in evidence in *Woman in a Dressing Gown*. As Hill suggests, there is a consistent foregrounding of intermediary objects and surfaces which obscure the spectator's vision of the action. Thus, the camera repeatedly shoots through windows, panelling, a china cabinet, even adopting 'impossible' positions to film from behind the cooker or out of a wardrobe.[9]

In one sense, such a strategy confirms the film's overall moralism. Thus, while Jim and Georgie enjoy their illicit lunch, the camera watches through a grilled window, moving off the action altogether to come to rest on a jungle'. Director Jack Lee Thompson was even blunter: 'We are saying, in effect, stop your silly whining, look at what it used to be like'.[12] In this respect, the film adopts a common ideological manoeuvre: legitimating the present by reference to the past, often distracting from the inadequacies of the present in the process.

As Ray Durgnat has commented, when seeking to influence people 'it is natural . . . to offer an attractive example of the desirable state of affairs, to demonstrate, in dramatic form, the benefits of its working'.[13] The problem the film then faces is the absence of conviction in its presentation of the desirability of the present. The contemporary reality offered by the film is that of a cold and bare housing estate, devoid of actual people. By contrast, Kennedy Street vibrates with human activity, shot in cluttered compositions and rich lighting contrasts. The strategy of the film may well be to demystify the romanticism attached to traditional working-class communities (borne at the expense of disadvantage and suffering), but the film's reliance on the conventions of 1930s proletarian drama and the employment of music-hall stars such as Stanley Holloway (cheerfully taking bets and singing) tends to undercut the negative impulse, bestowing an energy and vitality on the past which is entirely absent from scenes in the present. As with *Woman in a Dressing Gown*, the alternatives the film presents can be linked to the question of sexual desire. Tommy's sister, Hetty (Sylvia Syms), with her wish for a 'small business', represents the respectable aspirations of those who live in the street. She succumbs to the advances of local criminal Wilkie (Herbert Lom) but ultimately opts for decency in the form of policeman Frank (Frank Howard), now smug and self-congratulatory in his council flat bliss. As with *Woman in a Dressing Gown*, the extinguishment of fire and passion goes hand in hand with an 'inert, aimless contentment'. The image of the tree, allegedly symbolising the optimism of the film, evokes this irony nicely. In fact, it is a solitary tree, no longer growing wild, but strapped and hemmed in behind an encasing of wire fence.

The film's other failure of conviction derives from its attitude towards environmentalism. The logic of its contrast between past and present depends on Frank's assumption that 'bricks and mortar' would make a difference to people's behaviour; good housing wouldn't make people perfect but it 'might give them a chance to be people'. Now that people do, indeed, have 'decent houses' then the crime which was characteristic of Kennedy Street should no longer be necessary. But, as in the case of Basil Dearden's films, this logic of environmentalism is radically undercut by an emphasis on individual responsibility. Commenting on the 1930s gangster film, Colin McArthur has noted, 'There is a particular device, first used in *Angels with Dirty Faces* and later to become important in post-war phases of the genre, which seems to undercut any statement about the social origins of crime which the films purport to make. This device is to have a gangster and one of the establishment figures in the film (priest, policeman, lawyer) come from the same slum neighbourhood, suggesting . . . that the badness of the one and the goodness of the other are the result of moral choice rather than social conditioning'.[14] The same device is employed in *No Trees in the Street*.

Wilkie and Frank grew up in the same street and went to the same school, yet one became a criminal, the other a policeman. Tommy and Hetty are brother and sister, yet one ends up a murderer, the other a policeman's wife. Thus, it is entirely appropriate that Hetty should turn on Wilkie at the end to complain about the death of her brother: 'I used to blame the street. But it's you, and people like you. You kill us'. In effect, the blame for crime in the film becomes re-routed from the environment on to 'people like' Wilkie who malevolently lead astray the young. But, if 'people like' Wilkie are not the creations of their environment, as the film now suggests, then it inevitably consigns the contrast between past and present to irrelevance while the policeman's homilies to the youngster are exposed as the vacuous pieces of moralism they undoubtedly are.

Willis' next social problem screenplay, *Flame in the Streets* (1961), turned to race, focusing on the family disruption which results from a daughter's intention to marry a black man. But, like *Sapphire* before it, the logical progress of the film's promotion of reason is upset and finally comes to rely on non-rational means for a solution. The initial setting of the plot, however, is not the home but the factory. Pursuing the course of reason the film would wish to promote, trade union official Jacko Palmer (John Mills), confronts the prejudices of both management and workers alike by supporting the promotion of black fellow worker Gabriel Gomez (Earl Cameron), finally convincing a hostile union meeting to vote in his favour. The meeting over, Palmer's wife, Nell (Brenda de Banzie), appears in the hall to break the news of their daughter's forthcoming marriage. In the same room, that only minutes before had been the setting for Palmer's triumph of reason, we now see the lights go out (switched off by the caretaker) and Palmer's flowing rhetoric give way to stumbling inarticulacy: 'You find enough words at any other time, find a few now'. It is a turning-point in the movie. For despite the impeccable credentials of their daughter's suitor (a respectable school-teacher), neither Palmer nor his wife can rationally overcome their prejudice against the marriage. In order for a solution to be reached, the dilemma has to be displaced on to other issues and into a form with which the characters can cope.

In the first instance, this requires a relocation of the problem in terms of the family's own internal tensions (Willis' 'good, honest, fumbling people caught up in tiny tragedies'). As with *Sapphire*, it is the 'unfulfilled woman' who gives most vigorous voice to racial prejudice. Faced with this new family crisis, Nell remonstrates with her husband for his neglect and taking of her for granted, revealing her earlier intentions to leave him. Like Hetty in *No Trees in the Street*, Nell is characterised by desires of petty-bourgeois respectability and a fetish for order and cleanliness (her overriding ambition is to have 'a house with a bathroom'). The daughter's proposed marriage, by contrast, threatens contamination: 'I'm ashamed of you. When I think of you and that man sharing the same bed. It's filthy . . . digusting . . . It makes my stomach turn over . . . I want to be sick . . . You can't wait can you? You're no better than the whores in the high street. You can't wait to be with him . . . that's the truth. All you want is one thing'. As with *Sapphire*, the

This emphasis on middle-class values continues in later school movies, only now there is a move down the social scale and into the secondary modern. The success of *The Blackboard Jungle* (1955) was undoubtedly an influence here. Ronald Neame, for example, had attempted to set up a production of Michael Croft's *Spare the Rod* in 1954 but was dissuaded by the censor's demands for cuts in the script and warning of an 'X' certificate ('There will be riots in the classroom if this is made').[15] The success of *The Blackboard Jungle*, despite its 'X' certificate, revived interest in the project and a 'hotted-up' version finally hit the screen, with the help of some financing from Max Bygraves. Like the former film, its plot is organised around a new recruit to the teaching profession whose reforming zeal begins to reap success in a tough working-class school. Max Bygraves assumes the Glenn Ford role as the ex-naval instructor Saunders, committed to avoiding corporal punishment and making his teaching relevant (relating Julius Caesar to gangsters in the same way that Ford employs cartoons). The film's faith in liberal reform, however, does not enjoy an entirely smooth passage. Like the threat to Ford's family life in *The Blackboard Jungle*, it is the eruption of teenage sexuality which obstructs the forward march. Four girls in the class suggest to Saunders that he teach them about sex while a schoolgirl, Margaret, makes a clumsy attempt to seduce him.

Dramatically, such events represent a turning-point. As if sublimating sexuality into violence, Saunders turns against his surly class and resorts to violent punishment. Although he subsequently reasserts his liberal principles in preventing his sadistic colleague, Gregory (Geoffrey Keen), from beating two boys, it would appear that it is now too late. The schoolchildren break out in revolt and prepare to make a bonfire in the school hall. Just as 'understanding' could go 'too far' in *Violent Playground*, so the authority of the school must now reassert itself. As in *It's Great to be Young,* the headmaster requires that Bygraves resign ('When you opposed Gregory, you identified with the pupils against authority') and is supported in this action by the school inspector who had previously congratulated Saunders on the merits of his teaching. To this extent, the logic of the film matches that of *Violent Playground*: the liberal dream of reform has proved a failure, the rule of force, embodied in Gregory, must be reinstated.

But, just as it seems that all is lost, the film attempts to retrieve the situation. As the now sacked Saunders leaves the school, he passes the school assembly as the kids give voice to a version of 'Jerusalem'; two of the victims of his unjust punishment wish him farewell and a Merry Christmas; once outside, the children affectionately gather round, in stark contrast to the playground mayhem of the film's beginning; Gregory stops beating a youngster to the headmaster's commentary that it's 'never too late to learn'; Margaret apologises to Saunders, promising to 'be good next term'; while, in a final twist, a black schoolgirl, Olive, practically unnoticed in the rest of the film, appears with her racially mixed parents to thank him for the progress she has made. 'It makes the crowd happy', comments Sirk on his use of happy endings, but, 'to the few it makes the aporia more transparent'.[16] It is hard not to feel the same about *Spare the Rod*. For in its very excess, its rather

105

anxious overloading of endings, the film seems to mark a hiatus, rather than an organically developed conclusion. To 'the crowd', as Sirk suggests, this may provoke contentment; to 'the few' it undoubtedly confirms the liberal gloom.

A similar set of issues is raised in *Term of Trial* (1962); but, this time, the defeat of the liberal teacher would appear to be unequivocal. Like Saunders, Graham Weir (Laurence Olivier) is a sensitive and understanding teacher, committed to the 'progressive programme' of education, announced by the head at the film's beginning. By the end of the film, however, he has been dragged through the law courts on a charge of 'indecent assault ', assumed guilty by headmaster and pupils alike, and only succeeds in maintaining his marriage by giving in to deceit. What is at stake in Weir's demise is not just attitudes to education but a struggle between different sets of cultural values. As a Christian and pacifist (imprisoned during World War II as a conscientious objector), Weir represents spiritual and intellectual values at odds with the society around him. What cripples the two children who show most inclination towards learning is not economic disadvantage (the Taylor family, apparently, could 'buy and sell' Weir) but cultural deprivation. Thomson has to do his homework at school because of the lodger and the constant noise from the TV. Evicted from his own home while trying to study, his automatic response is to set fire to the lodger's 'big, flashy car'. Shirley Taylor's home is similarly constricting. Her father burps at the table, her mother is racially prejudiced, while her sister preoccupies herself with nail varnish and the sound of the wireless. Even Weir's own unhappy domestic life seems to reflect this conflict in values; while he spends his time with books in 'the library', his wife is content to spend hers in front of the box.

But what, above all, drags Weir down is not just the spiritual emptiness of the culture around him but its sordid preoccupation with sex. Weir's initial adversary, in this respect, is Mitchell (Terence Stamp), the 'disgusting and sordid young savage' whose sullen resistance defies all Weir's attempts at education. The struggle between the two makes itself concrete in relation to Shirley. While Weir seeks to cater to her mind, providing her with extra-curricular instruction, Mitchell's preoccupations are purely sexual. First seen passing round a pin-up during school assembly (to the accompaniment of 'To be a Pilgrim'), he subsequently photographs Shirley in the toilet, forces a kiss upon her in the corridor and makes a thinly-disguised sexual attack upon her in a deserted bombsite. As in *Spare the Rod*, it is Mitchell's sexual provocation which prompts the first setback to Weir's 'progressive programme'. Discovering the photograph of Shirley, he subjects Mitchell to a savage classroom beating, thus destroying his 'splendid record of non-violence'. In the process, he also helps unleash a further bout of violence. Mitchell himself takes revenge by smashing the windscreen of Weir's car, while his father and a friend attack Weir in the street. But, finally, it is not Mitchell but Shirley who ensures Weir's downfall. Like Margaret in *Spare the Rod*, she gives expression to her own sexual desire and attempts to seduce her teacher. Weir rejects her, but finds himself in court nonetheless.

The blame for this, however, does not attach so much to Shirley as the

Term of Trial (1962)

culture which makes her expect that innocent love should automatically be accompanied by sex. As Weir explains in court, what he felt for Shirley was 'tenderness, innocence, love . . . the things that God gives us before the filth of the world begins to take over'. What this 'filth of the world' implies is clearly spelt out in one striking scene prior to Weir's court appearance. Following his distracted walk down a city street, the film confronts us with a series of images of commercialised sex: teenagers in a coffee bar dancing to pop on the jukebox, shop displays of records, girlie mags and body-building manuals, a cinema hoarding for *The Ape's Revenge* with its dubious come-on of a woman, pierced through the breast with a sword. 'Everywhere he goes he is reminded of "sex" ', explains the accompanying publicity hand-out. 'It thrusts itself at him from the lurid covers of books: "sexy" songs reach him over the radio, and half-naked women peer at him from outside cinemas.'

Appropriately enough, when Weir takes the stand at his trial he does not denounce Shirley but the hypocrisy of a society which sees fit to judge him: 'It is exquisite irony that I should be condemned by a society which presumes itself more moral than I. A society endlessly titillating itself with dirty books and newspapers and advertising and television and the work of cynical and indifferent minds.' So deep-seated is the degeneracy of this culture that it does not matter that he is acquitted. His 'progressive' headmaster denies him promotion (favouring the teacher who had engaged in a casual pick-up in Paris) and suggests he should leave, his class show him an increased respect on the assumption that he'd 'got away with it', while his wife is only prevented from leaving him by his false admission of guilt. 'Who would have expected it of you', she marvels. 'Most people, apparently', comes his reply.

Weir's defeat in *Term of Trial* is not just that of a liberal educational philosophy but a whole set of moral and spiritual values as well, brought to its knees by the work of a cynical 'affluence'. Yet the film's conclusion is curiously ambivalent, as if it too has fallen prey to the very assumptions it seeks to oppose. At one level, the logic is straightforward: the sensitive and idealistic Weir is destroyed, incapable of survival save by the enactment of the culture's fantasy of sexual depravity. The 'upside-down' values of a commercialised society – making 'toughness and sexual prowess the supreme virtues of manhood' and sneering at 'gentleness and restraint' – are thus exposed.[17]

Yet in so far as the film manifests its own anxiety about the status of Weir's masculinity so, to a degree, is it hoist by its own petard. The characterisation of Weir is heavily marked by inadequacy (exacerbated, in turn, by the theatrical fussiness of Olivier's performance). He is dependent on drink, given to bouts of self-pity and derided by his wife for both his failure to earn more money and use of pacifism as a cover for cowardice. To some extent, his wife conforms to a type (already seen in *Sapphire* and *Flame in the Streets*), the 'unfulfilled woman' whose inability to have a baby and domestic frustration resurface as neuroticism. But by making Weir's wife French, rather than English as in the novel, the film also exudes a sensuality, characteristic of Simone Signoret's performances and partly reminiscent of *Room at the Top*, which cuts across such typing and reinforces a sense of Weir's own, rather than his wife's, failings. 'For God's sake, please stop being so bloody noble', she exclaims. 'Show some spark. Come and hit me. Go and get another woman. Do something human for a change.'

The suggestion thus set in motion is less that of Weir's nobility than his debilitating sexual inhibition. It is clear, for example, that he is attracted to Shirley but cannot allow himself to act on his desires. The consummation of their day in Paris together is thus 'converted' by the film into the surrogate necking of Mitchell and untroubled pick-up of a fellow teacher, Truman. As with *Spare the Rod*, the very excess of violence deployed against Mitchell suggests less a moral disgust than a disturbing sublimation of the desires upon which he cannot act (given emphasis, in turn, by the intercutting of the confrontation with Shirley who, strictly speaking, could not be expected to know what it is about). Simone Signoret suggests that her husband's refusal to sleep with Shirley amounts to no more than pure 'funk'. The irony of the film is that it seems to agree. For, by so 'objectifying' the lack of virility, or 'castration', of its hero, it reinstates the very version of masculinity it has been at such pains to dispute.

Modern mass culture is also a key element in *Some People* (1962). Just as *Term of Trial* had offered a pot-pourri of the new culture's symbols (jukeboxes and sex), so *Some People* begins with an equivalent montage of images from the 'affluent society'. Records, televisions, washing machines, jewellery and fast food dominate the shop windows while adverts invite us to

108

'enjoy immediate delivery' and 'credit with dignity'. A concluding sign announces that 'today's cigarette is a Bristol'. In so far as it is Bristol which provides the film's location, such a flourish amounts to no more than a joke, but it is, in another way, the key to the film's identification of the problem of youth. As director Clive Donner explained, the Bristol location was explicitly selected as a contrast to the more 'socially deprived' areas to be found in *Spare the Rod* and *Term of Trial*: 'It had to be made in a provincial city, not London. I didn't want to make it in a city where there was a traditional background of working-class problems, because I don't think that the subject we're considering in the film relates so much to traditional "bad areas" but much more to the housing estates and so forth: we didn't want a town like Jarrow.'[18] As such, the gang of youths upon whom the film focuses are in employment with money to spend on conspicuous consumption, most notably clothes and motorbikes.

What then characterises their situation is not unemployment, poverty or economic disadvantage but a kind of aimlessness, or 'money without responsibility', typical of the 'affluent teenager'. Sentencing them for speeding, a magistrate complains how 'monstrous' it is that boys of their age should so readily obtain motorbikes by means of HP. Deprived of their licences, the boys continue their purposeless behaviour: hanging around the bus station and eyeing up the girls, jeering at diners inside a city restaurant, loading a bookseller with books they don't intend to buy, throwing away a young sea-cadet's cap and glueing their faces to the window of a shop selling pornography. What appears to be absent is some kind of satisfactory outlet for their energies. The boys all play musical instruments but have nowhere to practise: they are thrown out of a youth club where Johnny (Ray Brooks) begins to play the piano while a vicar naturally resents their choice of his church as a locale for pop music and twisting. The 'salvation' of the boys then begins with the church caretaker and choirmaster, Smith (Kenneth More), offering them the use of his hall for rehearsals and subsequently encouraging them to enrol for the Duke of Edinburgh Award Scheme. As Smith explains, 'Some people have hardly any interest in life at all. They need a push . . . It's just that some people get a kick out of doing something a bit out of the ordinary line. It satisfies them and helps others. It's just really a question of keeping everybody busy.' In this way, the Duke of Edinburgh scheme holds out the prospect of reform to the boys, providing new aims and ambitions and keeping 'everybody busy'.

The process of reform, however, is not uniform and each of the boys displays a different response. To some extent, the film employs the duality already seen at work in *I Believe in You*. Bert (David Hemmings), the youngest and most innocent of the three, represents the basically 'nice boy' who quickly responds to the new challenges, constantly attending rehearsals (when the others stay away) and working on a canoe, despite a lack of support from Bill (David Andrews). As such, he epitomises the words of the title song: 'Some people think that kids are bad, well that's too bad. 'Cos they don't know the kids the way I do'. Despite appearances to the contrary (the bike and the leathers), Bert is not 'bad' but 'good'. Given the right circumstances this will show through. By contrast, Bill does not change and evades the net of reform. He is the first to tire of rehearsals, shows no enthusiasm for the Duke of Edinburgh scheme and is ultimately involved in wrecking the hall in which the group are rehearsing. The problem his character then poses for the film is that, in resisting reform, he ends up being typed in precisely the way the film is concerned to avoid with the other boys. Early on in the film, a youth club leader throws the boys out. Turning on Bert, he exclaims, 'I remember you . . . you're a trouble-maker . . . Get out . . . And take your pals with you. I'll not have Teddy Boys contaminating my boys and girls'. Bill responds angrily, 'Who are you calling Teds? If you want that sort of trouble, mate, I'll bring a gang of proper Teds up and we'll see.' Once outside, he is still complaining, 'They're all the same. Once you've disagreed with them, you're a Ted'.

Yet by the end of the film it is precisely such a reversion to the Ted label which marks the film's treatment of his character. Previously, the film had employed the image of a gang on motorbikes to undercut audience expectations: coming to a halt, one of the gang comments, 'This looks alright, dunnit', while Bill enters the church hall on his own to look for Jenny (Angela Douglas). The anticipated 'threat', which the imagery had initially suggested, thus fails to materialise. Later on, however, almost exactly the same image is used to confirm the stereotype: this time it *is* a 'gang of proper Teds' while Bill *is* a real 'trouble-maker', 'mindlessly' helping to destroy the contents of the church hall. Incapable of changing him, the film ends up by deploying the very 'folk devil' imagery of the Teddy Boy which it had initially sought to upturn.

Somewhere between the other two characters, we find Johnnie. For him, in particular, the experience of the group and the Duke of Edinburgh scheme entails a widening of cultural horizons. Rejecting the advances of the working-class girl and group's singer, Jenny, he strikes up a relationship with Smith's daughter, Anne (Annika Wills). With her he visits the theatre, eats out at a 'posh' restaurant and abandons the confines of the city for the open spaces below the Severn bridge. The film's second montage sequence seems to mark the change in emphasis. In contrast to the opening's brash materialism, the connotations of the second are more contemplative and spiritual. The shops are closed and a church appears in two shots; the jazzy soundtrack has been replaced by organ music. It is a Sunday morning and also a time for Johnnie to take stock. Whereas the pop group had established a kind of 'utopian' community of 'classless' youth – successfully integrating male with female, black with white, working class with middle class – the social divisions between Johnnie and Anne are not so easily resolved. Anne is going to college and she informs him that 'he won't be the last'. Johnnie is now forced to face questions about the nature of his future identity. As with Bill, it appears as if he too might revert to Teddy Boy type. Bill promises to 'save' Johnnie and following the destruction of the church hall the film dissolves from Smith's face, as he watches Johnnie leave, to a close-up of Johnnie's motorbike now being given a clean.

A subsequent scene, however, makes Johnnie's dissatisfaction with this alternative clear. He fights with Bill at the skating rink and demands to know what it's got to do with him if he likes the people at the club. A second possibility seems to lie in a *rapprochement* with his father who complains that children don't think their parents 'understand'. Forcing a drink upon him, he entices his son to play the bar piano (beginning with a rendition of 'My Bonnie Lies over the Ocean'). This traditionally working-class world of his father he chooses to reject as well. The only 'solution' open is to return to his friends at the club. The role of the real father is replaced by the surrogate father-figure, Smith, who speaks with him outside the hall and encourages him to go in. The camera then holds on Smith while Johnnie makes his way through the door, to be greeted by sounds of delight from those who are inside.

How far, in the film's terms, this represents a satisfactory resolution is open to question. The strategy of the film has been to effectively 'embourgeoisify' Johnnie, by introducing him to the tastes and values of the middle classes. However, by refusing to sanction the relationship between him and Anne, Johnnie is effectively denied an acceptance by the middle class (and even Johnnie's benign father-figure, Smith, displays a constant concern that his daughter might become too 'serious'). The result is that Johnnie is now stranded between the two classes, unable to fit in satisfactorily with either. The logic of the film is to intensify Johnnie's dissatisfaction with the limited life-chances afforded by his own family and class, with its connotations of cultural deprivation. In comparison to the tasteful elegance of the Smiths' home, Johnnie's is noisy and cluttered, dominated by the TV and an ineffectual father to whom he can't relate. On the other hand, the film then has very little to offer him, save the restricted community of the church hall with its 'magical' resolution of the real social divisions of class and race.

And, yet, there is a competing perspective which the film tries hard to deny. Bill, for example, rejects involvement with the Smiths because it requires that they 'conform and be happy'. The Duke of Edinburgh scheme allows for individuality only in so far as they join 'the team'. Such a position is, of course, undercut: Bill loses claim to individuality once he rejoins the Teddy Boy 'team' and behaves according to type. Yet it is also Bill who correctly predicts, despite Anne's denials, that her relationship with Johnnie 'won't work'. Of all the characters, he most clearly perceives the social and cultural divisions which continue to divide them. What he also puts into question is the automatic assumption of superiority in the values now pursued by Johnnie. What is implicit in his position, but not embodied in the film, is the worth of those values thrown up by working-class culture which may not necessarily conform to those of the middle class and may, indeed, represent a positive resistance. All the film shows Johnnie able to offer Anne, however, is 'respect' and the knowledge of how to shrink jeans in the bath. Victor Perkins' suggestion that 'Anne learns as much from Johnnie as he does from her' is hardly supported by the film overall.[19]

What is then characteristic of not only *Some People*, but *Spare the Rod*, *Term of Trial* and practically all of the Basil Dearden *oeuvre*, is a denial of worth and

111

validity to working-class forms of culture. Education and advancement derives from an assimilation of middle-class norms; the 'reform' of working-class youth from a contact with middle-class outsiders (teachers or youth workers) who occupy the parental role, either absent or weakly fulfilled by the children's own parents. Middle-class culture itself is hardly ever the subject of enquiry. The pattern persists with *To Sir, with Love*. Made as a film in the mid-1960s, it nonetheless looks back to the 1950s (when the original E.R. Braithwaite novel was published) in the organisation of its assumptions. Like *Spare the Rod*, it involves a new recruit to the teaching profession confronted by a hostile and threatening classroom. Like Saunders, Thackeray (Sidney Poitier) abandons the school curriculum (throwing the set books into the waste bin) and ultimately succeeds in winning over the pupils. His educational philosophy, however, is entirely middle-class in its attitudes, consisting primarily of 'suburban formality' (addressing the girls as 'Miss') and 'culture for the masses' (a trip to the museum). The role performed by Poitier, in this respect, is eloquent. He is both like the kids but not, a 'toff' yet at the same time ordinary. An immigrant from the colonies, with a background of poverty and manual labour, he functions as a mediator between what the kids currently are and what they might yet become. 'If you're prepared to work hard, you can do almost anything, you can get any job you want', he explains (a statement which is ridiculous even in the film's own terms since he himself is unable to get a job as an engineer).

For Jim Pines, such a characterisation represents part of a basically 'progressive' development in the cinema's representation of blacks in so far as the appearance of a black character is not automatically marked as a

To Sir, with Love (1966)

112

'problem'.[20] The price to be paid for such 'understatement', however, is an assimilation of the character to an entirely conformist and unthreatening set of values. Poitier has rejected his own black culture (substituting 'proper' English for his native patois) and completely internalised the manners and mores of the white middle-class world. The result, as Pines also suggests, is a kind of 'emasculation'. For in its determination *not* to make Poitier a 'problem', *To Sir, with Love* has removed the novel's theme of miscegenation, developed in the form of romance between the black and his white fellow teacher. And yet this is a relationship to which the film constantly alludes, through dialogue, editing and composition; so much, indeed, that its failure to bring it out into the open is tantamount to a 'structuring absence'.[21] The anxiety provoked by myths of black sexuality may have been avoided but the result is a characterisation replete with associations of inadequacy and impotence. This, in turn, reverberates against the programme of education he is promoting: the assimilation of respectable middle-class values by the kinds inviting a similar repression of energy and vitality.

However, it is *The Boys* (1962) rather than *To Sir, with Love* which probably stands closest to *Some People*. Basically a courtroom drama, the film's concern is not just the establishment of guilt and innocence but an inquiry into the defendants' status as representatives of modern youth. In effect, it is youth who are in the dock and their dress, lifestyle and apparent association with violence which are on trial.

The film's first section – the case for the prosecution – apparently confirms the dominant images of youth. 'I'll bring before you evidence of four hooligans on the rampage', announces the prosecuting counsel, Webster (Richard Todd), and, sure enough, the evidence of the witnesses confirms this. In the course of a series of flashbacks, we are shown Stan Coulter (Dudley Sutton) behaving suspiciously at the garage which is later to be robbed, the fighting of him and his friends at the bus stop and public toilets, their aggressive behaviour towards a bus conductor, toilet attendant, car-owner and old man queuing at the cinema and the mounting evidence of a plan for robbery. The pattern of the evidence is clear: the youths concerned are consistently identified as 'Teddy Boys'. Their behaviour is viewed as that of 'yobbos' and hooligans, mindlessly violent and inevitably escalating into more serious crimes such as robbery and murder. Much of the prosecution thus depends on the youths conforming to 'type', revealing the 'surly, aggressive and menacing' behaviour complained of by one witness. Up to this point, the film conforms to the model set by so many of its predecessors. The novel aspect of the film, however, is to go beyond this stereotyping and reveal the 'other side', the same events as seen by the boys themselves.

The turning-point, in this respect, is the scene which takes place between defence counsel Montgomery (Robert Morley) and the boys, once the prosecution is over. Drawing a parallel between his own stigmatism as a fat person and the labelling of them as Teds, Montgomery complains that they haven't told him a thing. He wants to know what they are 'really like behind the great tough act'. The defence is now able to proceed, revealing what the boys are 'really like' and challenging the prosecution image of mindless violence. 'No doubt you will wish to hear something of the violent and hooligan behaviour, my Lord', Montgomery announces to the court. 'They will go into the box and you will hear an unbiased account from their own lips. I'm going to show you this is a perfectly ordinary outing, as innocent and innocuous an occasion on which any boys of this age have organised an evening out for themselves on a barren Thursday night before payday'. As the boys themselves take to the stand, the film returns to the events already seen in flashback, only now in a manner that fundamentally alters their meaning.

The movement here is not towards relativism but complexity. Unlike *Rashomon*, the film does not offer incommensurate flashbacks which make it impossible to measure the 'truth' of what has happened. The events shown remain fundamentally the same; what is altered is the amount and type of information given about them. Three main strategies are involved: a) the addition of scenes to those we have already seen, b) the addition of the boys' own point-of-view shots, and c) the shooting of scenes from a different camera position. In the first set of flashbacks, the relationship to the boys had been primarily one of exteriority, as seen loosely from the point-of-view of the prosecution witnesses (only loosely because the film does not adopt subjective camera techniques). Through the addition of further narrative information, the inclusion of 'missing' point-of-view shots and adoption of alternative camera set-ups, the second set of flashbacks move closer to an interiority, providing a context and a reason for the events which had previously been denied. Thus, the events at the bus stop and on the bus assume a different significance by revealing how the fighting was precipitated by an argument over Stan's mother (dying from throat cancer) and how they would have apologised to the old lady they had knocked down, had it not been for the interruption of the bus conductor. In a similar fashion, it is now shown how the boys had intended to change a wheel for the car-driver before being chased off; while the apparent scuffling in the toilets had been inspired by the boys' innocent fantasies of acquiring wealth.

More particularly, a number of the scenes are now re-edited to include the boys' own point-of-view shots. The inclusion of such shots now reveals that Stan was looking at a pin-up, not the cashbox, at the garage, while, at the pub, it was a pair of girls visible in an upstairs window who were preoccupying the boys, not the lay-out of the garage. In other scenes, the inclusion of the point-of-view shots is accompanied by an absence of the witnesses' point-of-view shots and a re-positioning of the camera, usually from in front of the boys to behind. At the billiard hall, the owner's point-of-view shot of Stan is now replaced by Stan's point-of-view shot of him, as he advances menacingly towards him, intercut with close-ups of the billiard players as they look on in hostility. Whereas the conversation between the two men had previously been shot from behind the owner, now it is shot from behind Stan. This is repeated in other scenes. The second flashback of the car sequence removes the driver's point-of-view shot (previously used to introduce the boys), shoots the scene from behind the boys rather than in front as previously, and employs only one take, without the cut in to Billy

The Boys (1962)

(Ronald Lacey) being given money by the driver's sister. In the toilet scene, the attendant is introduced in a menacing point-of-view shot and for most of the time is shot from in front. Finally, in the sequence outside the cinema there are none of the point-of-view shots belonging to Lonsdale (Colin Gordon) which had been characteristic of the earlier flashback. Apart from one mid-shot of Lonsdale, the camera remains behind the boys and while the earlier sequence had employed cross-cutting to isolate Billy, he is now shot in a group context, where we can see the efforts of the others to bail him out. The logic of the changes is clear: by providing point-of-view shots and positioning the camera behind the boys our identification is structured in their favour rather than that of the witnesses. Rather than the boys appearing 'aggressive and menacing' it is now the prosecution witnesses who appear so.

Our sympathy towards the boys is further extended by the type of information now offered. Hitherto denied any social context, the boys' work and families are now introduced via details of their low-paid manual jobs, crowded high-rise homes and, in some cases, problematic family circumstances (Stan's mother is dying while his father is weak and ineffectual, Ginger is apparently fatherless, while Barney's parents are openly hostile to his dress). Thus, by the end of the defence, our perspective on the case has changed dramatically. Montgomery admits in court that much of the prosecution evidence was 'prejudiced and mistaken' while, in private, he shows doubt with respect to the boys' guilt.

The film's resolution then turns on the establishment of innocence or guilt and it is at this point the film faces problems. Webster is allowed to recall two of the boys to the stand, and, by careful calculation of their finances, manages to secure an admission of guilt. Once so established, the attention of the film diverts to the question of capital punishment and the propriety of sentencing Stan to death, a punishment to which he is liable because his crime was for gain, rather than pleasure, anger or revenge. As Montgomery demands of the court, 'Who will plead for the law?'

But what sense is then to be made of the sympathy generated for the boys in the film's second section, now that their guilt has been made clear? For Montgomery, the implication remains as before:

> I could say that any four boys – given the circumstances which involved my clients – might have done this dreadful, senseless deed, that any four boys consistently condemned by social and economic background, by their fellow citizens, by their very appearance took the inevitable next step – indulged in petty robbery, that this was a petty crime and that the killing was as foreign to their nature as killing a bird or a cat. I could say that these were no more than boys trying to have an evening out. I passionately believe this to be true.

However, the tenor of the judge's remarks quickly undermines this, returning to the conventional imagery of the film's beginning: 'It is impossible for me not to comment on the several acts of savagery to which you and the other accused have admitted: the wanton lawlessness, the contemptuous and wreckless disregard for public property and finally this bestial attack upon an old man'. As with the treatment of Bill in *Some People*, the liberalism of the film's second section, with its challenge to our expectations, is now undermined, while the 'prejudices' of the prosecution witnesses are reconfirmed. Thus, the witness who had warned Billy that he represents 'the sort of person who'll end up in prison' has his prediction borne out by events. The mistake of the prosecution was not in assuming behaviour, and an escalation into violence according to type, as presuming the robbery to have been premeditated rather than spontaneous.

But if condemnation of the youths appears to revert to their typing as Teddy Boys, hooligans and yobbos, the evidence of the second section, and Montgomery's defence, still remains problematic. For if these were just any four boys on an evening out then, by the logic of the film, all youths are equally potential murderers. As Cohen has noted, there is a tension in delinquent imagery between viewing delinquents as typical of a whole generation and delinquents as exceptional (the 'lunatic fringe').[22] The thrust of the film's second section is clearly to refuse the 'lunatic fringe' perspective, and any accompanying 'explanations' in terms of psychopathy or internal disorder. The boys are not exceptional, but quite ordinary. The resulting implication is that if these four boys can be involved in murder, then so can the rest of modern youth.

There is a further complication, however. For what the second section also makes apparent is the social and economic circumstance which led to their involvement in robbery and murder, the absence of money and demoralising scuffle over bus fares which finally prompted the break-in to the garage. In contrast to the complaints of the witnesses in the first section, that young people have too much money, the second section underlines their consistent anxiety about finance – the dependence on parents for gifts of cash, the lack of ready money for buying girls drinks or taking them to a dance, the resentments towards the better off and dreams of being wealthy. Barney (Jess Conrad) asks the others why he shouldn't be a company director able to afford a £2,000 car; while Billy has fantasies of winning the pools. Ginger (Tony Garnett) draws the plan of an imaginary flat for Stan and his mum, while Stan sourly accepts that the girls in the window are not for the likes of them: 'That's for the nobs'. In effect, the youths are not just any four youths but four working-class boys whose crime quite clearly relates to the economic disadvantages of their social position. Although the condemnation and justification of their behaviour provided by the film tends to disavow the significance of class (by appealing to either stereotypes of aggressive behaviour or their unexceptional characteristics) the implication of the second section is quite clearly to locate the boys within a structure of economic disadvantage. The sting in the movie's tail is that the only crime requiring punishment by death is murder for gain, with its grotesque sanctification of capitalist property relations and accompanying unequal distribution of wealth.

The film fails to make such a connection. Instead of demanding a more equal economic system it opts for a humanitarian appeal for legal reform. The evidence of the film, however, cannot disguise that the law is only a symptom of the real problems it has begun to uncover. As with *Victim* and the school movies, the most 'progressive' politics on offer is a minor accommodation (slightly more 'liberal') on the part of the dominant legal and ideological structures.

Exploitation
While most of the films so far discussed have represented a generally 'serious' concern to deal with social problems, there is also in evidence, during this period, a more straightforwardly 'commercial' attempt to 'exploit' the issues involved, looking back less to documentary and Ealing than to the more melodramatic offerings of Gainsborough, such as *Good Time Girl* (1947) and *The Boys in Brown* (1949) and an early 1950s 'social problem' film like *Cosh Boy* (directed by Lewis Gilbert, 1952). In one sense, it can be argued that all social problem films are 'exploitative', capitalising on some current social trend or phenomenon (Teddy Boys, Wolfenden) as part of their overall appeal. The more specific connotations of the 'exploitation' label, however, are those of the 'exploitation' of subject-matter (and, by implication, the audience) through a sensational, and often prurient, treatment.

Sensationalism is, of course, an essential component of the market strategy. Exploitation films are conventionally low-budget (dispensing with stars, minimising sets and elaborate camerawork), aimed at specific target audiences (usually male) and heavily reliant on a quick turn-over of capital. As such, they generally rate low in cultural prestige and are conventionally ignored or even reviled by the critics. *Beat Girl*, for example, – an 'exploitation hit de luxe' according to publicity – reminded the *Daily Herald* of 'how ghastly British films can be' while the *Daily Express* confidently concluded that it was a film which 'no one could like'.[23] *The Times* was more cautious, but displayed an appropriate cynicism about its methods: 'This is the sort of film that is made to a formula for a market that is eager and anxious for it. The idea is to get a popular singer – in this instance, Mr Adam Faith – concentrate on the "beat" generation and the jivers in cellars, set the action against a background of striptease, clubs and coffee bars, tack a perfunctory moral on the end, and sit back and wait for the click of money at the box-offices.'[24]

For the critic of *The Times*, such flagrant commercialism, and reliance on formulae, implies a *prima facie* condemnation, and, yet, for many contemporary critics it is precisely such 'formulaic' qualities which constitute the exploitation film's appeal. Pam Cook, for example, has suggested that the overt manipulation of conventions characteristic of the exploitation film undermines traditional formal invisibility and hence exposes the ideological meanings which such conventions embody.[25] In the case of *Beat Girl* and *That Kind of Girl* it is the manipulation of the 'happy ending' which is most transparent. As David Pirie has observed, the 'fascination' of *Beat Girl* derives from 'the sheer prurience of its contents which like so much popular English art from Milton to Hammer horror allows its audience to enjoy virtue in principle and vice in practice', while, according to Eric Shorter, *That Kind of Girl* is 'that kind of film' successfully combining both 'salacity and moral primness'.[26] Yet, in both cases it is the moral 'virtue' or 'primness' which is most unconvincing, imposed as a kind of *deus ex machina* and drawing attention to its own 'conventionality'.

At one level, for example, *Beat Girl* (1959) would seem to amount to no more than a familiar drama of repression. The relations of 'husband, family and home' enjoyed by Nicole (Noelle Adam) at the film's beginning are put under threat but ultimately reaffirmed by the reimposition of paternal authority and confirmation of family unity. But what is implied in the process of enacting this drama is somewhat different. For from the very beginning of the film, the associations accruing to home and marriage tend to suggest constraint. The attempts of Paul (David Farrar) and Nicole to embrace on the train are frustrated while the home to which they are travelling is large, austere and devoid of life. Paul's daughter, Jennifer (Gillian Hills), describes it as a 'morgue' while Nicole baulks at the 'living room's' barrenness. Appropriately enough, in this home of the 'living dead' there lies a 'coffin' in the corner. Although not containing the 'body' which Nicole suspects, it does contain Paul's model for the City 2000 – 'an almost silent place' in which 'noise, hustle and bustle . . . will be unknown'. As Paul explains, 'psychologists think most human neurosis comes from too much contact with other humans . . . in my city man can be alone'. And, yet, if there is neurosis it does not derive from too much contact, too much hustle

118

and bustle, but from its absence, as found in the death-like atmosphere of the home. By contrast, the world outside implies release. The coffee bar that Jennifer frequents (shot in cluttered compositions and with a quicker pace of editing) provides all the people, noise and energy which City 2000 would suppress.

The complication faced by the movie revolves around its female characters, whose roles begin to mingle the domestic expectations of wife and daughter with the 'perverse sexualities' of the world outside. Following the example of *Expresso Bongo* (1959), whose poster decorates the coffee bar wall, the film deploys a Soho location to run together the teen world of coffee bars with the illegitimate sexuality of the strip club. Nicole's role as wife and step-mother is dislocated by revelations of a past involvement in striptease and prostitution while Jennifer herself makes a visit to the strip club opposite the coffee bar. Through her exposure to a strip performance (loosely organised in terms of her point-of-view), Jennifer imports this role into the home, imitating her step-mother's past career, and stripping to please her fellow party-goers, who have 'taken over' the house. The implication of this eruption, however, is a descent into chaos. Jennifer returns to the strip club where she becomes implicated in murder. Her only escape-route is to cry for 'Daddy'. As with *Wind of Change*, state and paternal authority become fused. The police sergeant advises Paul to 'take over', explaining that if it wasn't for his pension he'd 'wallop her'. The film's closing shot reveals the family reunited as they turn their backs on the world of Soho. As *The Times* suggested, it is only a 'perfunctory moral'. The energy and vitality of the Soho world survives; the home still remains the source of repression.

A similar imbalance also marks *That Kind of Girl* (1963). Once again, the threat to normality materialises in the form of extra-marital female sexuality. Like *Shivers* much later, this takes the form of disease. Although not its source, it is Eva (Margaret-Rosa Keil) who ensures a rapid circulation of VD (passing it on, apparently, even by kissing). As with *Beat Girl*, diverse social phenomena are pulled together into one composite image of deviance, embracing beatniks, strip clubs, students and CND, all linked as one by the threat of sexual excess. Elliot (Peter Burton) meets Eva at a beat club and takes her to a strip show; Max (Frank Jarvis) accompanies Eva on an Aldermaston march (with all the attendant dangers of overnight stops!); while Keith (David Weston), who is a university student, seduces her at a bathing party. Also, as in *Beat Girl*, sexual promiscuity quickly degenerates into criminality: Elliot, for example, turns into a potential rapist and obscene phone-caller. The film's resolution is then dependent on bringing its sexuality under the rule of adult authority: the doctors whose medical diagnoses rapidly transform into moral denunciations, the police who capture Elliot and the Millers who confine Eva to the home, before finally sending her away and exorcising her threat once and for all.

Despite the denunciations, the film's 'exploitative' impulse also ensures a vitality to the club and seduction sequences which is entirely absent from the scenes at the home and the clinic. The latter are generally shot high-key to

119

produce an overly white and sanitary image. The club scenes, by contrast, tend to employ strong contrasts, dynamic angles, rapid cutting and a loud soundtrack. One sequence makes this opposition between exciting nightlife and domestic constriction quite apparent. Elliot takes Eva to a strip club as a preliminary to seduction. As Elliot takes a last look at the stripper's performance, there is a dissolve to the Miller home (where Eva is staying). The Millers are watching a television, compositionally dominant in the centre foreground of the frame. Facing the opposite direction from Elliot, it is as if they have turned their backs on the excitement represented by the club in favour of the 'safe' domestic viewing provided by the box. They yawn, turn off the set and go to bed. The logic of the film, then, is to endorse the moral superiority and social stability represented by the Miller family arrangements. Thus, by the end of the film we see Eva in a similar domestic set-up, listening to records, with Mrs Miller behind the telephone, in the position previously occupied by the TV (in fact, it's the same room, rearranged according to budgetary constraints!). But, as with *Beat Girl*, the Millers' home life has been endowed with few attractions compared to the world outside. It is, perhaps, not inappropriate that when Keith and Janet (Linda Marlowe) decide to get married, chastened by the disastrous effects of their contact with Eva, they conclude, 'If we're going to be unhappy . . . we'd better be unhappy together'.

Beatniks also provide the subject-matter for *The Party's Over* (1963). Although completed in 1963, the film did not appear in British cinemas until 1965 as a result of a censorship wrangle. 'The film was unacceptable for general release because it did not sufficiently condemn the socially undesirable behaviour it portrays', commented John Trevelyan. 'We cannot be sure it would not influence the young'.[27] Cuts, of about twelve minutes, were finally agreed on and, presumably, the addition of an opening voice-over making clear where the film's morality lay: 'This film is the story of young people who choose to become – for want of a better word – beatniks. It's not an attack on beatniks. The film has been made to show the loneliness and unhappiness and eventual tragedy that can come from a life lived without love for anyone or anything. Living only for kicks is not enough.'

This did not prevent the press from rising to take the bait: 'The film-makers say their work has a moral purpose: to show that depravity is not a good way of life', commented the *Express*: 'The usual excuse for parading obscenity.' 'To me it is not so much a shocking picture', continued Cecil Wilson in the *Mail*, 'as a sickening one and a shameful specimen of British youth to show the outside world'.[28] Not everyone, however, was quite so taken aback and it took the *Observer* and the *Telegraph* to strike a more appropriate note. 'The general atmosphere is about as outrageous as a teenage hop juiced up with chemical cider', complained a cynical Kenneth Tynan, while Eric Shorter sounded a note of regret. 'Why can't the English somehow put over a proper sense of impropriety?' he enquired, '. . . or did the censor rob the film of all its erotic and narcotic potency?'[29] Although the film undoubtedly merits a historical footnote for its attempt to bring necrophilia to the British screen, their conclusions are difficult to dispute.

To Sir, with Love (1966)

Yet, as the censor suspected, there is undoubtedly an ambivalence in the film's treatment of its young. Although it is *Beat Girl* which Durgnat suggests anticipated 'flower power', it is *The Party's Over* which is most cynical about the virtues of ambition and economic acquisitiveness.[30] This is most clearly expressed in relation to the American, Carson (Clifford Evans), who penetrates the world of the Chelsea bars in pursuit of his fiancée Melina (Louise Sorel). Carson represents 'the world we are conditioned to accept as normal'. He has worked his way up to the Vice-Presidency of a large corporation and is now 'scheduled' to marry the daughter of the boss. Through his contact with 'The Pack', his production-oriented puritanism begins to wane: 'I had everything mapped out. Well, I don't. As a matter of fact, I'm way off course'. Indeed, after being bedded by Nina (Catherine Woodville) he abandons his search for Melina and resolves to turn his back on business ('I've got to find something else to do'). But, of course, this is a luxury only available to the economically advantaged (compare with the fantasy of being a company director in *The Boys*). As Tynan observes, the film remains resolutely 'bourgeois to the core', chastely avoiding the details of economics which would explain how the principle characters support themselves.[31]

Nor can the film allow the beat life-style to emerge without criticism, for the beats themselves must also change, adapt and 'mature'. As with so many youth movies, one form of deviance (promiscuity, drug-taking) must

121

necessarily lead to something more serious. Melina falls to her death at a party. Assumed to be unconscious she is apparently raped (the cuts make this slightly obscure). Discovering the truth later, Phil (Jonathan Burn) atones by committing suicide. The party is now effectively over for the 'The Pack'. Yet the film is remarkably coy about where they should go. For having also rejected the conformist world of big business it leaves its characters in a limbo. Carson announces he wants to find a place called 'Stow-in-the-Wold'. His query, 'Does it really exist?', underlines the retreat into fantasy.

The other peculiarity which the film presents is in its treatment of the female character, Melina. In a sense, it is with her that the real conformity of the film lies, not in its final denunciation of the immorality of youth. For Melina is a kind of structured blank within the film's discourse: wan, anaemic and marionette-like in her movements. What seems to make her representation so difficult is that, unlike the other female characters, she has refused all the conventional female roles. She is neither daughter nor wife, having fled from both father and fiancé; yet neither has she adapted to the norms of the sexually promiscuous beat society (thus avoiding becoming a 'tart'). She is, according to Moise (Oliver Reed), a 'miracle' – a girl 'who says no'. Moise himself is determined that her 'miraculous' purity should not survive. It is thus that she becomes his other 'miracle' – 'the statue' which bleeds. 'The virgin is pure. Her soul can be loved precisely because her body has not been touched', writes Susan Griffin. 'But the virgin is punished by carnality'.[32] The retribution that Melina faces is thus not at the hands of her father (who finds her already dead) but of the beats. The disturbance she poses to both straight and 'deviant' society (both male) can only be resolved by humiliation and death.

Conclusion

In my introduction, it was suggested how films might be seen to perform an ideological role in their accounts and explanations of the social world. Now, it would clearly be in error to argue that the social problem film of the late 1950s and early 1960s simply and straightforwardly reproduced the dominant ideological attitudes and assumptions of the period. As has been indicated, there were often differences of emphasis and varying degrees of ideological coherence to be found in the films. On the other hand, it would equally clearly be mistaken not to recognise some measure of consistency amongst these films and some degree of inter-relation between the way they represented the world and the dominant ideological discourses of the period. It should now be possible to sum up some of the more general tendencies.

In Chapter One, for example, it was suggested how an ideology of 'classlessness' had been constructed out of the experience of 'affluence'. Although the theme of 'classlessness' was rarely explicit in the social problem film, it was nonetheless implicit in the way that problems were identified and explained. As Richard Dyer argues, the nature of 'the problem' is regarded as 'essentially the same' irrespective of 'social class or economic circumstances'. This is so, he suggests, even when 'the pheno-menal forms of class' may be present. Thus, while films such as *Sapphire* and

Victim do, indeed, sketch in the surface characteristics of class distinctions, they only do so in order to assert their ultimate 'irrelevance' to the issue at hand.[33] This rejection of the dimensions of class is equally clear in the treatment of youth. As Chapter One indicated, it was an inevitable consequence of the ideology of 'classlessness' that the problem of juvenile delinquency should be identified as primarily a generational, rather than class-specific, phenomenon. This is also the case with the problem film. On the one hand, many of the films stress the 'universal' nature of the youth problem by focusing on teenagers who are also socially and economically privileged (cf. *My Teenage Daughter*, *It's Great to be Young*, *Beat Girl*, *The Party's Over*, *That Kind of Girl*, *The Young Ones*, *The Wild and the Willing*). Although there may be some merit in refusing to see 'delinquency' as the sole responsibility of working-class youth, the problem is in the way that these films assume a representative status for their well-to-do youngsters and so remove the significance of social and economic divisions in their identification of youth as a grouping. This suppression of the dimensions of class is particularly prominent in those films which deal with teenagers from a variety of social backgrounds (e.g. *I Believe in You*, *Beat Girl*, *The Young Ones*). Here it is what young people have in common as young people which is stressed and so marked as more important that any of the differences (of class and status) which might otherwise be expected to divide them.

Even in those films, like *Some People*, which do acknowledge some degree of class division it is still not the economic relation which is considered significant. As with *Term of Trial* and *To Sir, with Love*, it is not economic disadvantage which handicaps the working-class youth ('affluence' has apparently seen to that) but rather cultural deprivation. But, even here, it is not the shared social condition which, in the end, is important but rather the differences of individual attitude. Films like *I Believe in You*, *No Trees in the Street* and *Some People*, for example, reveal a consistent concern to highlight distinctions between characters even though they may share a common social background. What is ultimately important in the identification of 'juvenile delinquency' is not economic divisions and conflicts but the quality of individual behaviour and attitude. This also helps explain both the stress given to and accompanying treatment of juvenile violence in so many of the films. For it is inevitable that, by undercutting the significance of class divisions and conflicts, the social problem film should render the violence of its characters not only 'irrational' and 'meaningless' but also unintelligible except in terms of the individual. If this violence has an explanation at all, it can only be in terms of the individual's own 'psychological maladjustment' (e.g. *Violent Playground*, *No Trees in the Street*) or 'psychopathy' (e.g. *The Blue Lamp*, *I Believe in You*).

This emphasis on juvenile violence can also be linked to the 'solutions' to the 'problem' of youth provided by the films. As was suggested in Chapter One, the amplification of the problem of teenage violence encouraged responses which were primarily punitive in intent. In the same way, the social problem film deploys an image of teenage violence in order to legitimate its own disciplinary solutions (cf. *The Blue Lamp*, *I Believe in You*,

Violent Playground, No Trees in the Street). This is not always the case of course. Many of the films, particularly those concerned with the 'cultural disadvantage' of teenagers, reveal a more liberal concern with re-education. Despite the apparent differences, there is also a basic similarity of attitude at work in both groups of films. Both groups, for example, effectively rely on a negation of the attitudes and values of the teenagers with which they deal. Thus, just as the more disciplinary films employ images of 'mindless violence' to deny meaning and rationality to the actions of their characters, so the more liberal films employ images of 'cultural barbarianism' in order to undermine the validity and integrity of forms of cultural expression by the kids.

As a result, while the latter films may reject the more directly punitive responses of the first group of films, they nonetheless share a common concern with social control. Here, it is not force which proves the most effective mechanism but an education which will encourage the acceptance and assimilation of middle-class norms of behaviour and attitude. The identification of homosexuality as a 'sickness' in films like *Victim* and *The Trials of Oscar Wilde* is similar. While this attitude may imply a rejection of more direct forms of legal control and punishment it still involves a denial of the validity of homosexual desire and a more oblique form of control, in the guise of 'treatment' and 'therapy'. As with the Wolfenden Report itself, the apparent leniency of the films with respect to homosexuality remains within the bounds of a commitment to a heterosexual norm, and thus the possibility, as with teenagers, of 're-educating' the 'deviant' back into it.

Indeed, it is this assumption of a sexual norm and corresponding concern with regulation that is probably true of all the problem movies. Although the ostensive problem may be juvenile delinquency or race relations, the implicit 'problem' is often that of sexual excess. As Chapter One suggested, the increasing number of married women at work, rising divorce rates and resulting preoccupation with the emotional health of children precipitated anxieties about family stability and 'declining moral standards'. The teenager often provided the convenient scapegoat for such anxieties by condensing the dangers of immorality and breakdown into a readily identifiable form. It was also this image of the sexual deviance of the teenager which was to recur in so many of the problem films. Despite some ambivalence here and there, what is also generally characteristic is a preoccupation with the control and stabilisation of sexuality within the regime of marriage. Characters are either punished for their expression of sexuality outside marriage or rehabilitated back into the family and marital norm. However, if an excess of sexuality outside of marriage represents a 'problem', so too does a deficiency within marriage. Stability of marriage and family depends not only on curbing extra-marital sexuality but on the use of sexuality as a 'cement' within marriage (hence the importance of the 'sexual mother-figure'). It is for this reason that the 'unfulfilled woman' in a film like *Sapphire* can also be seen to represent a 'problem'.

Three main conclusions can now be drawn. First, it is evident that the social problem films were only concerned with some problems rather than others. They only identified some issues and groups as problems while ignoring, or consigning to irrelevance, other more deep-seated problems (such as continuing economic inequality).[34] Second, by the way that they then treated these problems – refusing to acknowledge class divisions and conflicts, denying rationality to 'deviant' groups and emphasising the possibility of resolution, through either punishment or assimilation – they tended to conceal, or distract from, the socially structured determinants of the problems with which they dealt. As a result, the responsibility for social problems was shifted onto convenient 'outgroups' (usually the teenager) or isolated individuals.

Finally, it was because of such characteristics that these films, for all of their raising of problems, ended up confirming, rather than querying, a consensual view of the world. This was the result not only of what they did, or rather didn't, show, but of how such problems were then used to reconfirm a particular set of attitudes and assumptions. Images of teenage sex and violence, for example, not only functioned as indices of the 'problem' but also helped clarify the 'correct' standards of behaviour by which they were to be understood and judged. As Stanley Cohen suggests, 'the devil has to be given a particular shape in order to know what virtues are being asserted'.[35] Needless to say, such virtues were neither universal nor agreed upon but rather the definitions of 'virtue' subscribed to by only certain groups within society but made to appear, nonetheless, as if they were the virtues subscribed to by all.

Notes

1. Leslie Mallory, *Daily Herald*, 6 January 1961.
2. Ted Willis, *Woman in a Dressing Gown and Other TV Plays*, Barrie and Rockcliffe, 1959, pp.7–8.
3. Mallory, *Daily Herald*, 6 January 1961.
4. Willis, *Woman in a Dressing Gown*, p.8.
5. Edward Goring, *Daily Mail*, 5 October 1957.
6. Willis, *Woman in a Dressing Gown*, p.17.
7. Derek Hill, *Tribune*, 18 October 1957.
8. Paul Willemen, 'Towards an analysis of the Sirkian system', *Screen*, vol.13, no.4, Winter 1972/3. See also Robin Wood, 'Film Studies at Warwick', *University Vision*, no.12, December 1974.
9. For a discussion of 'impossible' camera positions see Stephen Heath, 'Narrative Space' in *Screen*, vol.17, no.3, Autumn 1976, pp.95–7.
10. As I have not been able to see the film I am relying on the published script. See Willis, *Woman in a Dressing Gown*, pp.154–5.
11. Willis, quoted in *Evening Standard*, 28 October 1961.
12. Jack Lee Thompson, quoted in *Kine Weekly*, 10 April 1958, p.29.
13. Raymond Durgnat, *A Mirror for England*, London, Faber and Faber, 1970, p.51. The 'hysteric' and 'contentment' quotations also derive from Durgnat.
14. Colin McArthur, *Underworld USA*, London, Secker & Warburg, 1972, p.39.
15. Board of Film Censors spokesman, quoted in the *Observer*, 4 June 1961.
16. Jon Halliday, *Sirk on Sirk*, London, Secker & Warburg, 1971, p.132.
17. Nina Hibbin, *Daily Worker*, 18 August 1962.
18. Quoted in V.F. Perkins, 'Clive Donner and Some People', *Movie*, no.3, 1962, p.23.
19. Perkins, 'Clive Donner and Some People', p.24.

20. Jim Pines, *Blacks in Films*, London, Studio Vista, 1975, p.117.
21. Richard Dyer, 'Victim: Hegemonic Project' in *Film Form*, vol.1, no.2, 1977 p.16, provides a convenient explanation. 'A structuring absence . . . refers to an issue, or even a set of facts or an argument, that a text cannot ignore, but which it deliberately skirts round or otherwise avoids, thus creating the biggest "holes" in the text.'
22. Stanley Cohen, *Folk Devils and Moral Panics*, Oxford, Martin Robertson, 1980, p.58–9.
23. *Daily Express*, 28 October 1960.
24. *The Times*, 31 October 1960.
25. 'Exploitation films and feminism' in *Screen*, vol.17, no.2, Summer 1976, pp.124–5. See also Aaron Lipstadt, 'Politics and Exploitation: New World Pictures' in Jim Hillier and Aaron Lipstadt (eds.), *Roger Corman's New World*, BFI Dossier no.7, London, British Film Institute, 1981.
26. *Time Out*, no.529, 6–12 June 1980, p.61 and *Daily Telegraph*, 31 May 1963.
27. Quoted in the *Observer*, 27 October 1963. The censor was also concerned about the script's change in setting from Paris to Chelsea, on the assumption that native British depravity was likely to set a more dangerous example.
28. *Daily Express*, 28 October 1963 and *Daily Mail*, 5 May 1965.
29. *Observer*, 9 May 1965 and *Daily Telegraph*, 7 May 1965.
30. Durgnat, *A Mirror for England*, p.139.
31. *Observer*, 9 May 1965.
32. Susan Griffin, *Pornography and Silence*, London, The Women's Press, 1981, p.21.
33. Dyer, 'Victim: Hegemonic Project', p.12.
34. Howard Becker, *Social Problems: A Modern Approach*, New York, John Wiley and Son, 1966. As Becker indicates, what is normally defined as a social problem is not necessarily the problem of a society as a whole, but rather of those groups with sufficient economic and political power to see their definitions of 'problems' legitimated. It is in this sense that the selection of some 'problems' rather than others for attention in the cinema is rarely ideologically innocent.
35. Cohen, *Folk Devils and Moral Panics*, p.75.

6

Working-Class Realism

I

It has become something of a commonplace to view the British cinema of the late 1950s and early 1960s in terms of a breakthrough, surfacing, first, as a series of documentaries screened at the National Film Theatre under the banner of 'Free Cinema' and bursting into full bloom with the appearance in commercial cinemas of *Room at the Top* and *Look Back in Anger* in 1959. What, above all, seemed to distinguish this new cinema was its commitment to 'realism', a determination to tackle 'real' social issues and experiences in a manner which matched, a style which was honest and 'realistic' as well. As Chapter Three suggested, such claims to 'realism' can, however, never be absolute. While it is in the nature of 'realism' to profess a privileged relationship to the external world, its 'reality' is always conventional, a discursive construction rather than an unmediated reflection. What then identifies a 'realist' innovation in the arts is less the quality of its relationship to an external referent than its place in the history of artistic conventions, its 'inter-textual' relationship to what has preceded. Realist innovations thus take place in a kind of dialectic with what has gone before, underwriting their own appeal to be uncovering reality by exposing the artificiality and conventionality of what has passed for reality previously. As Paul Willemen explains: 'Any change in the dominant tradition, any move "closer to reality", can only be achieved by rejecting the essential features of the previous tradition.'[1]

The 'realism' of the British 'new wave', in this respect, was no exception. By opting for location shooting and the employment of unknown regional actors, occasionally in improvised performances, it stood opposed to the 'phoney' conventions of character and place characteristic of British studio procedure. 'Tony Richardson, fighter for protest and fresh expression, despises studios', declared the publicity for *A Taste of Honey* (1961). 'They are artificial. They smack of artistic impotence. He will tackle any technical problem to leave them behind.'[2] By extending cinematic subject-matter to include the industrial working class it also opposed the British cinema's traditional marginalisation of such a social group. 'The number of British films that have ever made a genuine try at a story in a popular milieu, with working-class characters all through, can be counted on the fingers of one hand,' observed Lindsay Anderson. 'This virtual rejection of three-quarters of the population of this country represents more than a ridiculous impoverishment of the cinema. It is characteristic of a flight from contemporary reality.'[3]

In addition, this determination to put working-class characters on the screen implied a more general confirmation of the 'humane values' and the value of a 'socially committed' cinema. 'I want to make people – ordinary people, not just top people – feel their dignity and their importance,' explained Anderson.[4] 'The cinema is an industry . . . But it is something else as well: it is a means of making connections. Now this makes it peculiarly relevant to . . . the problem of community – the need for a sense of belonging together . . . I want a Britain in which the cinema can be respected and understood by everybody, as an essential part of the creative life of the community.'[5] Or as Richardson summed up, 'films should be an immensely dynamic and potent force within society'.[6]

While the debt to 1930s documentary, with its similarity of emphasis on ordinary people and social democratic values, is readily apparent, the relationship is not entirely straightforward. As Anderson explained, 'The essential difference between the Free Cinema approach and the Grierson approach was the Free Cinema wanted to be poetic – poetic realism, but poetic – whereas the Grierson tradition was always rather philistine. He sniffed at the word "poetic" and was concerned above all to make a social democratic contribution.'[7] To this extent, Willemen's observation that Free Cinema claimed to be filming 'reality' directly is misleading.[8] For Anderson, the key term in Grierson's definition of documentary ('the creative treatment of actuality') was 'creative' rather than 'actuality'; it was only through 'creative interpretation' that documentary was to be distinguished from mere journalism.[9] In the same spirit, he defended his own documentary, *Every Day Except Christmas*, against complaints that it lacked 'information' or 'social comment'.[10] It was thus Humphrey Jennings, of all the 1930s documentarists, that Anderson, and also Reisz, most admired, in so far as it was Jennings who was as much 'stimulated by the purely aesthetic potentialities of the medium as by its propagandist power'.[11] Two interlinked ideas were critical to this emphasis upon the 'aesthetic': a) the importance of the role of the artist and b) the conviction that the best 'realist' art should not remain at the level of mere reportage but should transform its material, as the earlier quotation suggests, into 'poetry'.

Implicit in the Free Cinema formulation were two related conceptions of freedom: on the one hand, a freedom from commercial constraint and, on the other, a freedom to give vent to a personal, or unusual, point of view or vision. As the programme notes to the second screening explained: 'All of the films have been produced outside the framework of the industry . . . This has meant that their directors have been able to express viewpoints that are entirely personal.'[12] Looking back on the movement, it was this element of personal freedom that Reisz considered the most important: 'We were not interested in treating social problems so much as we were in becoming the first generation of British directors who as a group were allowed to work freely on material of their own choosing.'[13] For Alan Lovell such a commitment to authorial self-expression highlighted one of the contradictions of the Free Cinema position: 'A central demand was that the cinema should be a medium where personal expression was possible . . . But the demand for realism limited that freedom since the director was necessarily constrained by the nature of the world he was trying to represent.'[14] But what this under-emphasises is the idea of 'poetry', the commitment to 'poetic realism' rather than just 'realism'. 'Independent, personal and poetic – these may be defined as the necessary characteristics of the genre', explained Anderson in his notes to accompany a Free Cinema revival.[15] It was, thus, 'poetry' which completed the Free Cinema equation: independence from commercial constraint and personal freedom of expression equals 'poetic' cinema.

The implication for 'realism', then, was that this should do more than merely duplicate the surface realities of working-class life. Karel Reisz was careful to distinguish 'sociological fact' from 'poetic truth' while Walter Lassally, cameraman for many of the Free Cinema documentaries and subsequent features, suggested that the 'remarkable thing' about the 'new wave' was not its 'strictly realistic view' nor its treatment of 'working-class problems' but its 'very poetic view of them'.[16] 'Even when it has been very realistic,' observed Anderson of his work, it 'has struggled for a poetic quality – for larger implications than the surface realities may suggest.'[17] For Anderson, the key to such 'poetry' lay in the fusion of form and content, style and theme, to create 'a whole greater than its parts.'[18] The evidence of the 'poetic' in the 'new wave' suggests something different: a disjunction or tension between form and content, or, more specifically, between narration and description.

'The locations seem rather arbitrary,' observes Pauline Kael in her discussion of *The Entertainer* (1960). 'They're too obviously selected because they're "revealing" and photogenic.'[19] 'Richardson, Reisz, Schlesinger and Clayton . . . are constantly obliged to "establish" place with inserted shots which serve only to strengthen our conviction that the setting . . . has no organic connection with the characters,' adds V.F. Perkins.[20] What is at issue in both these complaints is the apparent absence of narrative motivation in the 'new wave' employment of place, compared with 'classical' models of narrative film-making. Conventional narrative films tend to be characterised by a high degree of ordering and minimisation of 'redundant' detail, excluding those elements which do not perform a function within the overall narrative process. By contrast, what becomes a characteristic of the British 'new wave' is its deployment of actions and, especially, locations which are ostensibly non-functional, which only loosely fit into the logic of narrative development. For example, it is a characteristic of conventional narrative cinema to transform place into setting. Place as place is less important than its function in the narrative as a site for action. In many of the 'new wave' films, however, it is common to delay the fixing of a place as a locale for action, either by introducing places initially devoid of action (or characters) or by extending the number of 'establishing' shots involved in the introduction of a scene.

Examples of both types can be readily identified. In *Look Back in Anger*, for example, there is a dissolve from Alison to a pair of street musicians, whose role in the narrative remains obscure. It is only as they depart from the frame to reveal Jimmy and Ma Tanner that the location assumes a narrative significance. In *A Kind of Loving* (1962) there is a dissolve from the coffee bar to an overhead shot of a canal, and the factory chimneys behind, before the camera pulls down to reveal Vic, and hence establish the shot in terms of a setting for action. There is a similar aerial shot of Nottingham in *Loneliness of the Long Distance Runner* (1962). It is only once the camera moves to the left, passing a quarry, to reveal the two couples on the hill that the view makes sense dramatically. This emphasis on place prior to the presentation of a narrative action is writ large in the deployment of 'establishing' shots. Thus, in *Look Back in Anger*, there are four shots of the market, and the space around it, before its significance to the narrative is 'explained' by the appearance of Jimmy and Cliff. In *A Taste of Honey*, there are eight shots, lasting a total of twenty-seven seconds, of a street parade and the assembled crowd of onlookers before the scene is motivated in narrative terms by a cut to Jo. In *Saturday Night and Sunday Morning* (1960) there are two high-angle shots of the city and a back alley before Arthur is introduced at home in his bed. In *The Entertainer* there are three shots of a Punch and Judy show before Frank and Jean are identified, walking along the seaside promenade. The 'establishment' of place here, indeed, occurs in only the loosest of fashions: for it is, in fact, impossible to establish the precise (as opposed to merely general) spatial relationship between the couple and the Punch and Judy show, as revealed in the previous shot.

This detachment of place from action is intensified in the form of descriptive shots which form a complete sequence in themselves, what Metz has designated the 'descriptive syntagma', in which 'spatial co-existence' rather than 'diegetic consecutiveness' constitutes the principle of organisation.[21] Thus, in *The Entertainer*, there are eleven shots of the Blackpool illuminations, functioning as a self-sufficient sequence and 'interrupting' the narrative actions which precede and follow. The 'Sunday morning' sequence in *Some People*, already discussed, is similar. Unlike the two 'Sunday morning' shots in *Saturday Night and Sunday Morning*, which merely delay Arthur's introduction, this sequence is self-contained and does not motivate, even retrospectively, the location for Johnny's appearance at the sportsfield.

Similar in impulse to this use of descriptive shots is the multiplication of shots employed in following through a narrative action. Following the arrangement of a date with Ingrid, Vic, in *A Kind of Loving*, is seen running home in an extended series of shots. This begins with yet another shot of an industrial landscape before Vic enters the frame from the right; the camera pans right with Vic as he then runs down the slope of a hill towards the row of houses below, becoming smaller and smaller in the frame as he goes. There is a slight fade and then dissolve to a mid-shot of Vic, now in a cobbled street: the camera initially follows Vic but then holds, once again allowing him to decrease in size. A cut to a low-angle shot of some steps follows, with Vic, at first barely visible, running down them towards the camera. The

A Taste of Honey (1961)

camera pans with him as he crosses the street below but holds for a few seconds as he enters his house and then disappears from view altogether. At one level, it is apparent that the shots are an attempt to signify Vic's sense of elation; but, at another, it is equally clear that the real subject-matter of the shots is not Vic but the locations themselves. It is the places rather than the actions which are marked out by the style and command the viewers' attention. *A Taste of Honey* provides a further example. Jo is seen returning home from school in a series of seven shots (lasting nearly fifty seconds) before the sequence is infused with a narrative significance by the appearance of Jimmy.

Once again, it is place rather than action which assumes importance. Rather than place providing the setting for narratively significant action, it is insignificant action which provides the pretext for a visual display of place. Such an 'excessive' emphasis on place is also to be found in the title sequence of *Term of Trial*. The narratively significant action (the boy running to school) involves no less than fourteen shots. The boy himself is repeatedly dwarfed by the use of high-angle compositions, while the camera chooses to introduce a location before the boy can be seen or hold on to a space after he has left.

One explanation for such devices is clearly to be found in the films' concern for realism. In this respect, the apparent 'mismatch' between place and action can be seen as one means of inscribing a distance between these films and the overly contrived 'fictions' of Hollywood, with their tightly structured narratives and avoidance of 'residual' elements. By contrast, place

131

in these films is accredited an autonomy and 'integrity' outside the demands of the narrative, authenticating their claim, in so doing, to be more adequately 'realistic' (and 'outside' mere story-telling). Roland Barthes has discussed the role of objects and events in a fiction which are not 'used up' in the narrative process; providing neither narrative information nor character insight, it is, in effect, their function to signify 'reality', to furnish the 'effect of the real'. The shots of the market in *Look Back in Anger*, and of the carnival in *A Taste of Honey*, may be viewed in similar terms: 'It is the category of "reality" and not its contingent contents that is signified . . . the loss of the signified becomes the very signifier of realism.'[22]

Yet there is something more. For the meanings delivered by such shots do not stop at mere 'realisticness'. Take, for example, Jo's walk along the canal in *A Taste of Honey*. What is striking is not so much the 'reality-effect' as the artifice with which image and sound are organised. The shots are bound together by a soft and playful version of 'The Big Ship Sails', lingering dissolves (of three to four seconds each) bleed one shot into the next, careful compositions maintain a graphic continuity of line and mass. Thus, it is not the 'actuality' which impresses but the 'creative treatment'. As Paul Dehn put it at the time: 'The film's heroes are Mr Richardson and his masterly cameraman, Walter Lassally, who between them have caught Manchester's canal-threaded hinterland to a misty, moisty, smoky nicety. And they have found unforced poetry . . . among the mist, the moisture and the smoke.'[23] Note how three of the central terms of the Free Cinema aesthetic are neatly interwoven. The 'reality' of Manchester has been successfully 'captured' but, at the same time, transformed into an 'unforced poetry', the result of the film's real 'heroes', the director and cameraman. It is in this way that the tension between 'realism' and 'personal expression' is effectively resolved. For it is precisely through the production of a 'realistic surplus' that the film marks the authorial voice; the signification of 'reality' becomes, at the same time, the site of personal expression. It was because of such stylistic 'manipulation' that a number of critics (including those attached to *Movie* such as V.F. Perkins) had objected to the British 'new wave' films. For them the virtue of *mise-en-scène* in traditional American cinema was precisely its relative unobtrusiveness: style and technique amplified the themes of a film without distracting from the film's forward movement. By contrast, the style and iconography employed by the British 'new wave' is obtrusive; despite the claim to realism, the directorial hand is not hidden in the folds of the narrative but 'up front', drawing attention to itself and the 'poetic' transformation of its subject-matter. The implicit statement, 'this is reality', is so transformed into a stylistic assertion of a controlling eye/I. To adopt the phraseology of Steve Neale, the films are 'marked at a textual level by the inscription of features that function as marks of the enunciation – and, hence, as signifiers of an authorial voice (and look)'.[24]

It has been a common enough criticism of the 'new wave' films that, although about the working class, they nonetheless represent an outsider's view. Roy Armes, for example, argues that they follow the pattern set by

Grierson: 'the university-educated bourgeois making "sympathetic" films about proletarian life but not analysing the ambiguities of their own privileged position.'[25] Durgnat is even more scathing: 'the Free Cinema radicals are uninterested in the masses except as images for their own discontent.'[26] The importance of the point, however, is less the actual social background of the film-makers, none of whom ever lay claim to be just 'one of the lads', than the way this 'outsider's view' is inscribed in the films themselves, the way the 'poetry', the 'marks of the enunciation' themselves articulate a clear distance between observer and observed.[27] In the Free Cinema documentaries of Lindsay Anderson, for example, this is the result of the use of associative editing (a self-consciously 'artistic' patterning of images, in part influenced by Jennings) and, above all, of sound. As Bill Nichols suggests, *Every Day Except Christmas* (1957) is typical of a 'classical expository cinema' in which the primary principle of ordering derives from a direct address commentary.[28] It is in this voice-over commentary, delivered by an invisible narrator, that final authority resides, guaranteeing the coherence of the organisation of images and maintaining a privileged interpretation of their meaning (bolstered, in turn, by the class authority of the narrator's accent). What is absent is the voices of the workers themselves, or their interpretation of events, either reduced to inconsequential chatter or overlaid with a musical soundtrack (significantly classical rather than 'popular', 'high art' rather than 'low').

O Dreamland (1953) does not employ a narrator, yet is similarly 'authoritarian' in its use of soundtrack (the laughter of models, the song 'I Believe') to impose a privileged interpretation of events and create meanings (usually ironic) not contained in the images themselves. What, once again, is absent is the attitude or point-of-view of the characters themselves, strictly subordinated to the authorial point-of-view announced by the film's aesthetic organisation.

With the shift to feature film-making there is, however, a concern to 'fill in' the interiority which is absent from the documentaries. The films are conventionally organised around one dramatically central character, occasionally bestowed with interior monologue (*Saturday Night and Sunday Morning, Loneliness of the Long Distance Runner*) or 'subjective' flashbacks (*Loneliness of the Long Distance Runner, This Sporting Life*). Point-of-view shots, in turn, are occasionally employed in a way which amplifies this first person modality. While, as Stephen Heath suggests, the conventional point-of-view shot is, strictly speaking, 'objective' – 'what is "subjective" in the point-of-view shot is its spatial positioning (its place), not the image' – in some of the 'new wave' films it is the content of the image which is also 'subjective'.[29] When Colin and Mike turn down the volume of the television set in *Loneliness of the Long Distance Runner*, the image of the television spokesman is quite noticeably speeded up as he continues to mouth off in silent agitation. The image does not merely show 'objectively' what would be seen from the boys' point-of-view, but also their 'subjective' perception of the speaker's irrelevance and inanity. It was, indeed, this confusion of 'objective' and 'subjective' modes of narration in the film which made it impossible for Dilys Powell to decide whether she was a witness to what 'the central figure sees . . . or fact'.[30]

This use of point-of-view shots is less pronounced in other films, but is still, in part, in evidence. The shots of Arthur's fellow workers at the beginning of *Saturday Night and Sunday Morning* and the point-of-view shots of Vic in the coffee bar in *A Kind of Loving* may more closely conform to the conventional 'objective' viewpoint; yet by means of editing, composition and the postures of the characters there is a suggestion of something more: that these are indeed as Arthur and Vic 'see' (or, indeed, imagine) them, rather than as they would appear, strictly 'objectively'.

It has often been noted how such British films (especially *Loneliness of the Long Distance Runner*) were indebted to the French *nouvelle vague* (which provided the shorthand title by which the British films became known). Part of the influence, here, was undoubtedly in the adoption of these 'subjective' techniques. As Terry Lovell indicates, 'the subjective and objective worlds are fused' in the French *nouvelle vague*. 'Cartesian epistemology, egocentric and individualistic, is . . . reduced to absurdity. Egotisation of the world reaches the point of solipsism, where the ego submerges the world, and is in turn submerged in it.'[31] In the British 'new wave', however, such 'egotisation of the world' can only go so far. The subjective mode never becomes dominant but is always held in check by the 'objective' point-of-view and the authority of the inscribed authorial voice. Thus despite the dramatic prominence of the main character there are always scenes which exclude him or her (e.g. the scenes between Jack and Brenda in *Saturday Night and Sunday Morning*, between Ingrid and her mother in *A Kind of Loving*). Even apparently 'subjective' flashbacks contain shots of events which it would be impossible for the character concerned to have witnessed (e.g. the graveyard scene in *This Sporting Life*, the beating up of Stacey in *Loneliness*).

Such a superiority over the characters' own subjectivity is, of course, characteristic of the conventional film's employment of an omniscient camera, but, as Paul Willemen suggests, there is a distinction between such films and those which employ a first person narration: 'wherever conjunctions, overlaps, frictions, dislocations etc. occur in relation to the first person narration, the presence of another "person" is signified by a concrete mark'.[32] In this respect, the look of the camera is not merely anonymous but also 'authored', the look from the 'outside' is rendered 'visible'.

This is more generally true of the 'poetic' transformation of the subject-matter of the films, the foregrounding of the 'artistry' rather than the 'reality'. The shots of Vic running home in *A Kind of Loving* and the shots of Jo by the canal in *A Taste of Honey* reveal not so much an interest in their characters (their 'subjectivity') as their subordination to aesthetics, their visually pleasing positioning as 'figures in a landscape'. As Andrew Higson suggests, it is in the aerial viewpoints of the city, characteristic of practically all these films, that this 'enunciative look' becomes most transparent: 'That Long Shot Of Our Town From That Hill involves an external point of view . . . an identification with a position outside and above the city . . . the scope of the vision, the (near) perfection of the vantage-point is stressed: spectator and cameraman are masters of the world below'.[33]

But what then are the implications of this inscription of an 'outsider's' authorial view? It has become something of a commonplace of recent cultural criticism to argue that the introduction into art of 'new contents', such as working-class life, does not in itself guarantee radicalism: what is important is the treatment of such subject-matter. Walter Benjamin, for example, has pinpointed how the potentially disturbing images of photography can be rendered 'safe' by an assimilation into aestheticism:

Let us follow the . . . development of photography. What do we see? It has become more and more subtle, more and more modern, and the result is that it is now incapable of photographing a tenement or a rubbish-heap without transfiguring it . . . In front of these, photography can only say 'How beautiful' . . . It has succeeded in turning abject poverty itself, by handling it in a modish, technically perfect way, into an object of enjoyment . . . it has turned the struggle against misery into an object of consumption.[34]

The Loneliness of the Long Distance Runner (1962)

By codifying its images of cities and factories in terms of 'art' so the British 'new wave' runs a similar risk of transforming them into objects of 'comfortable contemplation'. 'Richardson has used the place and its objects as he uses people', commented Isabel Quigly on *A Taste of Honey*, 'moodily, lovingly, bringing beauty out of squalor'.[35]

But, what is also apparent is that it is only from the 'outside' that such 'squalor' can assume its fascination. Robin Wood suggests what might be at stake here: 'The proletariat . . . remains . . . a conveniently available object for projection: the bourgeois obsession with cleanliness, which psycho-analysis shows to be closely associated, as outward symptom, with sexual repression, and bourgeois sexual repression itself, find their inverse reflections in the myths of working-class squalor and sexuality.'[36] What is, indeed, striking about the 'new wave' films is how readily their treatment of 'kitchen sink' subjects ('working-class squalor') became attached to an opening up of the cinema's treatment of sex. Pascall and Jeavons' history of 'sex in the movies', for example, explains the 'breakthrough' of the 'new realism' in precisely such terms.[37] Riding on the back of the 'social commitment' to observe 'ordinary people', then, emerges a kind of sexual fascination with 'otherness', the 'exotic' sexualities of those it now has a licence to reveal, just as the Victorian 'social explorers', described by Mick Eaton, reported back 'the licentiousness of their objects of study'.[38] 'Audiences could identify with the people and places on screen', observes Nina Hibbin in her discussion of *Saturday Night and Sunday Morning*.[39] Yet the look which the films encourage is not so straightforward. 'Outside and above', marking a separation between spectator and subject, the pleasures delivered may well rely less on recognition than the very sensation of class difference.

Such a preoccupation with the sexual also intensifies the retreat into individualism, a concern with the inter-personal rather than social and historical. Once again, this can be related to the tension between narration and description. As the *Movie* critics suggested, the result is to create a disjunction between character and environment, a separation of the display of place from the forward momentum of the narrative. For them, however, the implication is a deficient 'psychologisation' of place; the use of environment fails to thematise the emotional and psychic states of the characters. By contrast, I wish to emphasise a different disjunction: that between character and the social relations they inhabit. It is not just that the images of cities and factories are devoid of narrative motivation (for it could have been possible to use such non-narrative 'inserts' to offer a productive counter-pull to the individualising logic of the narrative) but that they are also hypostasised into visual abstractions, and so emptied of socio-historical content.

Thus in so far as the city impinges on the lives of the characters, so the relationship between the two is de-socialised: the external, impersonal city, on the one hand, its powerless 'prisoners' on the other. It is also this quality

Saturday Night and Sunday Morning (1960)

which encourages the popularity of 'human' readings of such films: characters as representatives of a general 'human' condition rather than a concrete social situation. Take, for example, the shots employed in *Saturday Night and Sunday Morning* and *A Kind of Loving*, both of which initially 'mislead' the spectator's identification of character. In the final scene of *Saturday Night*, the camera picks up a couple in long shot while the voices of Arthur and Doreen are heard on the soundtrack; it is only when the camera pans left that it becomes apparent that the couple in shot are not Arthur and Doreen but another unknown and anonymous pair. In *A Kind of Loving* the camera picks out a solitary couple on the beach whom we assume to be Vic and Ingrid; it is only when the camera pulls back to behind an upstairs bedroom window (and we hear voices on the soundtrack) that we realise Vic and Ingrid are, in fact, inside and in bed. In both cases, the interchangeability of the couples is emphasised: the individual predicament is transformed into a general one. But it is also an abstract, peculiarly content-less, interchangeability. The generalisation implied can only make sense at the level of a diffuse universalism: a common identification on specific social grounds is explicitly blocked.

This blockage of access to the social is, in turn, intensified by the choice of narrative conventions. In common with classical narrative, the plots are conventionally organised in terms of one central character. Translation from the original novels and plays has generally involved a removal of 'auxiliary' characters and events and a tightening-up of the narrative thread (especially in *Saturday Night and Sunday Morning* and *A Kind of Loving*). Even in those films (e.g. *A Taste of Honey, Loneliness of the Long Distance Runner*) where there has been an expansion or addition to the original, the logic of the translation has been less complication than simplification of narrative motivation (the quarrel between Colin and his mother's 'fancy man' in *Loneliness*, for example). As a consequence, there is an ideology of individualism cemented into the narrative form: it is the individual's desires and motivations which structure the film's forward flow, the attainment or containment of these which bring the narrative to a close. Thus, despite the surface rhetoric of class war occasionally mouthed by Colin in *Loneliness of the Long Distance Runner*, his trajectory through the movie is basically an individual one, with his final act of defiance explained 'psychologically' by the death of his father. Arthur in *Saturday Night and Sunday Morning* is explicitly set apart as an 'outsider', counterpointed to the 'poor beggars' around him.

In contrast to the attempts of British wartime cinema to project a sense of collectivity on the screen, by loosening narrative form in favour of a more episodic structure and multiplying the number of dramatically central characters, the more tightly wrought narratives and dominant central characters of the British 'new wave' work against an expression of the collective experience of working-class life. Indeed, in so far as the organising principle of so many of the movies is upward social mobility (see the next chapter), so the desires and ambitions of the individuals are premissed upon an escape from one's class. This is particularly clear in *Sons and Lovers* (1960) and *Young Cassidy* (1965), both of which are indebted to the 'new wave' in terms of their choice of theme and style (in *Young Cassidy* the small and sickly Sean O'Casey, for example, becomes transformed into a rough and tough working-class hero as performed by Rod Taylor). Both Cassidy and Paul Morel in *Sons and Lovers* are possessed of 'special gifts' (artistic here but sporting in *This Sporting Life*) which can only find expression outside of their working-class backgrounds. Morel must desert his mining community for London; Cassidy must depart from Ireland (giving up 'everything' in the process). Escape as part of a class is impossible; only as individuals can both men achieve their salvation.

This emphasis away from collective experience and onto the individual is underlined by the treatment of work. Although it is work (and its place in the relations of production) which defines the working class as a class, it is significant how evasive the films become about actually showing their characters at work. Just as Eli Zaretsky has argued that capitalist development 'created a "separate" sphere of personal life, seemingly divorced from the mode of production', so the films of the 'new wave' reproduce such a 'divorce' between 'work' and 'life' by their concentration on the characters' 'personal lives', enjoyed during leisure not work (and, hence, the importance of shots of workers *leaving* the factory in *Saturday Night and Sunday Morning* and *A Kind of Loving*).[40] The scenes which do occur inside the factories only highlight this discrepancy. Arthur is seen momentarily working at the beginning of *Saturday Night*: otherwise, such scenes are

138

quickly retrieved for inter-personal drama by convenient interruptions of the work routine (a tea break, Arthur's need for first aid). Such an assimilation of the workplace into dramatic background is also in evidence in *A Kind of Loving*. In one striking ellipsis, the camera dissolves from Vic settling down at his desk after lunch to the girls in the typing pool preparing to go home. In one rapid stylistic manoeuvre, work is rendered invisible.

In so refusing to represent labour, the films also inhibit a perspective on character which might go beyond a notion of 'personal qualities'. For work is not outside and separate from the personal life at all, but a crucial determinant of how that personal life is expressed. Terry Eagleton, for example, provides an analysis of *Sons and Lovers* (the novel) which suggests how far the personal and emotional life of Morel's father is structured by the capitalist division of labour and his exhausting and oppressive experience of work.[41] Although this 'explanation' is a product of Eagleton's criticism rather than the novel itself, it can nonetheless be seen how the forms of the 'new wave' films would work against such accounts of their characters. Thus, in *Sons and Lovers* (the film) and *This is my Street* (1963), the domestic behaviour of the two husbands (Morel's father and Sid) is constructed in terms of 'personal inadequacy' rather than social location (in turn, the effect of an absence of the representation of work). While in *Saturday Night and Sunday Morning* there is a specific contrast between Arthur and those who have been 'ground down', there is little in the film itself which would provide an account of why they have been so reduced (e.g. predatory capitalism, alienating labour). The blame, instead, would seem to attach to the individuals themselves, either as willing victims or bearers of 'bad faith'. This tendency to reduce social relations to individual characteristics is more generally true of all the movies. Thus, in *Room at the Top*, class relations are converted into the personal tension between Joe Lampton and Brown; in *Look Back in Anger*, racism is reduced to the personally unpleasant behaviour of Hurst. Indeed, the very metaphor at the heart of *The Entertainer* ('the family as nation') embodies such a transposition.

But the virtual absence of labour in the 'new wave' films should not be read merely as some unfortunate omission, which a few days more shooting might have rectified; for it also reflects back on an aesthetic problem, the difficulty of actually presenting work within the confines of narrative realism. *The Kitchen* (1961), the one film of the period to make the organisation and experience of work its central concern, is illuminating in this respect. 'The world is full of kitchens', explains one character. 'Only they call some offices, call some factories'. The emphasis of the film is then towards typicality. The organisation of the work is characterised by mass production, a strict division of labour and a debilitating subordination to profit; the work-process is routinised, exhausting and unpleasant. Resisting the temptation to open out the original play, the action is almost completely confined to inside the kitchen, thus emphasising the dominance of work in shaping the physical and emotional existence of the characters. Such an emphasis on work also creates a formal problem of presentation for the film. On the one hand, the impulse of the movie is to reveal the shared, collective experience of work, its mechanical routines and enervating pace. On the other, it is in the logic of the form adopted to individualise the experience, fill in the psychology of characters and complement the non-dramatic tempo of work with the conflicts and climaxes of inter-personal relations. The result, as a number of contemporary critics observed, is a discrepancy between the film's representation of 'talk and work', or, more specifically, between the individualising actions of the narrative proper and the collective work routine, revealed in two extended montages (lasting over ten minutes of screen time) when conversation comes to a halt (replaced by a musical soundtrack).

The aesthetic interest of these two montage sequences is that they begin to propose an alternative formal approach to the representation of working-class experience in a way which would restore some of those elements which are 'repressed' in the other 'new wave' films. However, they remain no more than possibilities: in the end, it is in the logic of the framing narrative to retrieve a narrative significance and re-integrate the episodes by emphasising the individuality of actions (e.g. the use of close-ups of characters whom we can identify) as much as the collective experience. The first sequence, for example, includes two lengthy tracking shots (of about forty-three seconds each). In one way, they can be seen to anticipate the use of tracking shots by Godard in the car factory sequence of *British Sounds*.

There is a similar emphasis on noise and imprisonment (workers trapped behind equipment and utensils) and a sense of the general experience as the camera passes from one worker to another. But, in *The Kitchen*, such shots are also harnessed to a narrative purpose: bound in to the actions of individuals. Thus, the first tracking shot is motivated by the appearance of the kitchen owner, Marango, and his subsequent inspection of the work in progress, while the movement of the camera is halted as he engages in conversation with Kevin. Thus, while the film does begin to make the connection between character and work, noticeably absent in the other films, it still does so by shifting the balance in favour of individual pyschology rather than collective experience. Jonathan Miller suggested that this was the inevitable result of adaptation for the cinema: whereas a theatre performance allowed 'a single panorama', film tended to 'slice up the action into unrelated fragments'.[42] But such 'fragmentation' does not derive from any 'essential' differences between theatre and cinema: rather, it is the result of formal choices. Thus it is in the logic of narrative realism, with its concentration on inter-personal drama, that it should separate out the individual from the group, transform the collectivity into the sum of its individual parts. It was precisely for this reason that Eisenstein rejected both realism and classical narrativity (with its strong, individual protagonists) when he attempted to project the 'mass as hero' in films such as *Strike* and *Battleship Potemkin*.[43]

By contrast, the emphasis on the 'individual as hero' tends to transform the 'mass' into a 'mob'. Indeed, it is often the very condition of full individuality that characters should stand apart from, if not opposed to, the 'crowd' around them. It is precisely the individual/mob dichotomy that structures the treatment of industrial conflict in the 'new wave' which

140

influenced *The Angry Silence* (1960). Like work, strikes are a noticeable absence in most of the films of the 'new wave' (relegated to off-the-cuff references in *Saturday Night and Sunday Morning* and *Loneliness of the Long Distance Runner*) and has a similar effect of removing social and economic relations from the agenda. While *The Angry Silence* may restore the significance of industrial conflict to its characters' lives, it can only do so by reducing its strikers to a menacing and herd-like mob. A crucial element in this process is the idea of conspiracy, the manipulation of strikes by individual trouble-makers. Thus in the shooting of the mass meeting which decides upon the strike the film constantly draws our attention to the 'infiltrator', Travis. Following the works manager's comment that 'that crew down there will never get organised', the film cuts to the shop steward, Connolly, addressing the meeting. But although it is Connolly speaking he is actually relegated to the rear of frame; it is the profile of Travis which dominates the right foreground of the frame. It is this implication of influence, rather than an actual display, which characterises the whole of the scene. Travis says nothing during the meeting, but we are continually reminded of his presence by cuts to him in mid-shot or his position in the frame behind Curtis and Joe. When a vote is taken, it is his raised hand we see first; when the meeting comes to an end it is Travis on whom the camera dwells before dissolving to the next scene.

Without revealing how such influence is exercised, the dynamics of the strike are neatly reduced to a simple manipulation. As a result, it is entirely appropriate that we remain in the dark about the actual cause of the strike (although foregrounding industrial relations, the film is characteristically reticent about showing the experience and organisation of work) and, indeed, about the identity and motivations of the 'infiltrator' (seen arriving 'mysteriously' by train or making an unexplained phone call to London!). It also absolves the film from any responsibility to account for the behaviour of the strikers themselves. Conventions of narrative and character structure identification in favour of Curtis, the blackleg (and also the only character to whose home life we are privy). Our relationship to Curtis is thus premissed on interiority, our relationship to the strikers, on exteriority. The picket is seen from Curtis' point-of-view (shot in shaky, hand-held camera) while subjective techniques (rapid camera movement, tilts, distorted close-ups) are employed to signify his internal distress. The 'objective' view of the camera only reinforces this distance from the strikers: witness the final aerial shot of the men, penned in on all sides, looking like sheep. Although the film's 'solution' requires that the men should 'come to their senses' and abandon their strike, this remains as resolutely individual as all that precedes. The 'mob' remain as susceptible to manipulation as before; only now it is the 'approved' manipulator, Joe, who is pulling the strings, by his emotional and inarticulate appeal to the men outside the factory gates.

Treatment of the strikers in *Young Cassidy* is similar. Although this 1913 Dublin lock-out sequence does not shy away from showing police brutality, its overall effect is one of a generalised 'plague on both your houses' disdain for violence which then works against the strikers as much as the police.

141

Thus, just as the pickets had been viewed from Curtis' viewpoint in *The Angry Silence*, so here the camera assumes the viewpoint of the blackleg. In one particularly striking shot, the camera adopts his point-of-view as his cart comes falling down on top of him and into the river. The camera cuts to the cart hitting the water and then, perhaps inevitably, to the 'riotous mob' of strikers seen cheering above. However, once again, it is not so much collective action (and its significance for the Dublin working class) in which the film is interested as its relation to the individual-centred plot. Narratively, the scene becomes motivated in terms of its importance to Cassidy (his meeting with Daisy, its influence on his art). Appropriately enough, this detachment of individual from the mass is complete by the film's close, when Cassidy now calls upon his previous opponents, the police, to remove the 'mob' from a performance of *Shadow of a Gunman*.

While it may appear a little unusual, there is nonetheless a suggestive point of comparison here with the films of the Carry On series, begun at around the same time with *Carry On Sergeant* (1958). By contrast to the predominantly private dramas of the 'new wave', the setting for the Carry On comedies (at least to begin with) is the public world of the institution (National Service, the hospital, the school, the police force). Whereas the narratives of the 'new wave' are conventionally organised around one central character, the plots of the Carry On favour a multiplication of leading characters. As a result, the causal logic of classic narrativity is replaced by a more loosely motivated plot, less developmental than episodic. Gill Davies' distinction between the *Bildungsroman* and the picaresque is helpful here.[44] The former tradition, to which we might allocate the narratives of the 'new wave', 'entails the growth to maturity of a character through the accumulation of experience', thus reinforcing a 'linear plot with linear development'. The picaresque, by contrast, is more akin to the Carry Ons. Here 'the narrative is not so much a progression as an accretion. The beginning of the story is loosely justified, and it continues with a series of loosely connected, often repetitive events, ending at a more or less random point. The reader is presented with a series of tableaux of equivalent significance, sealed off from each other (except that some characters are carried through).' In the same way, the plots of the Carry Ons are weak in dramatic accumulation, functioning more as a thinly disguised pretext for the display of comic set-pieces (or tableaux) and ribald banter which are the real substance of the films. Continuity is maintained primarily by the consistency of character-types who carry us along the movie, and, indeed, across the series as whole (much as the characters do in the serial narratives of television soap opera).

Such an attenuation of classic narrativity and emphasis upon more than one character structures, in turn, a different attitude towards the collectivity. As Marion Jordan has suggested, a common theme of the films is the resistance by characters to institutions which would deny their sexuality, physicality and fun.[45] More particularly, there is in the earlier films a focus on those institutions which bear most heavily on working-class experiences. As

Parkin observes, the 'them' and 'us' attitude characteristic of certain forms of working-class consciousness refers primarily to the experience of authority relations, especially with petty officialdom.[46] And it is precisely the face-to-face authority represented by the National Service, the hospital, the school and the police on which the first Carry Ons focus. The result, as with other forms of social comedy, is a kind of enactment of 'utopian desire' in which such authority relations are subverted and 'they' (the individual authority-figures) have to submit to 'us' (the resistances of the group).[47] All the films end with a unified, collective effort (the winning of the tests by the misfit platoon in *Sergeant*, the do-it-yourself operation in *Nurse*, the disruption of the inspector's visit in *Teacher*, the capture of the robbers in *Constable*). In the process, the figures of authority become 'humanised' or submit to a collective rather than individual ethic. In both *Carry On Teacher*, and later *Cruising*, the authority figures (the headmaster, the captain) even forgo individual advancement in order to stay with the group. Of course, such communities are precisely 'utopian', binding together diverse social types through an 'imaginary' dissolution of real authority relations, just as there is much about the films that is conservative (especially their treatment of women and regressive attitude towards sexuality). The point being made is primarily a formal one: of how an attenuation of classic narrativity opens up a possibility for the positive representation of collective action. Despite the ostensive commitment to represent the working class, the British 'new wave', through their adoption of conventional narrativity and 'realism', tend to have the opposing effect, that is, the creation of an accentuated individualism.

Notes

1. Paul Willemen, 'On Realism' in *Screen Reader 1: Cinema/Ideology/Politics*, London, SEFT, 1977, p.47.
2. Press hand-out for *A Taste of Honey* in BFI Library. See also *Evening News*, 8 May 1961.
3. Lindsay Anderson, 'Get Out and Push' in Tom Maschler (ed.), *Declaration*, St Albans, MacGibbon and Kee, 1957, pp.158–9.
4. Lindsay Anderson, 'Free Cinema' in *Universities and Left Review*, vol.1, no.2, Summer 1957, p.52.
5. Anderson, *Declaration*, pp.160–1, 177.
6. Tony Richardson, 'The Man Behind an Angry Young Man' in *Films and Filming*, February 1959, p.32.
7. Interview in Eva Orbanz, *Journey to a Legend and Back: The British Realistic Film*, Berlin, Edition Volker Spiess, 1977, p.42.
8. Willemen, 'On Realism', p.51.
9. See Anderson's appreciation of *Listen to Britain*, *Observer* magazine, 18 January 1981, p.56. See also Anderson, 'Free Cinema', p.52. Grierson's definition of documentary can be found in Forsyth Hardy (ed.), *Grierson on Documentary*, London, Collins, 1946.
10. Anderson, 'Free Cinema', p.52.
11. Lindsay Anderson, 'A Possible Solution' in *Sequence*, no.3, Spring 1948, p.8.
12. Notes to *Free Cinema Programme 2*, 9–12 September 1956 (available in BFI Library).
13. Interview in Gene D. Phillips, *The Movie Makers*, Chicago, Nelson-Hall, 1973, p.186.
14. 'The Chequered Career of Karel Reisz' in *The Movie*, chapter 57, 1981, p.1127.
15. National Film Theatre notes, 15 August 1977 (available in BFI Library).

16. Karel Reisz, 'A Use for Documentary' in *Universities and Left Review*, 3, Winter 1958, p.66 and Barbara White, 'Interview with Walter Lassally' in *The Journal of the University Film Association* (US), vol.26, no.4, 1974, p.61.
17. Quoted in Elizabeth Sussex, *Lindsay Anderson*, London, Studio Vista, 1969, p.12.
18. Lindsay Anderson, 'Creative Elements' in *Sequence*, no.5, Autumn 1948, p.11.
19. Pauline Kael, 'Commitment and the Straitjacket' (1961) in *I Lost it at the Movies*, London, Jonathan Cape, 1966, p.71.
20. V.F. Perkins, 'The British Cinema' in Ian Cameron (ed.), *Movie Reader*, November Books, 1972, p.9.
21. Christian Metz, *Film Language*, New York, Oxford University Press, 1974, pp.127–8.
22. Roland Barthes, 'The Realistic Effect' in *Film Reader*, no.3, February 1978, p.134.
23. *Daily Herald*, 15 September 1961.
24. Stephen Neale, 'Art Cinema as Institution' in *Screen*, vol.21, no.1, 1981, pp.13–14.
25. Roy Armes, *A Critical History of British Cinema*, London, Secker & Warburg, 1978, p.264.
26. Raymond Durgnat, 'Brain Drains: Drifters, Avant-Gardes and Kitchen Sinks' in *Cinema*, no.3, June 1969, p.14.
27. Anderson was unapologetic about his 'upper middle-class characteristics' in *Declaration*, p.157. Karel Reisz also rejected any identification with Arthur in *Saturday Night and Sunday Morning*.
28. Bill Nichols, *Ideology and the Image*, Bloomington, Indiana University Press, 1981, p.196.
29. Stephen Heath, 'Narrative Space', *Screen*, vol.17, no.3, Autumn 1976, p.93.
30. *Sunday Times*, 30 September 1962.
31. Terry Lovell, 'Sociology of Aesthetic Structures and Contextualism' in Denis McQuail (ed.), *Sociology of Mass Communications*, Harmondsworth, Penguin, 1972, p.342.
32. 'The Fugitive Subject' in Phil Hardy (ed.), *Raoul Walsh*, Edinburgh Film Festival, 1974, p.84.
33. 'Space, Place, Spectacle' in *Screen*, vol.25, nos.4/5, July–October 1984, pp.18–19. The phrase 'Our Town from That Hill' derives from J. Krish, *Society of Film and TV Arts Journal*, Spring 1963.
34. Walter Benjamin, *Understanding Brecht*, London, New Left Books, 1973, pp.94–5.
35. *The Spectator*, 22 September 1961.
36. Robin Wood, *American Nightmare: Essays on the Horror Film*, Toronto, Festival of Festivals, 1979, p.10.
37. Jeremy Pascall and Clyde Jeavons, *A Pictorial History of Sex in the Movies*, London, Hamlyn, 1975, pp.155–7.
38. 'Lie Back and Think of England' in Eileen Phillips (ed.), *The Left and the Erotic*, London, Lawrence and Wishart, 1983, p.167.
39. 'Saturday Night and Sunday Morning' in *The Movie*, chapter 57, 1981, p.1124.
40. Eli Zaretsky, *Capitalism, the Family and Personal Life*, London, Pluto, 1976, p.30.
41. Terry Eagleton, *Literary Theory*, Oxford, Basil Blackwell, 1983, p.175.
42. Quoted in *New Statesman*, 27 January 1961.
43. Sergei Eisenstein, 'Through Theater to Cinema' in *Film Form*, New York, Harcourt, Brace and World Inc., 1949, p.16.
44. 'Teaching About Narrative' in *Screen Education*, no.29, Winter 1978/9, pp.59–60.
45. Marion Jordan in James Curran and Vincent Porter (eds.), *British Cinema History*, London, Weidenfeld & Nicolson, 1983, p.326.
46. Frank Parkin, *Class Inequality and Political Order*, London, Paladin, 1972, p.89.
47. Cf. John Ellis, 'Made in Ealing' in *Screen*, vol.16, no.1, Spring 1975. See also Richard Dyer, 'Entertainment and Utopia' in *Movie*, no.24, Spring 1977, in which the idea of community is identified in terms of a 'utopian sensibility'.

7

Working-Class Realism

II

If one movie had to be selected as the most eloquent of the dominant assumptions of the period, a strong contender would undoubtedly be *Left, Right and Centre* (1959). Affluence, consensus, political convergence, mass culture and the position of women are all neatly intertwined in its comic treatment of a Westminster by-election. The changes wrought by affluence and the advent of mass culture have irrevocably transformed the social order. The old aristocratic seat of Wilcot Priory has been 'handed over' to the masses who now flock to enjoy its rich variety of amusements (everything from fruit machines to 'sex in 3-D'). Lord Wilcot (Alastair Sim) has accommodated to this new order by an adoption of political 'neutrality', supporting his nephew's selection for a Tory candidature only in so far as it serves his 'sordid financial' ends. But if Wilcot Priory signifies a Tory adjustment to the post-war settlement, so this new social order has also rendered redundant the traditional rhetoric of socialism. 'Toryism means unemployment . . . poverty . . . destitution . . . starvation . . . despair', exclaims a Labour Party supporter. The camera meantime reveals a row of rooftops, a TV aerial attached to each chimney. The result for party politics is a complete absence of distinctions in policy. A Tory MP (one of the party 'intellectuals') mistakenly addresses a Labour Party rally, only to enjoy the same rousing reception he subsequently receives from a Tory meeting for exactly the same speech. As one elector sums up to a TV reporter, the result 'don't make no odds either way'.

What differences do exist between the parties are then a fabrication, usually the work of party agents who have a professional interest in creating confrontation where none in fact exists. Thus, while the 'convergence' of the two parties is dramatically highlighted by the two competing candidates falling in love – in a 'classless' alliance paralleled by the romance between upper-class model Annabel and 'physical culture expert' Bill Hemingway – it is the requirement of the party machines that they disavow their true feelings in favour of a dishonest display of 'fighting spirit'. 'She seems to be acting all the time,' worries Bill of the Labour candidate's performance. 'Of course, she is,' comes her agent's cheery reply, 'she's trying to win an election.'

What underlines such fraudulence is the contamination of politics by the

Left, Right and Centre (1959)

superficial values of television. Although the film's release predated the 1959 General Election by several months, it did successfully anticipate the advent of the 'TV election'.[1] On the spot reporters monitor the election's progress (usually stage-managed by the agents) while vox pop interviews reveal the uninterested attitude to it all. More particularly, the Tory candidate, Robert Wilcot (Ian Carmichael), is himself a TV celebrity, piloted to fame by a 'popular panel game', 'What on Earth was That?' Taking his leave from the programme in order to join the election, presenter Eamonn Andrews introduces footage of Wilcot's first TV appearance. Then, he was merely a 'naturalist', just returned from an Antarctic research expedition and inarticulate and maladroit in front of the camera. 'You've come a long way since then, Bob', observes Andrews, while Wilcot removes his glasses and flashes a mannered media smile at the audience. Previously outside of society, and at one with nature, Bob has now become 'socialised' into a world where triviality and insincerity have become the accepted norms. Devoid of political credentials, Wilcot's claim to public office relies solely upon the familiarity of his face 'in every home'. 'You could say the same for almost any detergent', observes his Labour opponent, Stella (Patricia Bredin). Television values have become at one with politics; the promotion of a politician no different from the selling of any other 'product'.

Stella herself is also the victim of 'illusory beliefs' which the film, in turn, 'exposes'. An LSE graduate, and committed to a career, she is dismissive of marriage and scornful of her boyfriend's encouragements to read *Woman's Dream* and its article on 'infant welfare'. Just as 'love' undercuts the false divisions of party politics, so does it also subvert her demands for independence. Through 'love' she becomes properly 'feminised' (seeing herself, as if for the first time, in the mirror, hair down and in a soft négligé) and reconciled to the loss of her career (i.e. her defeat in the election). It is not, after all, marriage she has been rejecting: merely marriage to the 'wrong' man.

This undermining of the 'independent woman' is also interlinked with an attack on commercialism in *The Battle of the Sexes* (1960). Hostility to industrialisation, anti-Americanism and misogyny entwine as a small family business of tartan manufacturers struggle, *à la* Ealing, against the chill wind of modernisation. Thrown into crisis by the death of the firm's paternalistic owner, the 'threat' to the firm's traditional methods is embodied in the form of the 'new woman': divorcee, 'castrator' and American 'industrial consultant' Angela Barrows (Constance Cummings), with her plans for mass production and the employment of synthetic fibres. Just as the American businessman endures a cruel humiliation at the hands of the canny Scots in Ealing's *The Maggie* (1953), so now Angela is faced with the wily intrigues of an old retainer, Martin (Peter Sellers). Successfully reduced to hysteria, she is conveniently deprived of her position on the grounds of a 'breakdown', a condition apparently 'common with women who undertake the burdens of business life'. Once so removed, the portrait of the erstwhile owner can be correctly positioned in a victorious re-assertion of paternal authority. Deprived of real power, Angela finds consolation in the strength that is properly 'feminine': 'man's greatest hazard – a woman's tears'.

The corrosive effect of the new 'materialism' is also at the heart of *I'm All Right Jack* (1959). Although much ink has been spilt on the film's anti-trade unionism and lack of even-handedness between management and workforce, there is a sense in which the film is only in part concerned with industrial relations, or, indeed, 'the widening gulf between management and workforce'.[2] For underneath the apparent divisions there is, at root, consensus: that is to say, the common self-interest and greed uniting all in the modern consumer society. *I'm All Right Jack* was, in fact, closely based upon the earlier Boulting film, *Private's Progress* (1956), in which this theme is already clear. Both films employ the same screenwriter (Frank Harvey, in collaboration with John Boulting after the novels by Alan Hackney), many of the same actors and, indeed, characters (Windrush, Cox, Tracepurcel, Hitchcock and Dai) as well as many features of plot. In both films Ian Carmichael plays Stanley Windrush, a university-educated innocent at odds with the corrupt and cynical world beyond. Just as he fails to secure a post in industrial management in *I'm All Right Jack*, so he fails his commission in *Private's Progress*; just as he joins the shopfloor in *I'm All Right Jack*, so he is relegated to the ranks in *Private's Progress*; just as he is manipulated by his uncle in *I'm All Right Jack*, so is he also set up by him in *Private's Progress*; and just as he is labelled 'ill' by the end of *I'm All Right Jack*, so is he also accused of 'cracking up' in *Private's Progress*. 'We need to get a clear picture of the sort of world we're all fighting for', declaims an army educational officer to an audience of visibly uninterested privates. Whatever the official rhetoric,

147

I'm All Right Jack (1959)

what is apparent from *Private's Progress* is that, for most of the characters, their primary preoccupation is the 'fight' to secure their own self-interest. Like the workers in *I'm All Right Jack*, the ranks are chock-a-block with dodgers and malingerers, stretching job details to the limit, skiving off to see *In Which We Serve*, and avoiding the completion of training via desertion.

Such diligent resistance to work and noble causes is matched only by the opportunism with which the officer class contrive to line their own pockets. As with *I'm All Right Jack*, Windrush's uncle, Tracepurcel (Dennis Price), takes advantage of his position to further his own acquisitive ends, masterminding an elaborate secret mission whereby he can appropriate a fortune in German art treasures. Thus, while the beginning of *I'm All Right Jack* suggests a break with the old via the exit of Sir John, the cynical drama of *Private's Progress* implies less of a change than might at first appear: it is, after all, the actor Victor Maddern, deserter and layabout in *Private's Progress*, who cheerfully welcomes this 'brave new world' with his well-known reversal of the V-sign. If there is a difference it is only in so far as the new commercialism and its worthless consumer items (such as 'Detto', the 'New Black Whitener') has encouraged hitherto unprecedented opportunities for economic self-advantage. In *Private's Progress*, Cox and Tracepurcel are, at least, brought to justice (just as, in the Boulting *Carlton-Browne of the F.O.*, the cynically self-interested machinations of the British colonial office are up-ended by a successful 'revolution'); in *I'm All Right Jack*, by contrast, not only do Cox and Tracepurcel go free, they receive the blessing of the court to boot.

Towards the end of *Private's Progress*, Cox (Richard Attenborough) arrives with a bag of money for Stanley. He does the same in *I'm All Right Jack*. In both cases, it is the bag of money which most eloquently underlines the theme which is at the core. In *I'm All Right Jack*, the bag is taken by Stanley as he joins a TV discussion of the film's strike, presided over by Malcolm Muggeridge (surely no accidental choice given his association with religious and spiritual belief). Finally appreciating the significance of what has happened to him, Stanley winds himself up to a denunciation of employers and workers alike, drawing on the film's title as he does so: 'Wherever you look, it's blow you Jack, I'm all right'. Requested by Muggeridge to stick to 'the facts', he reaches for the bag to reveal the money inside. Showering himself with notes, he explains, 'These are the only facts that interest anybody in this dispute. This is what they all want. This is all they want.' As if to prove his point, the studio audience now degenerate into a rabble, falling over each other and fighting in order to cop their share of the loot. Muggeridge in the meantime makes a discreet exit.

Although C.A. Lejeune considered the film's nudist camp scenes to have 'no real relevance to the film at all',[3] they are in this light crucial. For in the materialist free-for-all that is modern society, there is no room for the uncomplicated innocence which Stanley represents; for such a society it is Stanley, rather than its own values, who is 'mad'. Stanley's own solution is to go outside society and make a retreat 'back to nature'. As he is pursued by a group of energetic female nudists, a sign is there to remind us of the 'danger' existing 'beyond this point'.

To this extent, there is a kind of rural nostalgia implicit in the work of the Boulting brothers, a sort of forlorn regret for the fall from grace entailed by the advent of industrialism. Thus, while Sunnyglades nudist camp is associated with scenes of rural bliss (thatched cottages and horse-drawn carts) at the film's beginning, it is overhead shots of ugly factories, all smoke and grime, which initiate Stanley's entry into industry. 'From Burke's musings on the great trees of England to Leavis's on *The Wheelwright's Shop* the same image endures,' observes Tom Nairn. 'There is always a Village Green under siege from crass, irreverent materialism.'[4] Unlikely though it might at first seem, the Boultings are, in their fashion, the inheritors of this 'great tradition'. 'Crass, irreverent materialism' is also their target: 'the legend world' of 'Old England' its unfortunate victim.

This is also true of their later film, *Heavens Above* (1963). Based on an idea by Malcolm Muggeridge, who also makes another brief appearance in the film, the film underlines the impossibility of spiritual values and practical Christianity in a world which is dominated by commercialism and economic self-interest. As with *I'm All Right Jack*, the film's beginning contrasts the traditional rural imagery of England with the signs of the new commerce. 'England's green and pleasant land' gives way to a sign announcing the 'erection of houses, flats and maisonettes'; a large and forbidding factory is revealed behind a small boy fishing in Orbiston Parva's 'quiet backwater'. Just as *Left, Right and Centre* had shown political interests coming a good second to the attractions of the *News of the World*, *Spider Man from Mars* and Tommy Steele, the Sunday 'devotions' which preoccupy the citizens of *Heavens Above* are television, bingo, dancing to the jukebox and *From Here to Eternity*. The usurpation of spiritual by material values is summed up in the product upon which the livelihoods of Orbiston Parva depends: 'Tranquillax', the new commercialism's answer to the church's 'Holy Trinity', a 'three-in-one' restorative, combining a sedative, stimulant and laxative. This time it is Peter Sellers as the Rev. John Smallwood who plays the innocent let loose in a world he does not understand. Attempting to generate an authentic Christian spirit of charity and goodwill, he merely succeeds in alienating the whole community, who selfishly combine to reject him. As with Windrush in *I'm All Right Jack*, modern society can find no place for Smallwood's simple idealism, confining him to isolation as the church's first bishop of outer space. 'Idealism is neither here nor there', explains Durgnat, 'but a kind of lonely warbling in orbit.'[5]

Although, at first glance, it might seem an unlikely comparison, there is something of a similarity here with the films of the British 'new wave'. For what also emerges as a theme in these is the corrosive effects of a modern mass, commercialised culture. As Karel Reisz explained of *Saturday Night and Sunday Morning*: 'the film began to ask the question whether material improvements in people's lives weren't going to be accompanied by a spiritual crisis.'[6] The same could clearly be said of *I'm All Right Jack* or *Heavens Above*. There is, however, a specific inflection to the mass culture theme in the 'new wave' films; one which is, in turn, dependent on their commitment to a representation of the working class. As Chapter One suggested, the increasingly dominant image of the working class during the 1950s was one of change and decline. Modern mass production, increasing geographical mobility and urban redevelopment were breaking up traditional working-class communities, while the 'economic emancipation' of the working class was being bought at the expense of a cultural subjection to the hollow banalities of mass entertainment. The introduction of the working class on to British cinema screens thus occurred at a particular 'cultural moment' whose attitudes and assumptions were to structure the way that the working class were to be represented. As Alan Lovell has suggested, the 'views of the world' characteristic of Free Cinema resulted from 'preoccupations common among intellectuals in the second half of the fifties': 'a sympathetic interest in communities . . . fascination with the newly emerging youth culture . . . unease about the quality of leisure in urban society and respect for the traditional working class'.[7] This is particularly true of the two Lindsay Anderson documentaries *Every Day Except Christmas* and *O Dreamland*, both of which are eloquent of the 'structure of feeling' governing the representation of the working class in this period. On the one hand, there is the dignity and community represented by the traditional working class of Covent Garden; on the other, the mass degradation of the working class at the hands of an ersatz and commercialised culture.

For Anderson, *Every Day Except Christmas* was intended as a celebration: 'at the moment it is more important for a progressive artist to make a positive affirmation than an aggressive criticism'.[8] 'Only connect', it may be remembered, was Anderson's choice of title for his essay on Jennings, and like Jennings' *Listen to Britain* (1942), *Every Day Except Christmas* is concerned to stress the sense of community and interconnection both between the workers in the film itself and with 'us', the larger community beyond. The film's logic of exposition embodies this principle by following the pattern of the night's work as one job prepares for and then gives way to another. Although individuals are identified (e.g. Jenny, the flower-seller) it is the collective effort which is stressed, by inter-cutting the variety of people involved in any one task (be it packing, setting up a stall or portering) rather than dwelling on the individual action. This subordination of the part to the whole is underlined by the film's mismatching of sound and image. The voices we hear are not those of the people we see: the individual identity of the speaker is less important than the flow of the overall pattern. 'We all depend on each other's work as well as our own – on Alice and George and Bill and Alan and Sid and all the others who keep us going', intones the narrator at the film's close. Character and spectator so intertwined, the Covent Garden workers now proceed with their 'curtain call'.

If *Every Day Except Christmas* seems to draw on the example of *Listen to Britain*, it is surely Jennings' *Spare Time* (1939), and its discomfiting survey of working-class leisure, that suggests a precursor for *O Dreamland*. For where *Every Day Except Christmas* offers affirmation, *O Dreamland* provides 'aggressive criticism'; where *Every Day Except Christmas* bestows its 'ordinary people' with dignity, *O Dreamland* reveals their degradation. The film's choice of opening images, although undoubtedly ambivalent, is suggestive. A chauffeur is seen polishing a Bentley from a variety of viewpoints; the camera then pans away from the car and on to an empty gate. A group of people march past on their way, as a subsequent shot reveals, to the amusement park ahead. On the one hand, there is the 'old order', the 'traditional social set-up' of class and privilege under which the deferential worker labours to clean his master's goods; on the other, there is the 'new order', the economically liberated working class now laying claim to their new 'democratic' culture.[9]

It is not a development, however, which *O Dreamland* can view with equanimity. In 1948, Anderson had decried the 'moronic mass audience' for popular films and invited any critic who might doubt this to 'spend their Sunday evenings in front of cinema queues just looking at them'.[10] The invitation of *O Dreamland* is the same: to look at the 'moronic mass audience' in the arcade, as they gawp at a succession of model re-enactments of executions and torture and bow before the 'shiny barbarism' of the Magic Garden. Whereas *Every Day Except Christmas* intercut individual actions to emphasise collective endeavour, the editing of *O Dreamland* reduces its characters to an interchangeable mass. There is a continual ambiguity in the use of eyeline matches, such that it is impossible to be sure just who is looking at what. This is not important, however; what matters is the overall pattern of degrading spectacle and lethargic spectators. This disdain is further marked by composition, fragmenting the spectators' bodies and imprisoning them behind bars, as well as editing, whereby model dummies and spectators are intercut in the suggestion of a parallel.

However, it is in the use of sound that this attitude is most clearly expressed. 'The image speaks. Sound amplifies and comments', declared the Free Cinema's first programme note.[11] *O Dreamland* bears this out. In the absence of direct sound, the overlaid soundtrack is only loosely motivated by what we see, quite commonly providing the element which binds together the film's association of images. Thus, the raucous laughter of a model policeman is heard one shot before we can identify its source and then continues over the four succeeding shots. It quickly becomes something of a motif, punctuating the film at a variety of stages and accumulating thematic significance, mocking the spectators and underlining the debasement of feeling that has turned torture and suffering into objects of amusement. The ritualistic chant of a game of bingo is employed in a similar fashion, as is the popular song, 'I believe' (in contrast to the classical music employed by *Every Day Except Christmas*). Introduced as a record on the jukebox, the song, like the laughter, recurs throughout the film before reaching a climax at the film's close when the camera sweeps up and over the illuminated Magic Garden to the rousing accompaniment of the chorus, ''Cos I believe'. This final, carefully orchestrated, 'bravura' effect sums up well the film's meanings: the spiritual emptiness of a modern mass culture in which faith and belief amount to no more than a flickering of lights, surrogate art and romantic fiction.

Allison Graham suggests that the film should at least 'dispel any notion that Anderson romanticises the working class'.[12] Yet this is, in some ways, to miss the point. For the distaste for working-class leisure to be found in *O Dreamland* does not merely 'balance' the idealisation of working-class community in *Every Day Except Christmas* in so far as the attitudes at work in both are entirely consistent within the terms of the cultural viewpoint that animates them. A respect for the traditional working class and hostility to the corruptions of modern mass culture are not opposed but part of one and the same response to the economic and cultural developments of the 1950s. It is a tension, moreover, which is characteristic of the work of the 'new wave' as a whole.

152

The Blackpool amusements sequence in *A Taste of Honey*, for example, is practically a reprise of Anderson's *O Dreamland*. There is exactly the same emphasis on degrading spectacle and its culturally repellent mix of prurience, ghoulishness and pseudo-art (e.g. the grotesque tableau of Van Gogh's 'Fascination', 'now hanging in the Louvre Gallery in Paris'). Blaringly loud pop songs ('I'm gonna grab it. I'll have it. Why not, why not, why not?') punctuate the action, employing numbers already familiar from other films ('Baby, baby you're so square' is used in the youth club sequence in *The Entertainer*: 'Slip away' and, indeed, 'Grab it' are heard during the fair sequence in *Saturday Night and Sunday Morning*). Like *O Dreamland*, the characters themselves are made to look grotesque, stuffing themselves with food, matching their heads to model cavemen's bodies, disfiguring themselves in front of distorting mirrors. And, in a practical steal, there is a cut from the close-up of a woman's face to a model clown in a glass cage, linked by their mutually repulsive laughter.

This distaste for mass culture, however, is probably most in evidence in the treatment of television. Arthur (Albert Finney) returns home in *Saturday Night and Sunday Morning* to find his father absorbed by the television and its flow of vacuous adverts ('Bristol is today's cigarette', 'Silvikrin for lovely hair'). Attempting to capture his attention, Arthur recalls an accident in the three speed shop: 'This fellow got his hand caught in a press. He didn't look what he was doing. Of course, he's only got one eye, he lost the sight of the

Saturday Night and Sunday Morning (1960)

153

other looking at telly day in and day out'. In *Loneliness of the Long Distance Runner*, Colin's mother's 'fancy man' brings a television into the house which the family all gather round to watch (treated to yet more adverts); all except Colin (Tom Courtenay) who walks out of the room in disgust. In *A Kind of Loving*, Vic (Alan Bates) is prevented from attending a brass concert by his wife and mother-in-law; instead he must stay at home to watch 'Spot Quiz' and its parade of inconsequential competitors (e.g. a man whose hobbies include 'looking at people'). The television set also appears prominently in compositions in *The Entertainer*, while Archie (Laurence Olivier) is derided by a schoolgirl for never having made a TV appearance. In *Look Back in Anger*, it is the popular tabloids, rather than television, which inspire the most anger.

What is also significant, especially in the two sequences from *Loneliness of the Long Distance Runner* and *A Kind of Loving*, is the contrast which is assumed between modern mass culture and traditional working-class culture, 'male' values and 'female' values. In *Loneliness of the Long Distance Runner*, the death of Colin's father furnishes the family with a windfall. The resulting shopping spree is a kind of Cook's tour of modern consumer society as they trip from shop to shop, stylistically inter-cut with graphics of white stars, bursting forth on to the screen in a parody of advertising techniques. On their return, Colin is given his share of the pay-out (despite his reluctance to accept); turning his back on the television, he goes into his dead father's bedroom, looks at himself in the mirror, moves past his father's photograph and proceeds to set fire to one of the pound notes. In *A Kind of Loving*, the scene with the television is preceded by shots of the brass band in concert, including a cut in to Vic's father as he begins a trombone solo. In both cases, it is not that just modern mass culture is being criticised; it is also defined negatively in relation to traditional working-class culture.

Crucial to the idea of the traditional working class as it was developed in the 1950s and 1960s was the intimate relationship between work and cultural identity, the strong sense of identity and 'proletarian consciousness' characteristic of the 'occupational community' (in industries such as mining, for example).[13] By contrast, the characteristics which most pre-eminently defined the 'new' working class were less work than leisure, patterns of consumption and recreational pursuits. Thus, as Colin Sparks has observed of the work of writers like Hoggart, there is a significant absence of a discussion of work and trade unions in their consideration of patterns of working-class culture.[14] Here then is another explanation for the omission of work and industrial conflict in the films of the 'new wave'. For their representation of class is being made precisely at a time when the traditional working class is perceived as being in decline, supplanted by a modern working class whose identity is most tellingly revealed in consumption rather than production. Thus in *Saturday Night and Sunday Morning* it is Arthur's 'affluence' (instructed by his foreman not to let on to the others what he's earning) and 'conspicuous consumption' (removing his newly laundered jacket from the wardrobe, narcissistically knotting his tie in front of the mirror) which is highlighted: the significance of capitalist exchange

Look Back in Anger (1959)

rather than production. Appropriately enough, the one reference to a strike in the film occurs in conversation with the 'old-timer' whom Arthur meets in the traditional working man's club, not normally favoured by Arthur. Such an antithesis is also clear in *Loneliness of the Long Distance Runner*. Colin's father, trade unionist and strike-leader, is dead; Colin – who is 'like his father' – refuses to succumb to the blandishments of the new consumerism by burning its symbol (the pound note) in his memory. In the same way, it is the traditional working-class concert of the brass band – 'this substantial pocket of music, so untouched by the mass media', according to Brian Jackson in his study of working-class community – which Vic is prevented from attending by his night's viewing of television in *A Kind of Loving*.[15] In Stan Barstow's novel, it is a symphony concert he does not attend. Thus, while for the book it is the high versus low art opposition which is emphasised (as revealed in Van Huyten's education of Vic in classical music and Conroy's revelations of learning), for the film it is the traditional versus mass culture opposition which is stressed instead.

In *The Entertainer*, it is the traditional culture of the music hall which takes the place of *A Kind of Loving*'s brass band. Billy's patriotic pub performance of an old music hall song ('Don't let 'em scrap the British Navy') is followed immediately by Archie's lewd and tatty denigration of the patriotic spirit ('This was their finest shower'). A semi-naked Britannia, a mocking refrain of 'Land of Hope and Glory' plus an inverted V-sign (cf. *I'm All Right Jack*) complete the shoddy spectacle. Whereas Billy (Roger Livesey), singing without a microphone, is intercut with the appreciative group who join in the chorus, the audience for Archie's performance remain invisible (save for the applause of the self-seeking Cox's). 'The music hall is dying, and, with it, a significant part of England', explains John Osborne in his introduction to the play.[16] Billy's death on stage in the film thus marks the end of the traditional culture he represents, just as the death of Ma Tanner, the widow of a music hall entertainer, performs a similar function in *Look Back in Anger*. For Osborne, the music hall is 'immediate, vital and direct' and thus representative of a popular culture under threat from the new trivialities of mass culture.[17] It is for the same reason that both films also draw on jazz. Archie recollects the sincerity and emotion of a negress singing in a bar in *The Entertainer*; Jimmy escapes the 'phoniness' of the society around him by playing jazz trumpet in *Look Back in Anger*, making the claim that anyone who doesn't like jazz 'has no feeling for music or people'. Significantly, it is both music hall and jazz which Hall and Whannel use for examples in their defence of popular art against its 'corruption' into mass entertainment in *The Popular Arts*.

Something of a similar contrast, though less emphasised than in *The Entertainer*, can be found in *Saturday Night and Sunday Morning*. Arthur and his friends sit upstairs boozing to the accompaniment of a pop group's chorus: 'What do you want if you don't want money?'; meantime down below there is a traditional sing-song as the older clientele join in a version of 'Lily of Laguna'. In a similar fashion, the simple pleasures of Jo and Jimmy's romance in *A Taste of Honey* are counterpointed to the dance-hall jerkings of her mother and Peter (Robert Stephens), with its connotations of sexual deviance ('you know I like this mother-son relationship').

What is also in evidence in the two sequences from *A Kind of Loving* and *Loneliness of the Long Distance Runner* is not just the traditional versus mass division but the contrast between male and female. Whereas the brass band in *A Kind of Loving* is all-male, including Vic's father, the viewing of television is associated with women, Vic's wife and mother-in-law, whose preoccupations throughout the film are highlighted as shallow and consumerist. Ingrid (June Ritchie) is named after Ingrid Bergman, hasn't 'much time for reading' but can lovingly recall the details of a television soap opera ('Call Dr Martin') while her mother's horizons of interest wouldn't appear to extend beyond 'Take Your Chance' and new acquisitions for the home (a carpet, chest of drawers, curtains). In one striking shot, both mother and daughter are shot in mirror-reflection, drawing attention to both Ingrid's narcissistic absorption with appearance and the 'counterfeit' values by which they live (Mrs Rothwell is lamenting the fact that her daughter will be missing 'Spot Cash Quiz'). In a similar fashion, it is Colin's mother in *Loneliness of the Long Distance Runner* who leads the foray to the shops and argues with Colin over the use of the money that the death of his father has provided. Whereas the traditional working class (as represented by Colin's father) had generally been characterised in terms of a pronounced masculinity (male pride in tough and demanding work, militant trade unionism), the identification of the modern era is in terms of its opposite, the 'triumph' of female consumerism, as explained in Chapter One.[18]

One of John Schlesinger's films subsequent to *A Kind of Loving, Darling* (1965), emphasises the point. Diana (Julie Christie) functions as the metaphor for the trivial and shallow values of the consumer society, its slavish devotion to appearance rather than substance (cf. the opening sequence's covering of a poster for 'World Relief' by Diana's cover girl portrait). As with the other films, the 'shiny barbarism' of the new age is counterpointed to the literary and rural values of Southgate, whose death, like Billy's in *The Entertainer*, thus signifies the end of 'a certain flinty integrity . . . perhaps, for ever'. For some of these films, indeed, this ascendancy of the 'feminine principle' becomes tantamount to 'castration'. In *A Kind of Loving*, Ingrid becomes the 'preying mantis', described by Conroy; Vic, her 'victim' (seen under the cinema advertisement for the film of that name). Subordinated to an all-female household, Vic loses his potency, no longer making love to his wife. In *The Leather Boys*, Dot (Rita Tushingham) represents an even more exaggerated version of Ingrid, likewise devoted to the values of the mass media and consumerism (the pictures, 'True Romance' and dyed hair). As in *A Kind of Loving*, her husband's initial virility gives way to impotence and a retreat into a quasi-homosexual relationship with Reggie (Dudley Sutton).

This association of women with consumerism is underlined by the plot structures generally characteristic of the 'new wave' films. In all the films based on the work of Amis, Braine and Osborne, for example, the central theme and organising principle of the narrative is that of upward social mobility, of a working-class or lower middle-class character coming to terms with an upper middle-class milieu (cf. *Lucky Jim, Only Two Can Play, Room at the Top, Look Back in Anger*). Central to this process is the seduction of or marriage to a woman from a higher social class. This is also the case in *The Wild and the Willing, Expresso Bongo* and, as has already been noted, *Some People*. Indeed, as Blake Morrison suggests, in his discussion of the relevant literature, it is the combined connotations of the word 'class', as both social status and physical attractiveness, which underlines the ambivalent social/ sexual ambitions of the hero ('You've got real class' is actually Bongo's comment to Dixie in *Expresso Bongo*).[19] Even in those films where the hero remains within his class, it is still characteristic for the women to represent a 'respectability' or 'classiness' distinct from that of the male hero (cf. the suburban homes and lower-middle-class aspirations of Doreen in *Saturday Night and Sunday Morning* and Ingrid in *A Kind of Loving*). The result is that the women themselves can become something of a commodity, desired not so much for themselves as the economic advantages they represent (and, thus, a measure of the 'false' goals which the hero is pursuing).

This is nowhere clearer than in *Room at the Top*. For Joe (Laurence Harvey) the desire to have Susan (Heather Sears) is indistinguishable from his desire for what she represents (the sports car in which he first sees her). When he returns to the home of his uncle and aunt (the traditional Northern working class) to announce his impending marriage, the confusion in his motivations is transparent. 'I ask you about the girl and all you tell me about is her father's brass', complains his aunt. 'Sure it's the girl you want, Joe, not

157

the brass?', adds his uncle. As with the novel, it is the emotional and spiritual cost of this sacrifice of feeling to the pursuit of superficial, material values which is emphasised (his transformation into a 'successful Zombie' as the novel puts it). The use of a theatrical setting and emphasis on the parallels between theatrical performance and life outside (cf. Alice and Susan's performance as jealous lovers) foregrounds the problem of 'authenticity' faced by Joe. 'You don't ever have to pretend. You just have to be yourself', explains Alice to Joe (who does, indeed, become 'someone else' by his adoption of Jack Wales' name near the film's close). In contrast to Susan, Alice stands outside the complications of class ('self pity and class consciousness' were not part of her conception of Joe, explains the novel).[20] Alexander Walker pursues the point with respect to the casting of Simone Signoret and her absence of an English, 'classbound', accent. Sex and class so dissociated, she does not represent just 'one more conquest – among the English upper classes'.[21] This is reinforced by their 'escape' from the city and its corruptions to Alice's hide-out by the sea (a real location rather than the obvious set in which Joe and Susan make love). The 'naturalness' of their relationship is thus reinforced by an iconography of 'nature', contrasted to the social and economic pressures embodied in the city.

A similar contrast between the city and the country occurs in practically all the subsequent 'new wave' films. Colin and his friends enjoy a weekend in Skegness in *Loneliness of the Long Distance Runner*; Paul (Dean Stockwell) and Clara (Mary Ure) take an illicit holiday by the sea in *Sons and Lovers*; Frank (Richard Harris) takes Mrs Hammond (Rachel Roberts) and her children to the country in *This Sporting Life*; Vic and Ingrid take their honeymoon by the sea in *A Kind of Loving*; Jo, Geoff and a group of children abandon the city for the hills above in *A Taste of Honey*; Arthur and Bert (Norman Rossington) spend their Sunday afternoons fishing in the canal in *Saturday Night and Sunday Morning*. Similar rural scenes can also be found in *No Love for Johnnie*, *This Is My Street*, and *Some People*. In such films it is the city which represents entrapment. A favoured shot in many of the films is a high-angle view of the city as seen by the characters inside: Jimmy looks out on the street below from his bedsit in *Look Back in Anger*; Arthur looks down on the close in *Saturday Night and Sunday Morning*; Jo looks over the city in *A Taste of Honey*; as does Lewis in *Only Two Can Play*. In *This Sporting Life* and *Loneliness of the Long Distance Runner*, the characters observe the city from a hillside above. But the prospect of the characters so 'standing above' their environment is an impossibility, undercut by the enclosure and claustrophobia of the places from which they look or, in the case of the hill shots, the requirement that the characters return to the world below. In the same way, while it is in the country or by the seaside that the characters can most 'be themselves', they cannot remain in this 'natural state' but must return to the city to face the complications that bedevil their normal lives. Escape to the country or transcendence of their environment thus foreclosed, the characters must make some compromise with the world in which they live.

Such an adjustment is quite commonly marked by a rejection of fantasy. Archie must accept the destruction of his hopes for financial backing for his new show and face the prospect of impending imprisonment in *The Entertainer*; Jo's romantic retreat with Geoff comes to an end with the return of Jo's mother in *A Taste of Honey*; Vic's prospects of getting away are confounded by his marriage to Ingrid in *A Kind of Loving*; Billy (Tom Courtenay) must abandon his fantasies of going to London in *Billy Liar* and reconcile himself to family responsibilities and the realities of his life as a 'nobody'. The renunciation of fantasy is also at the heart of *Only Two Can Play*. Although the *Monthly Film Bulletin* objected that the introduction of Liz (Mai Zetterling) was unrealistic, it is precisely such an 'unreality', the eruption of fantasy into reality, that her character represents.[22] Her large American car, her foreignness (having come over to Britain with the 'free Norwegians') and defiance of regulation (parking where she shouldn't, knocking down the 'no waiting' sign) provides a precise fulfilment of the sexual fantasies for so long nurtured by Lewis (Peter Sellers). Inevitably the 'fantasy' must disappoint, must prove to be 'unworkable'. Chastened by his experience, Lewis now returns to his wife. Having learnt his lesson, the amorous overtures of his library customers are henceforth rejected.

As this would suggest, the rejection of fantasy and acceptance of compromise is closely related to the problem of sexual choice, the question of a female partner. As John Ellis suggests, 'In a society where roles are defined in terms of the masculine, the female becomes a problem. The masculine is assumed to be a set of positive definitions: actions towards a goal, activity in the world, aggressiveness, heterosexual desire. This implies an opposite: the feminine. However, the definition of this opposite remains a problem, and this problem is obsessively worked over in narrative fiction films . . . entertainment cinema depends upon the assumption of a masculine norm and the relentless demand to know what the female counterpart to that norm is.'[23]

This problem of a 'female counterpart' is structured into the 'new wave' films in the form of a dichotomy between two types of female characters. On the one hand, there are wives or potential wives; on the other, there are lovers and mistresses (e.g. *Look Back in Anger*, *The Entertainer*, *Room at the Top*, *Saturday Night and Sunday Morning*, *Only Two Can Play* and, to some extent, *A Kind of Loving* (where Ingrid is counterposed to the models in Vic's French girlie magazine). More generally, these divide into the virginal and/ or spiritual versus the sexually experienced and physical (this is most pronounced in *Sons and Lovers* and *Young Cassidy*). This can, in turn, be related to class in so far as it is normally the lower status female characters who provide the most intense physical satisfactions (e.g. *Saturday Night and Sunday Morning*, *Sons and Lovers*, *Young Cassidy* and, in part, *Room at the Top*). Conventionally, it is the former female characters whom the male hero chooses (or is forced to choose), the latter whom he rejects (though, in the case of *Sons and Lovers* and *Young Cassidy*, he rejects both in favour of an individual trajectory). Thus, despite the reputation for sexual explicitness (for some, even immorality), there is usually a moral and sexual conservatism in the endings of the films with their emphasis on marital and procreative sexuality.

Thus in *Look Back in Anger*, *The Entertainer* and *Only Two Can Play* the male characters engage in an adulterous affair (or at least attempts to in the case of *Only Two Can Play*) but ultimately return to their wives. In *Room at the Top* and *Saturday Night and Sunday Morning*, the male hero is punished by a beating (as is Morel in *Sons and Lovers*) and subsequently enters marriage, while Vic reconciles himself to marriage in *A Kind of Loving*. In three of these, the solution is explicitly linked to procreation: both Joe in *Room at the Top* and Vic in *A Kind of Loving* enter marriage because of the pregnancy of their partners, while Brenda returns to her husband in *Saturday Night and Sunday Morning* when she too becomes pregnant. The possibility of abortion is raised by a number of the films but rejected as a satisfactory alternative: Brenda's attempted abortion fails in *Saturday Night*; Jo rejects the possibility of one in *A Taste of Honey*; Alison is firmly reprimanded by her doctor for the suggestion of one in *Look Back in Anger*; while Jane's visit to the doctor in *The L-Shaped Room* makes up her mind to have the baby rather than terminate her pregnancy. Those abortions which do proceed are marked in purely negative terms for their refusal of parenthood, as in *Alfie* and *Darling*. Indeed, childlessness and/or sterility is conventionally linked to marital failure and adultery, as in *Only Two Can Play*, *This Sporting Life*, *No Love for Johnnie*, *Term of Trial* and *The Wild and the Willing*. 'Can't even someone of your age distinguish,' asks the professor in the last film, 'between a kiss taken from a woman who has no child of her own and adultery?'

While, then, it is in the logic of many of these films to reintegrate the characters into marriage there is, to some extent, a tension between the energies which the films release and the viability of the solutions they propose. In part, this derives from the split in female characters, whereby it is the characters who are eligible for marriage who are also the least physically exciting. Thus, in *Room at the Top*, Susan proves sexually disappointing to Joe by comparison with Alice while his marriage to her is specifically marked in terms of a loss. Vic likewise fails to find physical satisfaction with Ingrid in *A Kind of Loving*, unable to integrate the 'exotic' sexuality of his magazine into their relationship. In *Saturday Night and Sunday Morning*, the vivacity of Arthur's relationship with Brenda contrasts sharply with the fear-edged seduction of Doreen (Shirley Ann Field), shot in total silence with Doreen's words unheard (cf. Brenda's ability to vocalise her desire and pleasure). In *Sons and Lovers*, Paul Morel rejects the prospect of marriage to Miriam (Heather Sears) because of the failure of their sexual relationship to cement the bond of friendship that already exists between them. His resulting isolation, as with *Young Cassidy*, in part derives from the inability of the female characters to be both physical and intellectual partners. This is also the case, with a homosexual variation, in *The Leather Boys*. It is Pete's emotional and domestic relationship with Reggie ('looking after' him, bringing him cups of tea, listening to his troubles) which is the most personally satisfying; yet it is 'impossible' because of Pete's sexual need 'for a woman'. But Pete's marriage is also 'impossible' and the result is, once again, isolation, caught between the conflicting demands of heterosexual desire and personal and emotional fulfilment.

This Sporting Life (1963)

There is a similar tension in *A Taste of Honey*, only here it is the male characters who are split. It is with Jimmy (Paul Danquah) that Jo enjoys a physical relationship but it is Geoff, the homosexual, with whom she finds domestic harmony. The very impossibility of integrating the sexual and the domestic is underlined by Geoff's attempted advances which Jo rejects ('you're just like a big sister to me', she explains earlier). With physical pleasure apparently so divorced from marriage and domesticity, it is inevitable that those films which rely on marriage as a means of conclusion tend to imply less a positive endorsement than an emphasis on compromise and acceptance of constraint, the eschewal of fantasy already noted.

This would seem to be confirmed by the more general failure of the films concerned to project a compelling image of marriage outside of the main characters. The apparently 'ideal marriage' represented by Christine (Pat Keen) and David (David Marlowe) in *A Kind of Loving*, for example, is solid and respectable but hardly exciting, with David (an apparently 'good catch') showing all the signs of premature middle age (balding and bespectacled). Their smart but uninteresting modern flat is, indeed, more than a little reminiscent of *No Trees in the Street* (right down to the fenced-in tree growing in solitary confinement down below). Jack (Bryan Pringle) in *Saturday Night and Sunday Morning* is weak and easily deceived (seen reading a *Daily Mirror*, with its ironic headlines 'Be Proud of These Men' and 'He Was Once A

Bride', as his wife prepares to go out with Arthur); his recipe for marital harmony and the keeping of Brenda at home is the acquisition of a TV. Charles (Donald Houston) in *Room at the the Top* renounces his ambitions for 'a girl with no brothers and sisters and a nice little family business in the background' in favour of the solidly respectable June (Mary Peach) and her invalid mother. Maurice (Colin Blakely) and Judith (Anne Cunningham) in *This Sporting Life* (shorn of the novel's complications of pregnancy) merely provide a dull counterfoil to Frank's more intense physical and emotional entanglements with Mrs Hammond.

Families, where they exist, fare little better, generally marked by a 'decline in the status of the father'. Arthur's father in *Saturday Night and Sunday Morning* and Joe's surrogate father, his uncle, in *Room at the Top* have both been 'ground down' – 'dead from the neck up' in the description of Arthur's. Mr Morel (Trevor Howard) in *Sons and Lovers* is ignorant and weak compared to the strength and authority of his wife. Indeed, female domination of the household is complete in *A Kind of Loving*, *A Taste of Honey* and *Saturday Night* where Ingrid, Jo and Doreen all live with their widowed or separated mothers. In so far as the male heroes of these films then themselves enter marriage, they also risk a similar 'decline' or 'castration'. This has already been noted in *A Kind of Loving* and *The Leather Boys*, but consider also the case of Arthur in *Saturday Night and Sunday Morning*, only proposing to settle down once he has been beaten and put flat on his back in his sick-bed (in a kind of symbolic 'castration', in part similar to the end of *All That Heaven Allows*).

It is then the very problem of securing an adequate 'female counterpart' in which so many of the 'new wave' films trade, abandoning male heroes to isolation or imposing upon them 'solutions' which primarily consist of a compromise. This anxiety with 'female inadequacy' becomes highlighted in *Look Back in Anger* through Jimmy Porter's persistent railings against his wife's shortcomings and increasingly misogynistic attempts to awaken her from her 'beauty sleep' (indeed, she is asleep in bed on her first appearance, when Jimmy begins an attempt to make love to her). As Stuart Hall has suggested, it is through Alison (Mary Ure) that Jimmy (Richard Burton) gives expression to the anger that he feels for the world, whereby 'the sexual and human relationship between Jimmy and Alison is a metaphor for the social relationship between Jimmy and the world'.[24] Alison's 'pusillanimity' thus stands in for the absence of feeling and 'good, brave causes' characteristic, for Jimmy, of the modern world. But more specifically, Alison is upper class, the daughter of a retired colonel, and Jimmy's hostility to the upper classes, his personal class struggle, transforms into an abuse of his wife.

Just as the sexual mythologies surrounding race have led black males to 'get back at the white world' through a sadistic treatment of white women (most starkly summed up in Eldridge Cleaver's commitment to the rape of white women as an 'insurrectionary act'), so Jimmy is able to get back at the class system by his attacks on Alison and then seduction of Helena (Claire Bloom).[25] As Kate Millett suggests, what is at stake here is less the existence of class division, which remains impervious to individual enmity, than the reaffirmation of sexual hierarchy, the triumph of male 'virility' over female education and status.[26] 'There's nothing fey about Jimmy', as Alison chooses to put it. Thus, despite an initial resistance, Helena soon submits to Jimmy, accepting her 'proper place' – 'on her back' and in domestic servitude (taking up Alison's place behind the ironing board). Alison herself is effectively 'punished', even 'castrated', by the loss of her child (as had been wished upon her by Jimmy), only to return 'grovelling' and 'crawling' to her husband. Such punitive responses to 'female inadequacy' also occur in other films. Vic acts upon his father's advice (delivered from the 'natural' base of his allotment) to force Ingrid to live where 'she's bloody put', after she too has lost a child in *A Kind of Loving*. Robert (Dirk Bogarde) both asserts his virility and punishes Diana in *Darling* by first making love to her and then forcing her to return, in tears, to the unhappiness of her marriage in Italy.

Thus, while it may be argued that 'the image of active sexuality' in the British 'new wave' provided 'a resistance to refinement and repression', it should also be noted that such an image is primarily masculine.[27] Just as many of the original novels (*Room at the Top, Loneliness of the Long Distance Runner, A Kind of Loving, This Sporting Life*) were written in a male first person narration, most of the subsequent films assume a 'male norm', in their narrative organisation, employment of subjective techniques and patterns of identification. As Ken Worpole suggests of 'masculine style' in the working-class novel, the strengths are those of working-class virility and aggression, 'the celebration of individual resistance to arbitrary authority, its quick-witted repartee in response to authoritarianism', the weaknesses, 'the avoidance of engaging with the reality of personal and sexual relationships', the denial of their 'mutuality and reciprocity'.[28]

The dramatic and thematic subordination of the female characters which results is most clearly in evidence in *Sons and Lovers* and *Young Cassidy*. Kate Millett's observations on *Sons and Lovers*, the novel, would apply with equal ease to the film: 'The women . . . exist in Paul's orbit to cater to his needs: Clara to awaken him sexually, Miriam to worship his talent . . . and Mrs Morel to provide . . . enormous and expansive support.'[29] Janey Place's comments on *Young Cassidy* are almost identical: 'His mother must die for his development, the 'little tart' must answer his passion, the upper-class woman must encourage the art his own people reject . . . the intellectual woman must teach his mind and speak his feelings, and then he stands alone.'[30] The result, as Laura Mulvey suggests of the Western hero, who likewise resists the demands of social responsibility, marriage and family, is a 'phallic, narcissistic omnipotence.'[31] For the female characters, however, the 'solution' is firmly inside marriage. Clara's commitment to 'women's rights' in *Sons and Lovers* is radically undercut. Her speech at a political meeting assumes dramatic significance only in so far as it serves Paul's ends of seduction; her integrity as a speaker is undermined by her subjection to the controlling look of the male (the model and inspiration for Paul's sketch). Her feminism is thus revealed as an 'error' which she abandons in order to return to her unpleasant and brutish husband.

Such a narrative subordination of female characters to the male trajectory is more generally typical (cf. the disappearance from the plots of Brenda in *Saturday Night and Sunday Morning* and Alice in *Room at the Top*) but reaches its most pronounced articulation in *Alfie*, a film which can be seen as bringing to a stark conclusion the logic already implicit in the films of the 'new wave', especially *Saturday Night and Sunday Morning*. Like *Saturday Night and Sunday Morning*, *Alfie* is organised around a 'playboy' hero, devoted to a 'good time' and sexual pleasure, and resistant to 'settling down'. The price of his 'sexual freedom', however, is a complete subordination and denigration of the film's female characters. Writing on the nude portrait, John Berger has suggested that what transforms the representation of 'nakedness' into 'nudity' is the absenting of 'subject-ivity', both the exclusion of the female model's will and intentions and her 'activity as a subject' (as opposed to her status as 'object' in the grip of the look of the male).[32] The aesthetic organisation of *Alfie* is similar, ruthlessly suppressing the 'subject-ivity' of the female characters whom it presents. This is achieved, in the first instance, by an extension of the voice-over, characteristic of some of its predecessors, and the adoption of direct address by Alfie (Michael Caine). Whereas the voice-over leaves open the possibility of a disjunction between image and sound (as in the case of *Darling* where, significantly, it is the female voice-over of Diana which is marked as unreliable), the use of direct address in *Alfie* tends to ensure a harmony between the two, in so far as Alfie's commentary on the action becomes an element of its performance.

Although such direct address can run the risk of laying bare the 'illusion' of cinematic rhetoric (and is so employed by, say, Godard), the effect of its use in *Alfie* is less an 'alienation' of the spectator than an intensified complicity with Alfie's character, whereby it becomes impossible to separate Alfie's perception of events from the actual events themselves. Alfie's narration, indeed, occasionally employs the term 'we' (e.g. 'what she don't know is we won't be seeing very much more of her') as a means of reinforcement of the bond between character and spectator which the film assumes. Of course, there are stops and gaps in the use of direct address and voice-over, when a more strictly 'objective narration' begins to take over, but the 'separation' from Alfie which then results is kept firmly in check. Female point-of-view shots, for example, are conventionally refused, except in so far as they are initially motivated by a point-of-view shot of Alfie's. Even these are kept to a minimum by the film's adoption of relatively long two-shots and thus avoidance of the more standard procedure of reverse-field cutting. Furthermore, there are hardly any scenes in which we see the female characters without the presence of Alfie, and once their involvement with Alfie is over they are effectively disposed of by the narrative (cf. the disappearance of Annie). Given that the film's plot is loose and episodic, the appearance of a female character tends to imply less distinctiveness (stages of Alfie's development) than repetition (the continuing confirmation of Alfie's sexual prowess). In formalist terms, i.e. in terms of narrative function, one woman is as good as another and the film could quite easily be re-edited without causing any particular violence to its thematic continuity. Such an

Alfie (1966)

interchangeability of female characters is highlighted by one short montage sequence. It only consists of six shots yet manages to introduce four different women. They remain anonymous, it is their only appearance in the film, their narrative function no more than a confirmation that Alfie 'was having a beautiful little life' but couldn't 'see it'. 'Any bird that knows its (sic) place can be quite content', announces Alfie. For the film, it is quite evident that such a 'place' means either sexual or domestic subordination to Alfie (Annie neatly combines both roles, seen scrubbing the floor on her knees in front of Alfie's bed). The only female character apparently not bedded by Alfie in the film is 'abnormal': a female doctor ('queer job for a bird, innit?') whose swept back hair and glasses suggest repression.

The film does contrive the conventional moralistic conclusion: Alfie receives his come-uppance (a rejection from Ruby, the traumatic experience of the abortion intercut with his son's baptism) and, to that extent, appears to be moving towards a recognition of the hollowness of his existence (hollow for him, of course, not the women he's abused). But, like the exploitation films already discussed, the ending is itself hollow, undercut both by the complicity with Alfie's perspective that the film has maintained throughout and, as a result, the absence of any compelling alternative to Alfie's philandering. As with many of the 'new wave' films, the representation of husbands in the film is heavily marked by 'castration': Harry is either bed-ridden or in a wheelchair, entirely innocent of his wife's infidelity; Sadie's cuckolded husband is drab and uninspiring (bald, bespectacled and pipe-smoking, given to a study of gardening manuals while his wife is out with

165

Alfie); Humphrey, the surrogate father to Alfie's child, can only offer comfort and understanding to Gilda rather than a genuine excitement or passion. Indeed, to the extent that Alfie sets up home with Annie, so he too becomes 'poncified' (as his mates in the pub observe) and is forced to subsequently evict her. The new-found self-awareness which Alfie then discovers merely leaves him in limbo. In a previous discussion, I suggested there was something of a parallel between the British 'new wave' and the American 'film noir', in so far as both are marked by a weakness or fragility in their representation of the family.[33] The crucial difference, of course, is the absence in the films of the 'new wave' of strong female characters outside of home and marriage (the 'noir' femme fatale). Whereas 'film noir' foregrounds the insufficiency of marriage in relation to female desire, its inadequacy in the British 'new wave' is structured in relation to the male. The image of active sexuality, as *Alfie* suggests, is predominantly phallocentric.

What then of those films which do allocate a narrative centrality to female rather than male characters, most notably *A Taste of Honey*, *The L-Shaped Room* and *This is my Street*? Although two of these films place their female characters outside marriage, while the third (*This is my Street*) emphasises the woman's entrapment within marriage, the tendency is less to endorse a female self-direction than reaffirm the value of motherhood and reinsert their characters back into a network of family relations. The ending of *A Taste of Honey*, for example, necessitates a choice for Jo between Geoff and her mother. Although Geoff (Murray Melvin) is clearly more domestically skilled than Helen (Dora Bryan), it is in the logic of Jo's impending motherhood that Geoff should be the one to leave. Indeed, the conservatism of the film's treatment of homosexuality is that Geoff can only properly find himself in his relationship to Jo ('before I knew you, I didn't care much whether I lived or died') and the fantasy of being a father to her child. Yet it is precisely his homosexuality which blocks the possibility of wish-fulfilment, his adoption of a fulfilling parental role. Accordingly, he must be exiled once more by the film's close while Helena assumes her 'proper role' as a mother. The film ends with children dancing around a bonfire and brandishing sparklers (the flame of life). Excluded by the nature of his sexuality from procreation, Geoff observes the 'reconciliation' of mother and daughter before departing. This does, of course, avoid a conventional resolution in terms of a submission by the female characters to the male, or a re-imposition of the 'normality' of the patriarchal family. But what also undercuts this as a positive resolution is its association with compromise and a fatalistic acceptance. For what reunites mother and daughter is the repetitive cycle whereby Jo has, in effect, lived through the errors of the parent. Despite Helen's warnings to learn from her 'mistakes' and not get 'trapped', Jo has followed in her mother's footsteps by succumbing to a transitory passion and becoming pregnant outside of marriage. What then brings them together is less a positive resistance to other alternatives than a resigned acknowledgment of things as they are. The absence of a father and 'proper' family relations is thus one of the components which mark their adjustment as 'second best'.

The logic of *The L-Shaped Room* displays similarities. Although Alexander Walker praised the film at the time for its 'story of a girl with a mind of her own', its endorsement of the female character is hardly so straightforward.[34] 'Activity in the world', 'actions towards a goal' and 'heterosexual desire': these were the terms employed by Ellis in his identification of a 'male norm' in conventional narrative cinema. The substitution of a narratively central female character in *The L-Shaped Room*, however, does not lead to an equivalent set of values. Jane (Leslie Caron) is less positive than negative, less actively pursuing her goals than reacting negatively to events around her. She is attempting to escape both from her family and from the father of her child. Her decision to have the baby outside marriage is prompted less by a positive commitment to motherhood than a negative reaction to the doctor (opulent and uncaring) to whom she originally goes for an abortion ('Anything is better than your way'). Even her 'heterosexual desire' would seem devoid of an active libidinal component. Her pregnancy derived from a belated attempt to lose her virginity by a man for whom she had no love; her attempt at an affair with Toby (Tom Bell) involves more of a submission than a commitment (crying and in fear that 'everything will be all right'). This lack of positivity in her actions is reinforced by the socially displaced role she now occupies: a foreigner alone in a strange city and, subsequently, a resident in a house whose dominant characteristics are rootlessness and sexual 'abnormality' (prostitution, lesbianism, homosexuality and adultery). Although it is possibly the film's intention to imply the virtues which the house can provide nonetheless (the 'neighbours . . . that drew her back into life' as the novel's blurb puts it) it is clear that it can function as no more than a halfway house.[35] For both the 'role models' of female independence which it supplies are explicitly marked as unsatisfactory. On the one hand, there is the ageing lesbian, now alone and isolated, with no family to go to. On the other, there are the prostitutes in the basement whose lives are described as 'no worse' than a million years of purgatory. One of the prostitutes is also a foreign exile, sharing the same name as Jane, and threatening the fate which could also befall her namesake (who is, indeed, labelled a 'whore' by her housemate, Johnny). The speeches of both lesbian and prostitutes are linked to an abandonment of God, so it then becomes appropriate that Jane should secure a 'redemption' by giving birth to her child on Christmas Day. The 'holy family' so secured, she is now able to return to her home in a submission to the law of the 'father' (he has sent her the ticket) and abandon the social and sexual irregularity which characterises the house.

This is my Street (1963) comes closest to traditional melodrama, with its emphasis on family and domestic relations: 'a strange hybrid of kitchen sink and pre-war women's weekly', as David Robinson was to put it in his contemporary review.[36] The 'problem' of the film is once again the 'problem' of woman. The central female character, Margery (June Ritchie), is trapped in a marriage which she detests: 'I've got a lifetime sentence with Sid . . .

I cook for him, I sew for him, I sleep with him. Yet he's everything in a man I despise. I'm married to a man I don't even like.' Her 'solution' is to start an affair with the lodger, Harry (Ian Hendry), but it is a course of action which the film cannot sanction. Harry subsequently loses interest in her, she makes an attempt at suicide but then settles for a reconciliation to her lot, re-integrated into her role as mother. She refuses Harry's invitation to go to his club, preferring to go home. Meeting her daughter outside, she picks her up, hugs her and then carries her inside. 'The street settles down once again to its drab existence', as the publicity handout explains. The morality implicit in such a conclusion is 'doubled' by the film's treatment of Maureen (Philippa Gail), one of Margery's neighbours in the street. She is 'punished' for her extra-marital affair with a dentist by a car crash and resulting disfigurement to her face (also the film's reprimand for her narcissism). She is, however, 'saved' by the innocent affections of Charlie (John Hurt), whom she had previously rejected, but who still wants to take her out, despite the damage now done to her face. Although it is the female characters who are central, it is clearly the work of the film to confine them, re-establishing their 'proper place' within the 'normality' of family and marital relations.

What slightly dislodges this as a satisfactory conclusion is the ruthlessness with which the film then portrays its sexual relationships. Jane Feuer, for example, has suggested how TV soap operas, such as *Dallas* and *Dynasty*, may be deemed 'progressive' for their 'demystification' of the economic and financial relations underlying conventional notions of marriage for love.[37] By virtue of the persistence with which it reveals its female characters as the victims of a predatory male sexuality, based upon economics and power, there is something of a similar 'exposure' in *This is my Street*. Maureen 'sells' herself to the dentist for the presents he can provide; Margery is attracted to Harry for the economic advantages he possesses in comparison to her husband; while her boss at work promises her 'modelling' provided she supplies him with sexual favours. One short, but striking, scene sums up the predatory world in which the women find themselves. Maureen is eyed up by a customer at a club who slips her his card. Visiting the address, she is barely in the door when the man pounces on her, pulling off her dress and grabbing at her bra. His wife then appears with a camera, announcing there will be 'no problem with the money'. While it is undoubtedly the intention of the film to use such scenes to underline the dangers to its female characters outside the sexual regime of marriage and family, it does at the same time draw attention to the exploitative way in which they are used. Women's only asset in the film is their bodies (underscored by the film's own prurient camerawork); their only 'escape' in a world of female subordination through 'prostitution'. Harry explains to Margery that if she wants to get out of the street then she could – if she used her 'head'. What he, and the film, really imply is if she used her body.

The chapter began with a consideration of some comedies whose themes could be seen to overlap with those at work in the British 'new wave'. By way of a conclusion, I'd like to return to comedy and suggest how the 'position of women' also assumed a significance here. The intention, however, is not to provide a survey, merely to isolate a couple of examples whose characteristics are in some way distinctive. *She Didn't Say No!* (1958), for example, provides an unusual representation of the family; *Petticoat Pirates* (1961) one of women at work. Although in both cases the 'threat' represented by these abnormalities is 'contained', such a process is not as straightforward or punitive as might at first be expected.

She Didn't Say No!, for example, revolves around the 'problem' of Bridget Monaghan (Eileen Herlie), an unmarried mother with six children by five different fathers. What is unusual, however, is that this problem is not located in relation to either domestic or moral disturbance, as would conventionally be the case in the 'social problem' film. Bridget is financially independent and self-supporting, maintaining a well kept and ordered household. The first shot of the family at the dinner table is evenly lit and harmoniously composed with no indication of any abnormality. This is confirmed by Bridget's success in preventing her children from being taken into custody. The judge establishes that the children are 'well fed', 'clean and neat' and 'happy and contented' and dismisses the charge that their home is 'not morally sound'. The positive value attached to the family is underlined by the absence of 'normal 'domestic relations elsewhere in the community. Mrs Bates (Joan O'Hara) deprives her husband of his 'conjugal rights' while Mrs Powers (Betty McDowell) is unable to have a child of her own. Hogan (Patrick McAlinney) lives with his spinster sister while Casey (Niall MacGinnis) lives alone.

It is, indeed, these weaknesses in the community at large rather than the inadequacy of the Monaghan family itself which set in motion the demands for change. In the first instance, these are precipitated by the birth of twins to Mrs Bates, thus drawing attention to the paternity of the Monaghan twins. As with Wolfenden's attitude towards prostitution, the resulting anxiety is primarily focused on the problem of 'visibility'. The plan to move the Monaghan family elsewhere leaves the family intact but removes the embarrassment it causes to the wider community.

However, the real anxiety provoked by the family is its threat to lines of community continuity. The 'solution' thus required by the film is for the fathers to recognise their children in order to maintain the patterns of patrilineal inheritance: O'Casey and Powers are thus provided with heirs to their farms while Hogan is able to see his theatrical talents carried on by his daughter. The resulting break-up of the Monaghan family thus relies on conventional notions of maternal self-sacrifice, with Bridget acquiescing in so far as it is 'for the sake of the children'. To this extent, the plot's resolution might have been expected. What it cannot suppress, however, is the recognition that the necessity for such a solution does not derive from any internal instability in a family without a father but solely from a community organisation that is ordered according to the principle of father-right.

Petticoat Pirates approaches the 'problem' of women in relation to work and, in particular, their fitness to undertake jobs which are traditionally

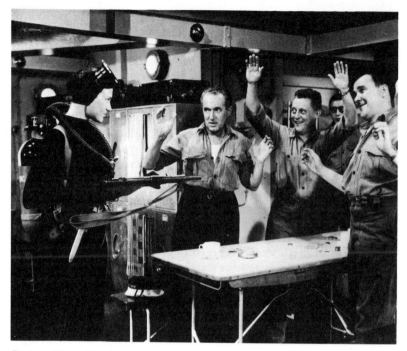

Petticoat Pirates (1961)

male. Like *Operation Bullshine* (1959), the film picks up on the popularity of service comedies in the period, developing their conventions by an accentuation of the role of women. But, whereas the comedy of *Operation Bullshine* derives from the incompetence of women to adapt to military circumstances (preoccupied with romance and appearance), the humour engendered by *Petticoat Pirates* results from their successful confounding of male expectations by proving their worth in taking over a warship. Prevented from crewing a battleship of their own by a male commanding officer's predictions of the 'chaos' which would result, an all-female crew set out to prove that there's 'not a single job that we couldn't do on board ship as well as any man' by first overpowering the male crew of the HMS Huntress and then putting out to sea. They successfully defy the men's own attempts to take back the ship, fight off a male-commanded warship sent to capture them and then play a vital role in NATO manoeuvres by 'torpedoing' the American flagship.

Male order is, to some extent, reassumed when most of the female crew become seasick during a storm on their return journey and the female captain is forced to call on the male crew for assistance. But it is only a temporary, and flagrantly contrived, 'recuperation'. The Lieutenant who has consistently opposed the female piracy admits that Ann (Anne Heywood) is 'the best captain' he has ever sailed with while the Commander-in-Chief (Cecil

170

Parker), who had previously opposed such 'feministic nonsense', now congratulates the women on their success and promises to make further representations on their behalf. Unlike *Operation Bullshine*, where the women's success in shooting down a German aircraft is marked as serendipity, women in *Petticoat Pirates* have successfully defied male expectations and proven their abilities in performing traditionally male roles.

In his discussion of American war movies which foreground the 'female group', Michael Renov suggests how female effectivity is characteristically 'neutralized' by the 'erotic dependency' of the female characters on 'male desire'.[38] While this would also be true of *Operation Bullshine*, the example of *Petticoat Pirates* is, once again, more complex. Unlike *Operation Bullshine*, where romance and marriage are constantly highlighted (indeed, much of its comedy derives from the women's competitive pursuit of a good-looking Lieutenant), home and family life are entirely absent from *Petticoat Pirates*. Romantic interest intrudes but not in a way which diminishes the women's pursuit of their goals. Ann, indeed, rejects Michael (John Turner), despite her attraction to him, once she realises his intentions to inveigle her into giving back the ship. The female crew enjoy flirtations with their captured male crew but this does not distract from their subsequent naval successes (achieved without help from the men).

'Erotic dependency', however, is not solely the product of narrative organisation but also of the look of the camera. Just as women in institutions (e.g. prisons, convents) conventionally provide the pretext for voyeuristic spectacle, *Operation Bullshine* and *Petticoat Pirates* contrive plot situations (women preparing for bed, taking a shower) whose guiding rationale resides in a subordination of the female body to an implicitly male gaze. What activity the women enjoy within the narrative is thus undercut by their reduction to objects of a male spectacle. While this is straightforwardly the case in *Operation Bullshine*, the use of such camerawork in *Petticoat Pirates* is partly qualified. Here, for example, the voyeuristic look of the camera is also given some attention. Charlie (Charlie Drake) is seen observing the women's gym exercises through a periscope. Our complicity with his look, and, indeed, its regressively infantile character, is rendered transparent by Charlie's direct addresses to camera. Moreover, the women themselves become aware of Charlie's gaze: his look is returned down the periscope and then the women as a group go downstairs to arrest him, effectively bringing him to task for his illegitimate 'peeping tom activities'. Second, while in *Operation Bullshine* the look of the camera is used to keep women 'in place', secure them in a system in which their only proper role can be as objects of male desire, *Petticoat Pirates* does not enforce the same divorce between female 'desirability' and traditionally male activity. Thus, while in *Operation Bullshine* the women who do not conform to the demands of erotic spectacle are signalled as 'abnormally masculine' (e.g. the female sergeant), the women in *Petticoat Pirates* are allowed to retain their 'femininity' at the same time as they assume male roles. As Ann makes clear to Michael, she wants to be both a 'beautiful woman' and a successful captain: it is only his male 'manoeuvring' which suggests that being 'beautiful' is sufficient in itself.

The positive values attached to the women's activities is reinforced by the persona adopted by the film's star comedian, Charlie Drake. As Krutnik suggests, the comedian conventionally figures as 'a locus of confusion', defiant of 'normal' expectations of identity and maturity.[39] By virtue of his diminutive stature, long hair and shrill voice, Drake makes problematic the relations of sexual difference, enjoying heterosexual courtship but also mistaken for a woman by male and female characters alike. In the same way, he is unable to find a clear-cut gender identification: on the one hand, he opposes the women's piracy, rallying the men to defiance, on the other, he supports them, helping fire a gun and wishing them 'good luck'. For Krutnik the resolution of the comedian's confused identity conventionally involves some sort of coming to maturity; if it does not, the comic hero remains outside the conventional social order, symbolised, in particular, by a rejection of women.[40] In Charlie's case, the difference is illuminating. He does achieve a form of social integration but in a way which leaves his ambivalent persona intact. Moreover, this is made possible, not by rejecting women, but joining them, as he cheerfully follows in the path of a group of marching Wrens. It may well be that this is only possible because Charlie is not a 'proper man'; the virtue of the film is that the yardstick of 'masculinity' no longer seems relevant.

In Chapter Five it was suggested how two of the most recurrent characteristics of the social problem film were their suppression of class divisions and conflicts and their preoccupation with the regulation of sexual excess. On the face of it, the working-class films of the 'new wave' would appear to provide a contrast. They take as their central focus working-class subjects and characters and show a consistent concern to deal with 'serious' and 'adult' sexual themes. It is certainly on this basis that they have been conventionally received and applauded for their energising effect on an increasingly ossified British cinema of the 1950s. It would clearly be both perverse and ungracious not to acknowledge some degree of validity in all of this. The films did, without doubt, introduce new themes and topics into the British cinema and exert a considerable influence on both contemporary film-making (including the social problem film) and many British films to follow. As Alan Lovell suggests, 'to gain a proper historical perspective on *Saturday Night and Sunday Morning* it should be seen with a film like Ealing's *The Titfield Thunderbolt* (1954) . . . *Saturday Night and Sunday Morning* destroyed the coyness and showed it was possible for the cinema to be responsive to contemporary social developments'.[41]

Yet there is also a danger that the critical acclaim which conventionally accompanies a consideration of these films may itself degenerate into little more than ritual obeisance. All too often, the mere display of the working class and sexual relationships on the screen is celebrated as a 'Good Thing' in itself, irrespective of the way they have actually been dealt with by the films concerned. What the preceding analysis has attempted to provide, by contrast, is precisely this: that is to say, some sort of assessment of the way in

The Loneliness of the Long Distance Runner (1962)

which these themes of class and sexuality have actually been worked through by the films and with what kind of ideological consequences. From this point of view, a number of similarities with the social problem film begin to emerge. In dealing with the working class, there is the same emphasis on individual rather than collective situations and the same emphasis on inter-personal rather than socially structured conflicts. There is a similar emphasis on cultural attitudes rather than political and economic relationships and, by virtue of the inscribed authorial distance, a common tendency to observe and judge characters from the 'outside'. Furthermore, while the films may move towards a greater sexual explicitness, there is still a continuing suspicion of sexual variety and fondness for morally conservative 'solutions', particularly in relation to female characters and the expression of their sexuality.

To this extent, there is considerable overlap with the work of the 'Angry Young Men'. While this has generally been regarded as a positive influence, a closer inspection of 'angry' attitudes reveals some problematic features. As Chapter One suggested, the 'anger' of this period was often politically ambivalent, prone to nostalgia and targeted primarily towards the super-ficiality of the modern age and its apparent figurehead, the female. In attempting to achieve 'the same sort of impact' as 'the Angry Young Cult' and in adapting so many of its key texts, it was, perhaps, inevitable that many of the same attitudes should survive. The other main influence was, of course, the New Left. In common with writers such as Richard Hoggart, there was an emphasis on the decline and corruption of the traditional

173

working class at the hands of modern consumer society and a corresponding focus on the quality of leisure, rather than work and political action. This affected, in turn, their response to more general perceptions of class relations. On the face of it, the films of the 'new wave' would appear to present a striking riposte to any complacent ideology of 'classlessness'.

At precisely the time the disappearance of class was being so loudly asserted, these films, at least, seemed to provide clear evidence to the contrary. And, yet, the relationship is probably more complex. Chas Critcher, for example, suggests how the fashion for 'working-class studies' which gripped the imagination of sociologists during the same period tended less to challenge the foundations of the 'withering away of class' debate than to refine and elaborate upon it.[42] In a similar fashion, many of the 'new wave' films were less concerned with a re-assertion of the continuing gap between capital and labour than with exploring the changing conditions of working-class life in the face of affluence and consumerism, the observation of, as Alan Lovell puts it, 'a working-class world being transformed by increased wealth'.[43] As with the New Left itself, many of the economic changes wrought by 'affluence' were taken for granted; it was the value of their moral and cultural effects which were open to question. Politically, this tended to lead to a representation of the working class as largely inert and conformist: it is only individual members of the class who are able to rise above or rebel against this general condition. Industrial action and organised political activity are absent and, by implication, increasingly redundant. 'The class war' might not be quite over in Macmillan's sense, but it certainly has become contained and constricted.

The same could not be said, however, about the 'sex war'. In common with the writings of the 'Angry Young Men' there was more than a streak of misogyny running through the films and a failure to acknowledge the changing social and economic role of women in British society other than as consumers. If, as the Birmingham Feminist History Group suggest, these changes had called for 'a new view of the role of women and their place in the family', there was little to suggest this in the films of the 'new wave'.[44] All too often, they were content to abandon their female characters to the confinement of familiar domestic and marital roles and even inflict a 'punishment' on those who chose to stray beyond. In terms of a history of the British cinema this clearly did not represent quite the major 'breakthrough' that is sometimes suggested, while, placed in social and historical context, it could be seen to be confirming, rather than querying and challenging, the dominant ideological assumptions about a 'woman's role'.

To this extent, the films appear to occupy an ambivalent space. While they undoubtedly assisted in 'opening up' the British cinema with their innovatory contents and more socially enquiring attitudes, they were, in the end, something less than radical. This can partly be attributed to the debt which they owed to the 'Angry Young Men' and, to a lesser extent, the New Left. As Chapter One suggested, the ideas and politics which they inherited from these groups were still shaped and structured by the dominant discourses of 'affluence'. While they may have countered many of their

174

conclusions, they did not, at the same time, fundamentally break with their underlying assumptions, continuing to remain within, as it were, the same ideological problematic, or field of play. The organisation of the film industry also played its role. As Chapter Two suggested, the fact that the films were made at all was dependent upon the industry's openness to innovation in the face of economic decline. But, at the same time, the innovations which the industry allowed were still subject to constraints. These were not only economic (the continuing monopoly control of distribution and exhibition) but also, as Chapter Three argued, aesthetic. As a result, many of the ideological attitudes characteristic of the films resulted from a dependence on the formal conventions of mainstream commercial film-making. Whether these films could have actually departed significantly from these conventions and still remained financially viable is, of course, unlikely.

Notes

1. According to Colin Seymour-Ure, '1955 was billed in advance as "the first TV election", but 1959 qualifies more aptly for the name'. *The Political Impact of Mass Media*, London, Constable, 1974, p.209.
2. Quoted from Anthony Aldgate, 'Vicious Circles: I'm All Right Jack' in Jeffrey Richards and Anthony Aldgate, *Best of British: Cinema and Society 1930–70*, Oxford, Basil Blackwell, 1983, p.120.
3. *Observer*, 16 August 1959.
4. Tom Nairn, 'The English Literary Intelligentsia' in E. Tennant (ed.), *Bananas*, London, Blond and Briggs, 1977, p.65. See also Raymond Williams, *The Country and the City*, London, Paladin, 1975, for a discussion of the recurrence of pastoral myths.
5. Raymond Durgnat, *A Mirror for England*, London, Faber and Faber, 1970, p.236.
6. Eva Orbanz, *Journey to a Legend and Back: The British Realistic Film*, Berlin, Edition Volker Spiess, 1977, p.58.
7. Alan Lovell and Jim Hillier, *Studies in Documentary*, London, Secker & Warburg, 1972, p.142.
8. Lindsay Anderson, 'Free Cinema' in *Universities and Left Review*, vol.1, no.2, Summer 1957, p.52.
9. The phrase 'traditional social set-up' is Anderson's in Tom Maschler (ed.), *Declaration*, St Albans, MacGibbon and Kee, 1957, p.160.
10. Lindsay Anderson, 'A Possible Solution' in *Sequence*, 3, Spring 1948, p.9.
11. Programme notes, 5–8 February 1956 (available in BFI Library).
12. Allison Graham, *Lindsay Anderson*, Boston, Twayne, 1981, p.51.
13. See explanation by David Lockwood of 'proletarian traditionalism' in 'Sources of Variation in Working-Class Images of Society' in Martin Bulmer (ed.), *Working-Class Images of Society*, London, Routledge & Kegan Paul, 1975, pp.17–18.
14. Colin Sparks, 'The Abuses of Literacy' in Cultural Studies and Theory, *Working Papers in Cultural Studies*, 6, University of Birmingham, Autumn 1974.
15. Brian Jackson, *Working-Class Community*, Harmondsworth, Penguin, 1972, p.39.
16. John Osborne, 'Note' to *The Entertainer*, London, Faber and Faber, 1957.
17. Ibid.
18. For a discussion of this 'masculine culture of work' see Andrew Tolson, *The Limits of Masculinity*, London, Tavistock, 1977.
19. Blake Morrison, *The Movement: English Poetry and Fiction of the 1950s*, Oxford, Oxford University Press, 1980, p.69.
20. John Braine, *Room at the Top*, Harmondsworth, Penguin, 1961, p.139. The phrase 'successful Zombie' can be found on p.123.

21. Alexander Walker, *Hollywood England: The British Film Industry in the Sixties*, London, Michael Joseph, 1974, p.47.
22. *Monthly Film Bulletin*, February 1962, p.21.
23. John Ellis, *Visible Fictions*, London, Routledge & Kegan Paul, 1982, p.48.
24. Stuart Hall, 'Jimmy Porter and the Two-and-Nines' in *Definition*, February 1960, p.100.
25. See Eldridge Cleaver, *Soul on Ice*, London, Panther, 1970, p.26.
26. Kate Millett, *Sexual Politics*, London, Virago, 1981, p.36.
27. The phrase is Andrew Higson's in his defence of the 'new wave' films against my original objections to their 'sexual reaction'; see 'Critical Theory' and 'British Cinema' in *Screen*, vol.24, nos.4/5, July–October 1983, p.88.
28. Ken Worpole, 'The American Connection: The Masculine Style in Popular Fiction' in *New Left Review*, no.139, May–June 1983, p.94. Worpole includes the work of Alan Sillitoe in this discussion.
29. Millett, *Sexual Politics*, p.247.
30. Janey Place, *The Non-Western Films of John Ford*, Secaucus, NJ, Citadel Press, 1979, p.218.
31. 'Afterthoughts . . . Inspired by *Duel in the Sun*', *Framework*, 15/16/17, Summer 1981, p.14.
32. John Berger, *Ways of Seeing*, Harmondsworth, BBC/Penguin, 1972, p.54.
33. 'Working-Class Realism and Sexual Reaction: Some Theses on the British New Wave' in James Curran and Vincent Porter (eds.), *British Cinema History*, London, Weidenfeld & Nicolson, 1983.
34. *Evening Standard*, 15 November 1962.
35. Lynne Reid Banks, *The L-Shaped Room*, Harmondsworth, Penguin, 1962.
36. *Financial Times*, 31 January 1964.
37. Jane Feuer, 'Melodrama, Serial Form and Television Today' in *Screen*, vol.25, no.1, January–February 1984, p.14.
38. Michael Renov, 'From Fetish to Subject: The Containment of Sexual Difference in Hollywood's Wartime Cinema' in *Wide-Angle*, vol.5, no.1, 1982, p.24.
39. Frank Krutnik, 'The Clown-Prints of Comedy' in *Screen*, vol.25, nos.4/5, July–October 1984, p.14.
40. Ibid. p.57.
41. Alan Lovell, 'The Chequered Career of Karel Reisz' in *The Movie*, Chapter 57, 1981, p.1126.
42. Chas Critcher, 'Sociology, Cultural Studies and the Post-War Working-Class' in John Clarke et al. (eds.), *Working-Class Culture: Studies in History and Theory*, London, Hutchinson, 1979, p.16.
43. Lovell, 'The Chequered Career of Karel Reisz', p.1126.
44. Birmingham Feminist History Group, 'Feminism as Femininity in the 1950s' in *Feminist Review*, no.3, 1979, p.50.

Conclusion

Texts and contexts are indivisibly interrelated . . . and to conceptualise them as discrete is to render full analysis impossible.[1]

The aim of this study has been to provide an analysis of selected film texts – the British social problem film, the working-class films of the 'new wave' – in relation to the social and economic context of their production. Strictly speaking, its focus has not been the relations between film and society (or text and context) in general, but rather the more specific interconnections between film and ideology. This has involved a double focus. On the one hand, the study has attempted to provide an explanation of why the films assumed the ideological characteristics which they did, of how they were shaped and influenced by the context in which they were produced. It is for this reason that the study begins with a consideration of, first, the economic, political and ideological relations characteristic of British society during the period of the production of the films; second, the specific economic and industrial relations in which they were made and, finally, the dominant, aesthetic conventions upon which they drew. The subsequent discussion of the films themselves then proceeds to consider how their representations of class, youth, sexuality and race, in particular, may be understood in relation to these varying forms of influence.

On the other hand, the study has not simply been concerned with 'origins' but also with 'effects', that is to say, with how the films were themselves 'effective' in shaping and influencing ideological attitudes and perceptions during this same period. This is a concern which is interrelated with, but nonetheless distinct from, the first. What the study has *not* suggested is that the ideological 'effectivity' of the films can be simply accounted for in terms of the sum of their social and economic determinations. Equally, it has obviously not suggested that the meanings which these films produce are then completely 'autonomous', with no determinate connection to other social relations at all. While the emphasis on the 'specificity' of the text may have provided a welcome antidote to the more reductionist forms of sociological explanation, it has, on the other hand, tended to encourage a rejection of sociological analysis *per se*. What this study has attempted, then, is to maintain a proper respect for the specificity, or productivity, of the film text without then severing it from its social context. Its argument is that an understanding of the social and historical context of a film's production is still *necessary* to any satisfactory account, and certainly assessment, of a film's ideological role even if it does not then provide a *sufficient* explanation of all of a film's ideological characteristics. In this respect, the analysis does not

177

This Sporting Life (1963)

suggest that the films concerned simply 'reflected' or reproduced the dominant ideological attitudes and assumptions of the period. It indicates how the films were themselves active in the construction of ideological meanings and with results that were often less consistent and coherent than the 'dominant ideology thesis' may sometimes be taken to imply. On the other hand, it does suggest a significant degree of interconnection between the films and more generally available ideological discourses.

The issues and the topics with which the films dealt, and the attitudes and the values which they promoted, were not the creations of the cinema alone but were also identified and elaborated upon outside of the cinema (in political speeches and writings, government reports, novels and plays). To this extent, any adequate assessment of the ideological significance of the films does not depend on an inspection of the films alone but also a consideration of their interrelation and attachment to more general forms of social definition and explanation. Moreover, although the films may have displayed a degree of variation and complication in their views of the world, this did not, in the end, amount to a radical diversity of outlook. Certain perspectives on the social world tended to predominate while others were excluded or rendered marginal. The issue of class, for example, was either suppressed or conceived in such a way that its significance was undercut. Sexual attitudes were explored, but only within certain limits or boundaries. What is significant, then, is not just the ideological homogeneity, or otherwise, of the views which the films displayed, but also the *range* of views and the *boundaries* in which these operated. What the study has suggested is that, even allowing for the shifts and innovations in theme and attitude which many of the films registered, the cinema of this period still remained constricted and constrained, bound to certain limits, in the attitudes which it promoted and view of the world which it suggested. The 'new' British cinema, in this respect, was neither as novel nor, certainly, as radical as has sometimes been claimed. Indeed if, as Bogdanor and Skidelsky suggest, the 'age of affluence' is now more properly seen as one of 'illusion', then the films of this period would also appear to have played their part.

Note

1. Andy Medhurst, 'Victim: Text as Context' in *Screen*, vol.25, nos.4/5, July–October 1984, p.35.

179

Select Filmography

This filmography provides credits and selected critical commentary on the films discussed in the text. It also includes some data on films not discussed in the text but which are nonetheless relevant to the argument. The selection of critical commentary has been designed to give some impression of how individual films were received at the time and, in some cases, how they have been subsequently assessed. I have tried to give a generally fair picture of the balance of opinions, though the selection is inevitably slanted in favour of those comments most directly relevant to the text.

Abbreviations

cert: certificate

dist: distributor

p.c: production company

p: producer

d: director

sc: script

ph: photography

ed: editor

a.d: art direction

m: music

THE BLUE LAMP   (1950)

Cert – A *dist* – Rank *p.c* – Ealing *p* – Michael Relph *d* – Basil Dearden *sc* – T.E.B. Clarke, from story by Ted Willis *ph* – Gordon Dines *ed* – Peter Tanner *a.d* – Tom Morahan *m* – Ernest Irving 82 mins.

Jack Warner (*P.C. George Dixon*), James Hanley (*P.C. Andy Mitchell*), Robert Flemyng (*Sgt Roberts*), Bernard Lee (*Inspector Cherry*), Dirk Bogarde (*Tom Riley*), Patric Doonan (*Spud*), Peggy Evans (*Diana Lewis*), Frederick Piper (*Mr Lewis*), Betty Ann Davies (*Mrs Lewis*), Dora Bryan (*Maisie*), Norman Shelley (*Jordan*), Gladys Henson (*Mrs Dixon*).

1950 was the year of *The Blue Lamp*. Kindly P.C. Dixon is brutally shot dead by a hysteric teenage thug who wanted to be tough. Thereafter, the cop-delinquent confrontation became obsessive. (Raymond Durgnat, *A Mirror for England*, Faber, 1970, p.137)

The Blue Lamp makes a great advance by centring itself on an institutional job of work, the first of the post-war Ealing films to do so. The presentation of the force corresponds to that of the service organisations in the war films. Several later films follow this pattern . . . This provides a strong structure which can accommodate a composite picture of society and also firmly contain the threats of sex and violence. These can themselves become 'problems' which the jobs set themselves to cope with, as in *The Blue Lamp,* while the protagonists can sublimate their own energies in their work and their institutional routine. (Charles Barr, *Ealing Studios,* Cameron & Tayleur/ David & Charles, 1977, p.91)

CAGE OF GOLD (1950)

Cert – A *dist* – Rank *p.c* – Ealing *p* – Michael Balcon *d* – Basil Dearden *sc* – Jack Whittingham, from story by Whittingham and Paul Stein *ph* – Douglas Slocombe *ed* – Peter Tanner *a.d* – Jim Morahan *m* – Georges Auric 83 mins.

Jean Simmons (*Judith*), David Farrar (*Bill Brennan*), James Donald (*Dr Alan Kearn*), Harcourt Williams (*Dr Kearn Sr.*), Gladys Henson (*Nanny*), Herbert Lom (*Rahman*), Gregoire Aslan (*Duport*), Madeleine Lebeau (*Madeleine*).

The story is an unmitigated novelette in which Miss Simmons, David Farrar and James Donald struggle vainly with two-dimensional characters and women's magazine dialogue. (*Daily Mail*, 22 September 1950)

Cage of Gold is virtually the last Ealing film to give a decent part to a woman (old ladies aside) . . . Mainly through the actress, there is a real sense of the attractions of the less respectable life and the spiritual limitations of what Judy settles for, but the film loads the dice heavily the other way . . . What she settles down to, then, is life in a large, enveloping dark house, with her baby son, her old Nanny . . . and her worthy husband. Also, at the top of the house, there is her aged father-in-law, bed-ridden, demanding but lovable, a constant reminder of the right values. (Charles Barr, *Ealing Studios*, pp.150–1)

POOL OF LONDON (1951)

Cert – A *dist* – Rank *p.c* – Ealing *p* – Michael Balcon *d* – Basil Dearden *sc* – Jack Whittingham, John Eldridge *ph* – Gordon Dines *ed* – Peter Tanner *a.d* – Jim Morahan *m* – John Addison 85 mins.

Bonar Colleano (*Dan*), Susan Shaw (*Pat*), Renée Asherson (*Sally*), Earl Cameron (*Johnny*), Moira Lister (*Maisie*), Max Adrian (*Vernon*).

Pool of London is closely modelled on Dearden's earlier picture, *The Blue Lamp*, telling the same sort of melodramatic crime story in a realistic setting

– the river landmarks, the workings of the customs officers and river police. A third element is provided by the abortive love of the coloured sailor for the London girl . . . This is the film's least successful element. The relationship is treated as an interlude which can have no outcome, but is not handled with the feeling or sympathy which would justify its part in the film. (*Monthly Film Bulletin*, February 1951, p.229)

If only one film could be preserved for posterity, to illustrate the essence of Ealing . . . this would be a good choice, with its clear-cut embodiment of Ealing attitudes to women, violence, social responsibility and cinematic form. (Charles Barr, *Ealing Studios*, p.190)

I BELIEVE IN YOU   (1952)

Cert – U *dist* – Rank *p.c* – Ealing *p* – Michael Relph *d* – Basil Dearden *sc* – Relph, Dearden and Jack Whittingham, from the memoir *Court Circular* by Sewell Stokes *ph* – Gordon Dines *ed* – Peter Tanner *a.d* – Maurice Carter *m* – Ernest Irving 95 mins.

Cecil Parker (*Phipps*), Celia Johnson (*Matty*), Harry Fowler (*Hooker*), Joan Collins (*Norma*), George Relph (*Mr Dove*), Godfrey Tearle (*Mr Pyke*), Ernest Jay (*Mr Quayle*), Laurence Harvey (*Jordie*), Ursula Howells (*Hon Ursula*).

The film is a true story within the limits of the commercial cinema: that is to say, it keeps with unusual fidelity to the material of its original, often using incidents without changing them in any way, but it adds a romantic central theme and a melodramatic climax. (Dilys Powell, *Sunday Times*, 9 March 1952)

The fault of the film lies in the delinquents . . . Dearden and Relph have fallen into the old Shakespearean trap of making their lower-class characters either comical or eccentric. There is no fear nor grittiness in their slums. There is no shame in their poverty. (*Daily Herald*, 2 March 1952)

THE GENTLE GUNMAN   (1952)

Cert – A *dist* – Rank *p.c* – Ealing *p* – Michael Relph *d* – Basil Dearden *sc* – Roger Macdougall, from own play *ph* – Gordon Dines *ed* – Peter Tanner *a.d* – Jim Morahan *m* – John Greenwood 86 mins.

John Mills (*Terence Sullivan*), Dirk Bogarde (*Matt Sullivan*), Elisabeth Sellars (*Maureen Fagan*), Barbara Mullen (*Molly Fagan*), Robert Beatty (*Shinto*), Eddie Byrne (*Flynn*), Joseph Tomelty (*Dr Brannigan*), Gilbert Harding (*Henry Truethorne*), James Kenney (*Johnny Fagan*).

The film is a drearily safe piece condemning IRA terrorism during the 1940 blitz. The original play, by Roger Macdougall, may have been a serious study of pacifism and the moral ironies of war (for historically it's arguable that the British were quite as brutal to the Irish as the Nazis to occupied Europe). But his script as filmed, becomes a plea to the Irish not to blow up London, a plea so untopical that, despite the IRA's post-war fits, one supposes that Relph and Dearden were trying to persuade boys who thought it tough to use coshes that the really tough boys (who used guns) preferred being gentle ... (Raymond Durgnat, 'Two on a Tandem', *Films and Filming*, July 1966, p.30)

THE WEAK AND THE WICKED   (1953)

Cert – A   *dist* – Associated British-Pathé   *p.c* – A Marble Arch Production *p* – Victor Skutezky   *d* – Jack Lee Thompson   *sc* – Thompson and Ann Burnaby in collaboration with Joan Henry, from Henry's original book *Who Lie in Gaol*   *ph* – Gilbert Taylor   *ed* – Richard Best   *a.d* – Robert Jones *m* – Leighton Lucas   88 mins.

Glynis Johns (*Jean Raymond*), John Gregson (*Michael*), Diana Dors (*Betty*), Jane Hylton (*Babs*), Sidney James (*Sid Baden*), A.E. Matthews (*Harry Wicks*).

In every film I do I hold on to something, some social problem. Now, if you say 'Should the audience always see social problems?', no, not in a million years. The cinema is a mass medium for world audiences – there's nothing wrong with a Bob Hope/Bing Crosby picture. They're not trying to show any big social problem, but I personally must. (Jack Lee Thompson, *Films and Filming*, April 1963, p.6)

The treatment of this story provides an unfortunate example of the malaise with which so much British script-writing is afflicted nowadays. The basic situation is promising, for we are introduced to two widely differing aspects of the penal system. The first prison, Blackdown, is stern and bleak and the discipline is strong (there is no sadism, however), and the second, The Grange, is intended to depict the more constructive elements of the system: a 'prison without bars' where the prisoners are helped to prepare themselves for a free life once more. But against these backgrounds are paraded a prize collection of familiar feminine character types (alternately comic, sad and hysterical) – two-dimensional creatures, observed without insight or real compassion. The introduction of raucous comedy into several of the flashbacks, which involve shoplifting and the planning of murder, also seems in dubious taste in such a context . . . The facile ending, reuniting Jean and Michael, provides a final glib compromise with reality. (*Monthly Film Bulletin*, January 1954, p.22)

O DREAMLAND (1953)

A Sequence Film   *d* – Lindsay Anderson *Camera and assistance* John
Fletcher 12 mins.

O Dreamland emerged in the context of what Anderson later described as 'the
blissful dawn of the New Left'. In that context it would be taken quite simply
as a particularly vehement protest against what passes for popular
entertainment in the consumer society. The listless trippers are the
oppressed, exploited victims of a spiritually nihilistic system . . . But like all
Anderson's films *O Dreamland* contains far more of him than of any
movement with which he was associated. (Elizabeth Sussex, *Lindsay
Anderson*, Studio Vista, 1969, p.25)

The film's personal quality arises not from its point of view but out of the
disproportion between the feeling generated and the subject that generates
the feeling. The intense exasperation revealed isn't easy to justify. (Alan
Lovell, *Studies in Documentary*, Secker & Warburg/BFI, 1972, p.140)

PRIVATE'S PROGRESS (1956)

Cert – U *dist* – British Lion *p.c* – Charter Films *p* – Roy Boulting
d – John Boulting *sc* – Frank Harvey and John Boulting *ph* – Eric Cross
ed – Anthony Harvey *a.d* – Alan Harris *m* – John Addison 102 mins.

Richard Attenborough (*Cox*), Dennis Price (*Bertram Tracepurcel*), Terry-
Thomas (*Major Hitchcock*), Ian Carmichael (*Stanley Windrush*), Peter Jones
(*Egan*), William Hartnell (*Sgt Sutton*), Victor Maddern (*Pte George Blake*),
Kenneth Griffith (*Pte Dai Jones*), Miles Malleson (*Mr Windrush*), John Le
Mesurier (*Psychiatrist*).

The general irreverence of this film is in itself welcome; it is prepared to tilt at
almost any target – the boredom and futility of army routine, the corruption
of high-ups at the War Office, class-consciousness, all kinds of incompetence, intrigue and official absurdity. All that one wishes is for the humour
to have more edge. There is material here for real satire, but writing and
direction choose the less demanding level of affable farce. (*Monthly Film
Bulletin*, April 1956)

IT'S GREAT TO BE YOUNG (1956)

Cert – U *dist* – A.B./Pathé *p.c* – Marble Arch *p* – Victor Skutezky
d – Cyril Frankel *sc* – Ted Willis *ph* – Gilbert Taylor *ed* – Max Benedict
a.d – Robert Jones *m* – Ray Martin, Lester Powell, John Addison 93 mins.

John Mills (*Dingle*), Cecil Parker (*Frome*), Jeremy Spenser (*Nicky*), Dorothy

Bromiley (*Paulette*), Brian Smith (*Ginger*), Wilfred Downing (*Browning*), Richard O'Sullivan (*Lawson*).

For its salvation, this flimsy story ... should either have been told realistically or as a roaring musical ... farce. That Ted Willis (Author) and Cyril Frankel (Director) have mixed both methods and fallen between two stools turns it into a roaring musico-realistico-farcico failure. (Paul Dehn, *News Chronicle*, 1 June 1956)

I found the Angel Hill kids of Angel Hill Grammar School quite nauseating, and their jazz-mad form-master ... only a little less so. But they had the large preview-audience, usherettes and all, fairly rolling in the aisles. (Isabel Quigly, *Spectator*, 8 June 1956)

MY TEENAGE DAUGHTER   (1956)

Cert – A *dist* – British Lion *p.c* – Everest Pictures *p./d* – Herbert Wilcox *sc* – Felicity Douglas, from her own story *ph* – Max Greene *ed* – Bunny Warren *a.d* – Denis Johnson *m* – Stanley Black 100 mins.

Anna Neagle (*Valerie Carr*), Sylvia Syms (*Janet Carr*), Kenneth Haigh (*Tony Ward Black*), Norman Wooland (*Hugh Manning*), Wilfrid Hyde White (*Sir Joseph*), Julia Lockwood (*Poppet Carr*).

Now that literature has its novels of the discontented, and the theatre has its *Look Back in Anger*, it is not too sanguine, I suppose, to hope that British films will get around to recognising the dilemma on their doorstep. *My Teenage Daughter* is an attempt to describe The Problem. It succeeds only in skinning the grape. (Kenneth Pearson, *Sunday Times*, 24 June 1956)

It's the British answer to those American movies about children who go wrong because of the shortcomings of their Mums and Dads. In a typically British way it takes place in a nice house in London's semi-swish Hampstead Garden Suburb. In a typically British way 'Mum' is a respectable widow with a respectable job in a respectable publishing firm. All ever so nice! Anna refuses to marry again ... But that leaves Sylvia without a Dad to spank her when she's naughty. So Sylvia goes to the bad ... in a typically British respectable way. (F. Jackson, *Reynold's News*, 24 June 1956)

YIELD TO THE NIGHT   (1956)

Cert – X *dist* – A.B./Pathé *p.c* – Associated British *p* – Kenneth Harper *d* – Jack Lee Thompson *sc* – John Cresswell and Joan Henry, based on the book by Joan Henry *ph* – Gilbert Taylor *ed* – Richard Best *a.d* – Robert Jones *m* – Ray Martin 99 mins.

185

Diana Dors (*Mary Hilton*), Yvonne Mitchell (*MacFarlane*), Michael Craig (*Jim Lancaster*), Marie Ney (*Governor*), Geoffrey Keen (*Chaplain*), Liam Redmond (*Doctor*).

Miss Dors was called upon to act the part of a cold-blooded murderess awaiting execution, and gave a credible, sympathetic performance. It was Lee Thompson's most satisfactory film at that time, with an unusually partisan approach for a British film, firmly siding with the anti-capital punishment lobby. (George Perry, *The Great British Picture Show*, Paladin, 1974, p.185)

The most important thing about *Yield to the Night* is not so much its quality as a film, as the exceptional nature of its attempt. Here is a British picture which is daring enough to take as its theme the last few days in the life of a murderess condemned to be hanged: and brave enough to suggest that the whole business is not one that reflects the utmost credit on society. Given the treatment it deserves, this subject would be almost intolerable, savage, terrifying and salutary. *Yield to the Night* is intermittently tense, and makes some good points, but it lapses too often into clichés of characterisation and style, and the final tableau, with Geoffrey Keen as the daddy-knows-best prison padre, beats a painful retreat into conformism. (Alberta Marlow, *Sight and Sound*, vol.26, no.1, Summer 1956, p.35)

EVERY DAY EXCEPT CHRISTMAS   (1957)

dist – Ford of Britain *p.c* – Graphic *p* – Leon Clore
d/sc – Lindsay Anderson *ph* – Walter Lassally *ed* – Bill Megarry
sd – John Fletcher *m* – Daniel Paris 20 mins.

The film was trying to revitalise that sense of community that seems to inspire the British people only in time of war. Using many of Jennings' methods, Anderson succeeded in creating symbols of affirmation in the peace-time context . . . *Every Day Except Christmas* is a youthful film: the last of Anderson's Songs of Innocence and the last film he was ever to make in quite this optimistic spirit of unqualified delight. (Elizabeth Sussex, *Lindsay Anderson*, p.34.)

Every Day Except Christmas is an extremely soigné, effective, romantic documentary of a rather old-fashioned kind. (John Russell Taylor, *Directors and Directions*, Eyre Methuen, 1975, p.80)

THE FLESH IS WEAK   (1957)

Cert – X *dist* – Eros *p.c* – Raymond Stross Productions
p – Raymond Stross *d* – Don Chaffey *sc* – Lee Vance
ph – Stephen Dade *a.d* – John Stoll *m* – Tristram Cary 88 mins.

John Derek (*Tony Giani*), Milly Vitale (*Marissa Cooper*), William Franklyn (*Lloyd Buxton*), Martin Benson (*Angelo Giani*), Freda Jackson (*Trixie*), Norman Wooland (*Insp. Kingcombe*).

Sex melodrama giving the lowdown on the men behind the streetwalkers of London's West End. Its script, compounded of fact and fiction, is frank but, although it ruthlessly exposes the white slave traffickers, it does not entirely absolve their victims. The two sides to the problem are fairly faced. Milly Vitale wins sympathy as a girl who allows her desire for creature comforts as well as the dictates of her heart, to lead her from the path of virtue. Its supporting characters . . . ring true and the atmosphere is convincing. Despite its subject, or maybe because of it, it's quite a woman's film. Outstanding British X certificate offering. (*Kine Weekly*, 25 July 1957)

A crudely melodramatic film dealing with, but not one feels very gravely concerned about, the real life problem of organised prostitution. There is some rather loose and high flown talk regarding a change in the law and licences for the streetwalker but in the main the film has to do with the downfall of a Graham Greene-style boy gangster, played with appropriate menace by John Derek. The direction is brisk and there are some lively impersonations by Vera Day, Shirley Ann Field and Patricia Jessel among les girls. (*Monthly Film Bulletin*, September 1957, p.114)

LUCKY JIM (1957)

Cert – U *dist* – British Lion *p.c* – Charter *p* – Roy Boulting
d – John Boulting *sc* – Patrick Campbell, from the novel by
Kingsley Amis *ph* – Max Greene *ed* – Max Benedict
a.d – Elliott Scott 95 mins.

Ian Carmichael (*Jim Dixon*), Terry-Thomas (*Bertrand Welch*), Hugh Griffith (*Professor Welch*), Sharon Acker (*Christine Callaghan*), Jean Anderson (*Mrs Welch*) Maureen Connell (*Margaret Peel*).

Kingsley Amis's novel was a tough, funny and irascible piece of contemporary social comedy. The Boulting brothers' screen version broadens the comedy into farce, introduces a few elements of its own (a final slapstick car chase, a solemn boxer dog), and turns the whole thing into an amiable joke in the line of *Private's Progress* and *Brothers in Law*. The characters have lost contact with redbrick reality (compare, for instance, Jim's relationship with Margaret Peel in the novel and film) and in the process the book's social satire has been jettisoned. *Lucky Jim* has become broader, milder and softer; from the screen version, with its thoroughly traditional humours, one would never suspect that the novel had become the symbol of a new movement in English fiction. (*Monthly Film Bulletin*, November 1957, p.135)

WOMAN IN A DRESSING GOWN   (1957)

Cert – A *dist* – A.B./Pathé *p.c* – Godwin–Willis–Lee Thompson Production
p – Frank Godwin and J. Lee Thompson *d* – J. Lee Thompson
sc – Ted Willis *ph* – Gilbert Taylor *ed* – Richard Best *a.d* – Robert Jones
m – Louis Levy 94 mins.

Yvonne Mitchell (*Amy*), Anthony Quayle (*Jim*), Sylvia Syms (*Georgie*),
Andrew Ray (*Brian*), Carole Lesley (*Hilda*), Michael Ripper (*Pawnbroker*).

I have been waiting a long time for a really honest picture about ordinary
British people, and yesterday I saw it at last. (Leonard Mosley, *Daily
Express*, 19 July 1957)

They have accomplished one of the rarest of all achievements in the cinema –
the true, complete, and wholly convincing portrait of a woman. (*The Times*,
7 October 1957)

Women in a Dressing Gown is neo-unrealist: a little suburban story with
unsuitable gloss, and a kitchen sink performance by Yvonne Mitchell that
reminded me of Hermione Baddeley in one of her turns in an Ambassador's
revue. (Lindsay Anderson, *New Statesman*, 12 October 1957)

Sensitivity and sincerity have no place in this film. (Derek Hill, *Tribune*,
10 October 1957)

VIOLENT PLAYGROUND   (1958)

Cert – A *dist* – Rank *p* – Michael Relph *d* – Basil Dearden
sc – James Kennaway *ph* – Reginald Wyer *ed* – Arthur Stevens
a.d – Maurice Carter *m* – Philip Green 108 mins.

Stanley Baker (*Truman*), Anne Heywood (*Cathie*), David McCallum (*Johnny
Murphy*), Peter Cushing (*Priest*), John Slater (*Sgt Walker*), Clifford Evans
(*Heaven*), Moultrie Kelsall (*Superintendent*), George A. Cooper (*Chief
Inspector*), Brona Boland (*Mary Murphy*), Fergal Boland (*Patrick Murphy*).

A gripping, thought-provoking, sociological melodrama . . . which does
not preach yet clearly proves that the law must be upheld and that most
delinquents are victims of environment.(*Kine Weekly*, 9 January 1958, p.166)

It is NOT a serious study of juvenile delinquency. It is a gangster film of the
'crazy mixed-up kid' variety, and all its psychology and reform business is
simply thrown in as a gimmick. (Nina Hibbin, *Daily Worker*, 1 March 1958)

As the story progresses all attempts to discuss any genuine social problems
are abandoned in favour of a melodramatic and improbable climax. (*The
Times*, 3 March 1958)

THE YOUNG AND THE GUILTY   (1958)

Cert – A *dist* – A.B./Pathé *p.c* – Welwyn Films *p* – Warwick Ward
d – Peter Cotes *Original story and sc* – Ted Willis *ed* – Seymour Logie
a.d – Terence Verity *m* – Sydney John Kay 67 mins.

Phyllis Calvert (*Mrs Connor*), Andrew Ray (*Eddie Marshall*), Edward Chapman (*Mr Connor*), Janet Munro (*Sue Connor*), Campbell Singer (*Mr Marshall*), Hilda Fenemore (*Mrs Marshall*).

I want to make a film about real people experiencing real problems – the type which audiences of all sorts recognise as similar to their own problems . . . The star-studded cast and expensive locations featured in some recent 'spectaculars' have merely served to highlight the truth and naturalism to be found in the rival story, the human problem one, when that appeared on the cinema screen. (Peter Cotes on his decision to move from television to film direction, *Films and Filming*, March 1958, pp.9–10)

It is difficult to imagine exactly what the producers of *The Young and the Guilty* hoped to achieve in adapting Ted Willis' slight but accomplished television play to the more demanding requirements of the larger screen. Neither as an experiment in low-budget production, nor as a modest entertainment, can the result be regarded as satisfying . . . a well-meaning film which has sadly misfired. (*Monthly Film Bulletin*, May 1958, p.60)

In the old-fashioned British cinema, adolescent sex remains innocent or delinquent . . . Ted Willis' screenplay for Peter Cotes' *The Young and the Guilty* has it that the two amorous teenagers are really and innocently in love and unjustly suspected by their elders of precocious activities like heavy necking. Shame on you, you older generation, you. (Raymond Durgnat, *A Mirror for England*, p.193)

SHE DIDN'T SAY NO!   (1958)

Cert – A *dist* – A.B./Pathé *p.c* – A Sergei Nolbandov Production
p – Sergei Nolbandov *d* – Cyril Frankel *sc* – T.J. Morrison, Una Troy,
from the novel *We are Seven* by Una Troy *ph* – Gilbert Taylor
ed – Charles Hasse *a.d* – William Kellner *m* – Tristram Cary 97 mins.

Eileen Herlie (*Bridget Monaghan*), Perlita Neilson (*Mary Monaghan*), Wilfred Downing (*Tommy Monaghan*), Ann Dickins (*Poppy Monaghan*), Niall MacGinnis (*James Casey*), Patrick McAlinney (*Matthew Hogan*), Jack MacGowran (*William Bates*), Joan O'Hara (*Mrs Bates*), Ian Bannen (*Peter Howard*), Hilton Edwards (*The Film Director*), Liam Redmond (*Dr Cassidy*), Ray McAnally (*Jim Power*), Betty McDowell (*Mrs Power*).

All the humour to be evoked from the subject of illegitimacy is here unmercifully bludgeoned, and a jolly musical score insists what a gay affair it all is. The direction is heavily unsubtle and the playing coyly emphatic. As an entertainment, the film is mediocre as well as mildly offensive. (*Monthly Film Bulletin*, July 1958, pp.91–2)

A QUESTION OF ADULTERY   (1958)

Cert – A *dist* – Eros *p.c* – Connaught Place *p* – Raymond Stross
d – Don Chaffey *sc* – Anne Edwards *ph* – Stephen Dale
ed – Peter Tanner *a.d* – John Stoll *m* – Philip Green 84 mins.

Julie London (*Mary*), Anthony Steel (*Mark*), Basil Sydney (*Sir John Loring*), Donald Houston (*Mr Jacobus*), Anton Diffring (*Carl Dieter*), Andrew Cruickshank (*Dr Cameron*).

Dan Sutherland's play *Breach of Marriage*, itself hardly a well-argued discussion of the problem of artificial insemination, has here been given the full catchpenny treatment by the producer-director team responsible for *The Flesh is Weak*. As an entertainment the film is unlikely to appeal to anyone other than the emotionally retarded. Its dramatics are cheap, its presentation lurid, and any attempt at balance non-existent. Students of the bizarre will no doubt find the rape scene intercut with a climactic flamenco dance to their taste. (*Monthly Film Bulletin*, July 1958, p.90)

CARRY ON SERGEANT   (1958)

Cert – U *dist* – Anglo Amalgamated *p.c* – Insignia Productions
p – Peter Rogers *d* – Gerald Thomas *sc* – Norma Hudis, from *The Bull Boys* by R.F. Delderfield *ph* – Peter Hennessy *ed* – Peter Boita
a.d – Alex Vetchinsky *m* – Bruce Montgomery 83 mins.

William Hartnell (*Sgt Grimshawe*), Bob Monkhouse (*Charlie Sage*), Shirley Eaton (*Mary*), Eric Barker (*Captain Potts*), Dora Bryan (*Nora*), Bill Owen (*Corporal Copping*), Kenneth Connor (*Horace Strong*), Charles Hawtrey (*Peter Golightly*), Kenneth Williams (*James Bailey*).

Carry on Sergeant provides for any appetites not yet sated with army farce, in a film commendably brisk and played with great determination. (Penelope Houston, *Observer*, 21 September 1958)

A cheerful and unpretentious romp. (Nina Hibbin, *Daily Worker*, 20 September 1958)

From the moment of its launch, the public took to *Carry on Sergeant* as though it belonged to them. It was not peddling luxury or magic or stars and made no pretence at superiority. They saw *Carry on Sergeant* . . . as being part of themselves, a mate who showed them how to laugh at the problems and the people who pestered . . . and bossed them. The humour was the sort of humour they used themselves in pubs and clubs. Critics may call it corny, and lots of it was, but it was legitimate and true working-class humour. (Kenneth Easthaugh, *The Carry-On Book*, David & Charles, 1978, p.30)

ROOM AT THE TOP   (1959)

Cert – X *dist* – Independent/British Lion *p.c* – Remus
p – John and James Woolf *d* – Jack Clayton *sc* – Neil Paterson, from the novel by John Braine *ph* – Freddie Francis *ed* – Ralph Kemplen
a.d – Ralph Brinton *m* – Mario Nascimbene 117 mins.

Laurence Harvey (*Joe Lampton*), Simone Signoret (*Alice Aisgill*), Heather Sears (*Susan Brown*), Donald Wolfit (*Mr Brown*), Ambrosine Phillpotts (*Mrs Brown*), Donald Houston (*Charles Soames*), Raymond Huntley (*Mr Hoylake*), John Westbrook (*Jack Wales*), Allan Cuthbertson (*George Aisgill*), Mary Peach (*June Samson*).

One feels that a whole new chapter is about to be written in motion picture history . . . I can say for myself that the only shock I felt was the shock of recognition, the shock of recognising ordinary, tawdry people on the screen in an extraordinarily bitter, adult drama, and the shock of realizing how rarely this has happened before. (Arthur Knight, *Saturday Review*, 11 April 1959)

Room at the Top was the real eye-opener for me – the real proof that something had happened in the cinema. For here was a British film which, at long last, got its teeth into those subjects which have always been part and parcel of our lives, but have hitherto been taboo subjects on the prissy British screen – male ambition in all its ruthlessness, and sex in all its earthy compulsion. It is savagely frank and brutally truthful. (Leonard Mosley, *Daily Express*, 3 April 1959)

The film is much better than the novel . . . But, more than that, it is one of the bravest and best British films in years . . . The way it tells the story of how Joe Lampton . . . made good has earned it an X certificate. Not for meretricious horror or peek-hole sex: but for sheer, blatant honesty . . . The sex is there, in torrents. The horror is there, and of course, the down-to-common-earth words. This is in no sense a U story. But it is real and straightforward, and rings true. In this case at least, and at last, the X certificate looks like a badge of honour. (Derek Monsey, *Sunday Express*, 25 January 1959)

Working-class audiences will recognise British Lion's *Room at the Top* . . . as unsatisfactory. They will be quick to spot the false characterisation of its 'hero', especially as everything else about it is remarkably true to life . . . The main character isn't typical at all . . . Joe Lampton is a working-class cad . . . Now, its unhappily true that some working people have corrupt social ambitions. But in a film that sets out to explore class relations and sex relations between classes, it is a trick to select an immature, over-sexed, unprincipled climber as the main representative of the working class. (Nina Hibbin, *Daily Worker*, 26 January 1959)

Joe, indeed, is more of a cad than a card . . . Joe's private class war is, to a certain extent, justified by the behaviour of his natural enemies. Still, perhaps such people exist . . . (*The Times*, 26 January 1959)

PASSPORT TO SHAME   (1959)

Cert – X   *dist* – British Lion *p.c* – United Co-Productions *p* – John Clein *d* – Alvin Rakoff *sc* – Patrick Alexander *ph* – Jack Asher *ed* – Lee Doig *a.d* – George Beech *m* – Ken Jones 91 mins.

Diana Dors (*Vicki*), Eddie Constantine (*Johnny*), Herbert Lom (*Nick*), Odile Versois (*Malou*), Brenda de Banzie (*Aggie*), Robert Brown (*Mike*).

The plot is naturally far from pretty, but nevertheless vividly reveals the tricks of London's white slave traffic. Its principal characters ring true, yet it artfully cushions the sensational with romance, and the climax is salutary as well as thrilling. The title and subject, plus 'heaven-sent' publicity provided by the Wolfenden Report, should procure it considerable audiences. (*Kine Weekly*, 5 February 1959)

This wildly incredible story, introduced as a social document by Fabian of the Yard, must be the most wholeheartedly absurd prostitute drama yet. Motivations are mysterious and characterisations grotesque. Connoisseurs of the bizarre may relish some of the production's most ambitious moments, notably the conclusion, which features Herbert Lom scattering hundreds of bank notes from a blazing brothel in an endeavour to hasten the approaching firemen. (*Monthly Film Bulletin*, March 1959, p.35)

CARRY ON NURSE   (1959)

Cert – U   *dist* – Anglo Amalgamated *p.c* – Nat Cohen and Stuart Levy *p* – Peter Rogers *d* – Gerald Thomas *sc* – Norman Hudis *ph* – Reg Wyer *ed* – John Shirley *a.d* – Alex Vetchinsky *m* – Bruce Montgomery 86 mins.

Shirley Eaton (*Dorothy Denton*), Terence Longdon (*Ted York*), Wilfrid Hyde White (*Colonel*), Kenneth Connor (*Bernie Bishop*), Charles Hawtrey (*Hinton*), Hattie Jacques (*Matron*).

Carry on Nurse . . . makes the jokes you might expect – and a lot more you have, judging by previous experience of British comedy, no business to expect . . . It brings with it a welcome breath of good, vulgar music-hall fun. (Dilys Powell, *Sunday Times*, 8 March 1959)

The censor is making progress. Already this year we have seen the fiercest dialogue and most realistic love-scenes ever to be made in a British film: in *Room at the Top*. Now the censor takes another step – towards the kind of gag that can be heard any night of the week when Max Miller is performing in music-hall but not up to now in the cinema. (John Waterman, *Evening Standard*, 5 March 1959)

Carry on Nurse is 'significant' only as a signpost (or if you like, tombstone) to popular taste. This hospital farce is a fantasy on sex . . . A nurse is shown climbing on a table so that patients may study her legs; a young man who has had an operation grabs a nurse and embraces her on the bed; script and director rely for laughs on nurses' endeavours to undress men and supervise their baths; the final gag plumbs a new low in vulgarity. (Campbell Dixon, *Manchester Guardian*, 9 March 1959)

One can only suppose that the Censor has given *Carry on Nurse* a U Certificate because its non-U smut is of a sort which appeals chiefly to children. Doubtless the 8–12's will flock to see this hospital farce . . . in order to scream with happy laughter at lavatory jokes about bed-bottles, bowel movement, belches, bottoms, toilet-rolls, flatulence and vomiting . . . There is, of course, nothing wrong about a film company having a bash at sexual innuendo for adults only, if they think it will pay off . . . but there is surely something very wrong with a Board of Censors who will permit such stuff to be passed as fit entertainment for an uninstructed child . . . I found its unsmutty sketches so tedious and its final joke so hoary that I would sooner be certified than see it again myself. (Paul Dehn, *News Chronicle*, 6 March 1959)

The picture begins with a pubic shave, continues with a ceremony involving a suppository, settles down to some steady vomiting, wakes up with a scene full of toilet-paper streamers . . . The humour of these situations may largely be lost on people who have successfully completed their toilet training, but the phenomenal popularity of *Carry on Nurse* would suggest that they are not in the majority. (*Time*, 26 June 1960)

In 1969 Roger Manvell contrived to write a survey of 'New Cinema in Britain' – in effect the whole of post-war British cinema – without making any reference at all to the *Carry On* series and granting the horror cycle a single, disdainful footnote. Whatever one's estimate of the achievement of these series, I don't think that such a selective perception of the field, selecting for respectability, is critically defensible. The popular impact of these series indicates that they offered satisfactions which other British films had ceased to: at their strongest, in the late 'fifties, they were outlets for forces which mainstream British cinema had increasingly rejected as vulgar or shocking. (One can see the new 'adult' cinema of around 1960 as a more conventional attempt to achieve an integration). (Charles Barr, *Ealing Studios*, p.58)

NO TREES IN THE STREET (1959)

Cert – X *dist* – A.B./Pathé *p.c* – Allègro *p* – Frank Godwin
d – J. Lee Thompson *sc* – Ted Willis, from his own play
ph – Gilbert Taylor *ed* – Richard Best *a.d* – Robert Jones
m – Laurie Johnson 96 mins.

Sylvia Syms (*Hetty*), Herbert Lom (*Wilkie*), Joan Miller (*Jess*), Melvyn Hayes (*Tommy*), Stanley Holloway (*Kipper*), Liam Redmond (*Bill*), Ronald Howard (*Frank*).

Intended as a piece of social realism, it emerges as a heavy-handed thick-eared melodrama. There are all sorts of moral remarks about the bad old days and about environment creating criminals, but author Ted Willis seems to be merely using these to cloak a spot of sex and violence. (Anthony Carthew, *Daily Herald*, 6 March 1959)

What do these proud friends of the left imagine they're doing with a production which tells a story of a pre-war East End environment corrupting its inhabitants 'lives' and then ends with a complacent glance at today's living standards and a sharp word to the young that they've never had it so good? Flat, empty characterisations, meaningless plot twists, and treatment which thumps home every point with gross insensitivity do little to suggest that either writer or director has any confidence in the inherent dramatic values of the subject. Anyone really concerned with putting a true picture of working class life on the screen would hardly be so desperate to pack in the clichés. (Derek Hill, *Tribune*, 13 March 1959)

I am bored by the endless stream of motion pictures designed to explain to me how and why juveniles become delinquent. (Fred Majdalany, *Daily Mail*, 6 March 1959)

SAPPHIRE (1959)

Cert – A *dist* – Rank *p.c* – Artna *p* – Michael Relph *d* – Basil Dearden
sc – Janet Green *ph* – Harry Waxman *ed* – John Guthridge
a.d – Carmen Dillon *m* – Philip Green 92 mins.

Nigel Patrick (*Hazard*), Michael Craig (*Learoyd*), Yvonne Mitchell (*Mildred*), Paul Massie (*David*), Bernard Miles (*Harris*), Olga Lindo (*Mrs Harris*), Earl Cameron (*Dr Robbins*), Gordon Heath (*Paul Slade*).

Without fear of trespass I can say . . . that the film takes the colour problem very seriously, and if it arrives at no hard conclusion, at least has fair arguments to advance on both sides . . . It catches the real feel of London, and is acted . . .with a distinction not customarily found in thrillers. It is a thriller, though . . . and a very good one indeed. (C.A. Lejeune, *Observer*, 10 May 1959)

The traditional 'quality' cinema has given us a series of problem pictures dealing with, for example, race prejudice (*Sapphire*), homosexuality (*Victim*), and education (*Spare the Rod*). Their method is to devise a number of stereotypes to represent every possible attitude to the matter in hand; they have no success in their attempts to pass these stereotypes off as human beings. These pictures are particularly offensive in assuming that their holy platitudes are too loftily intellectual to be accepted by audiences unless the pill of wisdom is sweetened with spurious excitement. Thus in *Sapphire* and *Victim*, Basil Dearden and his scriptwriter Janet Green have produced thriller-problem films which work neither as thrillers nor as examinations of a problem, and particularly not as films. (V.F. Perkins, 'The British Cinema', *Movie* no.1, 1962, p.9)

The tragedy is set in motion by David's decision to marry her (and give up his scholarship in Rome) because she is pregnant; and her pregnancy is, of course, the result of her (not his) unashamed sexual licence . . . She is punished both by her violent death and by her suppression from the narrative . . . She is a sexually attractive and independent young woman who gets her come-uppance just at the moment when she seems poised to achieve her ambition. Her racial origins, foregrounded by the deceptive appearance of her body, seem to be a particularly insidious and racist metaphor for yet another elaboration of the patriarchal myth of female duplicity. (Carrie Tarr, '*Sapphire*, *Darling* and the Boundaries of Permitted Pleasure', *Screen*, vol.26, no.1, January/February 1985, pp.55–6)

LOOK BACK IN ANGER   (1959)

Cert – X *dist* – Associated British-Pathé *p.c* – Woodfall
p – Gordon L.T. Scott *d* – Tony Richardson *sc* – Nigel Kneale, from the play by John Osborne *ph* – Oswald Morris *ed* – Richard Best
a.d – Peter Glazier *m* – Chris Barber and his Band 101 mins.

Richard Burton (*Jimmy Porter*), Claire Bloom (*Helena Charles*), Mary Ure (*Alison Porter*), Dame Edith Evans (*Mrs Tanner*), Gary Raymond (*Cliff*), Glen Byam Shaw (*Colonel Redfern*), Donald Pleasence (*Hurst*).

A bare plot outline is incapable of indicating the qualities of *Look Back in Anger*: they derive from the impetus of Jimmy's anger, the power of its expression, the honesty with which the writing hacks its way through an emotional jungle. Nigel Kneale's adaptation, technically an extraordinarily clever one, sacrifices the claustrophobic tensions of the play, the long speeches in which Jimmy Porter defines his aggressions, but gives more weight to the personal drama. Tony Richardson, directing his first feature, has given it a tough, vital style which represents something new in British cinema. His cameraman, Oswald Morris, has responded to the challenge of the 'intimate' subject with harsh, realistically lit exteriors and extensive and imaginative use of close-up. All in all, from 'the best young play of its generation' has invigoratingly come the best young (British) film of our generation. (*Monthly Film Bulletin*, June 1959, p.68)

How long does it take a sensational, shocking, and timely play to become easily digestible and mildly dated? Answer: the time it takes to transfer it from the stage to the screen. (Leonard Mosley, *Daily Express*)

Look Back in Anger is a play about the young by a young man seething with rage at social inequalities and life's injustices. Take out the frenzied hate, which suggests at times that Jimmy Porter is a schizoid or a paranoic, and what would be left? Not much more than boy-meets-girl, boy-loses-girl, boy-gets-girl, with a romp in the hay in between. (Campbell Dixon, *Daily Telegraph*, 27 May 1959)

LEFT, RIGHT AND CENTRE   (1959)

Cert – U *dist* – British Lion *p.c* – Launder and Gilliat *p* – Frank Launder, Sidney Gilliat *d* – Sidney Gilliat *sc* – Sidney Gilliat, Val Valentine *ph* – Gerald Gibbs *ed* – Geoffrey Foot, Gerry Hambling *a.d* – John Box *m* – Humphrey Searle 95 mins.

Ian Carmichael (*Robert Wilcot*), Alastair Sim (*Lord Wilcot*), Patricia Bredin (*Stella Stoker*), Richard Wattis (*Harding-Pratt*), Eric Barker (*Bert Glimmer*), Gordon Harker (*Hardy*), Moyra Fraser (*Annabel*), William Kendall (*Pottle*), Jack Hedley (*Bill Hemingway*).

This is a political comedy entirely, and carefully, devoid of political references. The most daring of its conclusions is that the platitudes of one side are undistinguishable from those of the other, and it finds it more profitably amusing to turn to Alastair Sim. (Penelope Houston, *Sight and Sound*, Summer/Autumn 1959, p.162)

Launder and Gilliat's political comedy is less a satire on the British electoral system than an attempt to find humour in the influence of television on politics. The script, eschewing parody and caricature, extracts its mild quota of laughs from the periphery of apathetic voters, inadequate supporters and commercialised stately homes. (*Monthly Film Bulletin*, August 1959, p.109)

Left, Right and Centre opens with a series of cheap sneers at the British electorate for failing to take a serious interest in politics . . . (and) never stops pointing a scornful finger at working class characters who express a similar apathy or cynicism. The Socialists are represented as being coarse, ignorant in matters of manner and accent, considerably more violent than their opponents and fighting a largely meaningless battle. (Derek Hill, *Tribune*, 24 July 1959)

OPERATION BULLSHINE   (1959)

Cert – U   *dist* – A.B./Pathé *p.c* – Associated British/Frank Godwin
p – Frank Godwin *d* – Gilbert Gunn *sc* – Ann Burnaby, Rupert Lang,
Gilbert Gunn *ph* – Gilbert Taylor *ed* – E.B. Jarvis *a.d* – Robert Jones
m – Laurie Johnson 84 mins.

Donald Sinden (*Lieutenant Gordon Brown*), Barbara Murray (*Private Betty
Brown*), Carole Lesley (*Marge White*), Ronald Shiner (*Gunner Slocum*),
Naunton Wayne (*Pym*), Dora Bryan (*Private Cox*).

Made in the now very familiar pattern of army farce, *Operation Bullshine* is a
stereotype of such service comedies with the addition of large numbers of
underclad starlets. Only Dora Bryan and Peter Jones are genuinely funny,
whilst Gilbert Taylor's colour photography gives some zest to the stumbling
production, which never successfully resolves the problem of whether to be
a comedy of errors or a barrack-room farce. (*Monthly Film Bulletin*, August
1959, p.110)

Operation Bullshine is one more in the latest series of comedies devoted to
explaining life in the services. This one takes a rather inexpert and only
mildly lascivious look at a group of A T S stationed on an ack-ack site during
the war. All (except the inimitable Dora Bryan) are pretty. All are seen
dressing and undressing and doing PT. (*Sunday Express*, 5 July 1959)

I'M ALL RIGHT JACK   (1959)

Cert – U   *dist* – British Lion *p.c* – Charter *p* – Roy Boulting
d – John Boulting *sc* – Frank Harvey, John Boulting, Alan Hackney,
from the novel *Private Life* by Alan Hackney *ph* – Max Greene
ed – Anthony Harvey *a.d* – Bill Andrews *m* – Ken Hare 105 mins.

Ian Carmichael (*Stanley Windrush*), Peter Sellers (*Fred Kite*), Dennis Price
(*Bertram Tracepurcel*), Margaret Rutherford (*Aunt Dolly*), Richard Attenborough (*Cox*), Terry-Thomas (*Major Hitchcock*).

Nowadays there seem to be two sacred cows – Big Business and Organised
Labour. Both are deep in an open conspiracy against the individual – to force
us to accept certain things for what in fact they are not . . . Certainly a great
deal has changed since we used to be Angry Young Men before the war.
Social disparities have largely been abolished, people are infinitely better
off . . . we are told from on high that we have never had it so good . . . But at
the end of this huge revolution we are not so sure that the losses have not
been as great as the gains. For example, the tendency to think of people not as
human beings but as part of a group, a bloc, a class. (The Boulting brothers,
Daily Express, 14 August 1959)

The Boultings tell us we are a shower . . . Our only interest is in grabbing as much money as possible for as little work as possible . . . With the anger that makes a true satirist, they go for the false values that have stained the fifties. (Anthony Carthew, *Daily Herald*, 14 August 1959)

This is a picture made from no standpoint, other than the shoulder-shrugging confidence that everything is fair game . . . They take no risks, because they face no issues squarely: they hurt no one, because one jibe cancels out another. (Penelope Houston, *Sight and Sound*, Summer/Autumn 1959, p.163)

I asked some of the actors how they felt, as trade unionists, about making an anti-trade union film. 'It's not really that at all', they said. 'It's good fun, and it guys everything – bosses as well.' The Boulting brothers were very enthusiastic. 'It's a really contemporary theme', said Roy. 'We enjoy making fun of the Establishment: the trade unions are part of the Establishment.' He claimed to be deeply in touch with working-class tastes . . . In touch with the working class? I asked a technician what he thought. 'It's making working people out to be fools', he said. (Nina Hibbin, *Daily Worker*, 28 February 1959)

It is typical of *I'm All Right Jack* that that splendid actor, Miles Malleson, should be employed here momentarily shelling peas in the nude. (William Whitebait, *New Statesman*, 22 August 1959)

BATTLE OF THE SEXES   (1959)

Cert – U   *dist* – British Lion/Bryanston   *p.c* – Prometheus
p/sc – Monja Danischewsky   *d* – Charles Crichton, based on
James Thurber's short story *The Catbird Seat*   *ph* – Freddie Francis
ed – Seth Holt   *a.d* – Edward Carrick   *m* – Stanley Black   84 mins.

Peter Sellers (*Mr Martin*), Constance Cummings (*Angela Barrows*), Robert Morley (*Robert MacPherson*), Jameson Clark (*Andrew Darling*), Moultrie Kelsall (*Graham*), Alex Mackenzie (*Robertson*).

The first independent production to appear under the Bryanston banner, *The Battle of the Sexes* will come as something of a disappointment to anybody looking for genuine native material, originally conceived and executed. Though traces of Thurber remain visible, Monja Danischewsky's script concentrates on obvious humour – stock Scottish types, routine tradition-versus-automation skirmishes – and eschews the rigorous discipline of satire for easy-going, Ealing-inherited burlesque. (*Monthly Film Bulletin*, February 1960, p.18)

Masquerading as a comedy, the film was an unconsciously depressing account of the deep-rooted British unwillingness to contemplate change. (Robin Cross, *The Big Book of British Films*, Charles Herridge, 1984, p.96)

It's not basically about sex. It is about tweed. (Alex Walker, *Evening Standard*, 25 February 1960)

THE SHAKEDOWN   (1960)

Cert – X   *dist* – Rank /Alliance *p.c* – Ethiro *p* – Norman Williams
d – John Lemont *sc* – Leigh Vance, John Lemont *ph* – Brendan J. Stafford
ed – Bernard Gribble *a.d* – Anthony Inglis *m* – Philip Green 92 mins.

Terence Morgan (*Augie Cortona*), Hazel Court (*Mildred Eyde*), Donald Pleasence (*Jessel*), Bill Owen (*Spettigue*), Robert Beatty (*Jarvis*), Harry H. Corbett (*Gollar*).

This tentative and equivocal effort to cash in on the Wolfenden Report remains undistinguished for good or ill. There is enough nudity for an X Certificate, but it is all very prim; enough action to maintain interest, but no tension; routine coshings, but no sadism; cheap settings, but not shoddiness. Except for the error, or possibly box-office stratagem, of giving someone as good-natured and refined of speech as Terence Morgan a vice spiv's role, everything is fairly competently done. (*Monthly Film Bulletin*, February 1960, p.26)

THE ANGRY SILENCE   (1960)

Cert – A   *dist* – British Lion *p.c* – Beaver *p* – Richard Attenborough, Bryan Forbes *d* – Guy Green *sc* – Bryan Forbes, based on the story by Michael Craig and Richard Gregson *ph* – Arthur Ibbetson
ed – Anthony Harvey *a.d* – Ray Sim *m* – Malcolm Arnold 95 mins.

Richard Attenborough (*Tom*), Pier Angeli (*Anna*), Michael Craig (*Joe*), Bernard Lee (*Connolly*), Alfred Burke (*Travers*), Geoffrey Keen (*Davis*).

Beaver Films was a new production company set up by Richard Attenborough and Bryan Forbes within the Allied Film Makers framework. *The Angry Silence* was chosen as their first project. The film's treatment of a strike immediately provoked controversy, especially in the labour movement. The Trades Council in Ipswich, where some of the film had been shot, for example, passed a motion of boycott against the film. The Miners Union in South Wales called on cinemas and miners' welfare institutes not to show the film. 'This sort of Fascist behaviour is just what the film is about', responded Attenborough. 'Mob rule by a few scheming Communists.' (*Sunday Despatch*, 17 April 1960)

Humbly and most sincerely I salute . . . the courage and, yes, the genius of Richard Attenborough and a brilliant new team of British film-makers who have produced a story that will shock you and shame you, make you laugh but more often bring you to tears – a topical, controversial, vitriolic masterpiece. (Donald Gomery, *Daily Express*, 11 March 1960)

A film of rare quality and impressive realism . . . *The Angry Silence* is not a biased film. It tells its story with honesty and with understanding. It has about it the clear ring of truth. (*The Times*, 14 March 1960)

The film purports to be an attack on conformity. But it is entirely conformist itself. It accepts the conformist image of Communists, shop-stewards, wildcat strikes and sheep-like workers, and ends by gloating over the violence it sets out to condemn. Above all, *The Angry Silence* sees people in terms of a mob to be manipulated – and in this it is a direct reflection of the way the makers of the film see their audience. For although the film ostensibly condemns those who manipulate, it is, in itself, a thorough-going exercise in manipulation. There is no attempt to work honestly at communicating the truth of human experience. One eye is always on the shock effect to be produced on the back stalls. (Albert Hunt in Denys Thompson (ed.), *Discrimination and Popular Culture*, Penguin, 1964, p.111)

The strikers are apathetic, ignorant, irresponsible, easily driven, infested with thugs and on the point of degenerating into a yelling mob . . . we do seem to be in the presence of a right-wing denunciation of the collective spirit as equivalent to sheep-like acquiescence in mob violence. (Raymond Durgnat, *A Mirror for England*, pp.72–3)

THE LEAGUE OF GENTLEMEN   (1960)

Cert – A   *dist* – Rank   *p.c* – Allied Film Makers   *p* – Michael Relph
d – Basil Dearden   *sc* – Bryan Forbes, from the novel by John Boland
ph – Arthur Ibbetson   *ed* – John Guthridge   *a.d* – Peter Proud
m – Philip Green   113 mins.

Jack Hawkins (*Hyde*), Nigel Patrick (*Race*), Roger Livesey (*Mycroft*), Richard Attenborough (*Lexy*), Bryan Forbes (*Porthill*), Kieron Moore (*Stevens*), Terence Alexander (*Rupert*), Norman Bird (*Weaver*), Robert Coote (*Bunny Warren*).

It was a more wry, disenchanted kind of comedy than Ealing would have made . . . It maintained Ealing's unflagging belief that the amateurs could outwit the experts, the irregulars could defeat the authorities; and the aggressive band of shady customers, all keeping up a pretence of respectability under Supremo Jack Hawkins, appeared in retrospect to be mirroring Britain's buoyant acquisitive society in the 1960s . . . *The League of Gentlemen*, with its target of quick capital gains, was the ideal comedy for a boom-time economy. (Alexander Walker, *Hollywood England*, Michael Joseph, 1974, pp.103–4)

SONS AND LOVERS (1960)

Cert – A *dist* – 20th Century-Fox *p.c* – Company of Artists
p – Jerry Wald *d* – Jack Cardiff *sc* – Gavin Lambert, T.E.B. Clarke, based
on D.H. Lawrence's novel *ph* – Freddie Francis *ed* – Gordon Pilkington
a.d – Tom Morahan, Lionel Couch *m* – Lambert Williamson 100 mins.

Dean Stockwell (*Paul Morel*), Trevor Howard (*Morel*), Wendy Hiller
(*Gertrude Morel*), Mary Ure (*Clara Dawes*), Heather Sears (*Miriam Leivers*),
William Lucas (*William*).

Sons and Lovers is one of the most moving, compassionate, understanding and
genuinely human films I have ever experienced . . . With sympathy and full-
in-the-face frankness *Sons and Lovers* plots the course of the young man's
progress as he sails through the stormy seas of young manhood. His
encounters with the problems of sex – a rock upon which he comes close to
foundering – are told with delicacy, skill and great tenderness. (Leonard
Mosley, *Daily Express*, 4 June 1960)

Not to mince words, the film version of D.H. Lawrence's *Sons and Lovers* is
something of an act of desecration. It is Lawrence not only de-gutted, but
stuffed and mounted. It is Lawrence pre-packaged – in the usual, time-
encrusted Hollywood tradition of 'shooting the classics'. (Clancy Sigal, *Time
and Tide*, 2 July 1960)

OSCAR WILDE (1960)

Cert – X *dist* – 20th Century-Fox *p.c* – Vantage *p* – William Kirby
d – Gregory Ratoff *sc* – Jo Eisinger *ph* – Georges Perinal
ed – Tony Gibbs *a.d* – Scott MacGregor *m* – Muir Mathieson 98 mins.

Robert Morley (*Oscar Wilde*), Phyllis Calvert (*Constance Wilde*), John Neville
(*Lord Alfred Douglas*), Ralph Richardson (*Sir Edward Carson*), Dennis Price
(*Robert Ross*), Alexander Knox (*Sir Edward Clarke*).

The first, by five days, of two neck-and-neck versions of the Wilde story to
reach the screen, *Oscar Wilde* was still being edited up to a couple of hours
before the press show. Unfortunately the hasty circumstances of its arrival
can neither excuse nor account for the funeral pace of the film itself, which
has the extraordinarily stiff and stagy look of some tea-cup screen drama of
the very early Thirties. Nor has the director, Gregory Ratoff, succeeded in
what must surely be his primary object, to give a living portrait of Wilde.
Like the entire film, Robert Morley's performance is external, cautious and
afraid. (*Monthly Film Bulletin*, July 1960, p.93)

THE TRIALS OF OSCAR WILDE   (1960)

Cert – X *dist* – Eros *p.c* – Warwick/Viceroy *exec.p* – Irving Allen, Albert
R. Broccoli *p* – Harold Huth *d/sc* – Ken Hughes
ph – Ted Moore *ed* – Geoffrey Foot *a.d* – Ken Adam, Bill Constable
m – Ron Goodwin 123 mins.

Peter Finch (*Oscar Wilde*), John Fraser (*Lord Alfred Douglas*), Yvonne
Mitchell (*Constance*), Lionel Jeffries (*Marquis of Queensberry*), Nigel Patrick
(*Sir Edward Clarke*), James Mason (*Carson*).

In retrospect its implications that medicine, not the law, was the suitable
means of treatment for offenders like Wilde stands out for what it was, a
piece of 1960-ish special pleading just before the reform of the law, as
recommended by the Wolfenden Report of 1957, was put into effect. The
contemporary pressures put on public opinion in 1960 to 'accept' homosexuality as less a crime than a condition probably account for the film's
omitting the grotesque side of Wilde's character so that, despite Finch's
excellent and unsentimentalized performance, he seemed at times to be
simply a decent family man who preferred stimulating small talk in cafés to
dull nights at home. (Alexander Walker, *Hollywood England*, pp.158–9)

THE ENTERTAINER   (1960)

Cert – X *dist* – British Lion/Bryanston *p.c* – Woodfall/Holly
p – Harry Saltzman *d* – Tony Richardson *sc* – John Osborne,
Nigel Kneale. Adapted from the play by John Osborne
ph – Oswald Morris *ed* – Alan Osbiston *a.d* – Ralph Brinton
m – John Addison 96 mins.

Laurence Olivier (*Archie Rice*), Joan Plowright (*Jean*), Brenda de Banzie
(*Phoebe Rice*), Alan Bates (*Frank*), Roger Livesey (*Billy*), Shirley Ann Field
(*Tina*), Thora Hird (*Mrs Lapford*).

I thought *The Entertainer* was the most encouraging film ever to come out of
a British studio . . . *The Entertainer* was never directly concerned with
politics. It was much more concerned to say something about the quality of
life in England. This is where the film really succeeds. It brilliantly observes
the decaying quality of English social life. (Alan Lovell, *Tribune*, 19 August
1960)

Because some of the intellectual Teddy Boys are saying 'brilliant' I am going
to say what I think of this film . . . *The Entertainer* is badly made . . .What
ever the film of *The Entertainer* is about, it is not about anything remotely
connected with aesthetic or intellectual or emotional truths. (Derek Monsey,
Sunday Express, 31 July 1960)

It is amateurishly directed. Its script limps along like a lame dog and never misses a lamp-post on the way. (Leonard Mosley, *Daily Express*, 26 July 1960)

BEAT GIRL (1960)

Cert – X *dist* – Renown *p.c* – Renown *p* – George Willoughby
d – Edmond T. Greville *sc* – Dail Ambler *ph* – Walter Lassally
ed – Gordon Pilkington *a.d* – Elven Webb *m* – John Barry 85 mins.

David Farrar (*Paul Linden*), Noelle Adam (*Nichole*), Christopher Lee (*Kenny*), Gillian Hills (*Jennifer*), Adam Faith (*Dave*), Shirley Ann Field (*Dodo*), Peter McEnery (*Tony*).

He did not really understand what these kids were all het up about or hepped-up about, but if they wanted a film about beatniks, whoever or whatever they were, he would give them it. For good measure, he was going to have some scenes in a strip-tease club which he thought everyone would understand, even the squares. (Thomas Wiseman on George Minter's decision to make a film 'for the kids', *Evening Standard*, 14 August 1959)

With Soho strip-tease, Teddy Boys, 'pop' songs, jiving in Chislehurst caves, a sports car chicken run, stepmother trouble, a wife with a past, teenage tantrums, and a race to save a Bardot-like heroine from the clutches of a rogue with two 'plane tickets to Paris, this film is nothing if not eclectic. (*Monthly Film Bulletin*, November 1960, p.154)

SATURDAY NIGHT AND SUNDAY MORNING (1960)

Cert – X *dist* – British Lion/Bryanston *p.c* – Woodfall
p – Harry Saltzman, Tony Richardson *d* – Karel Reisz *sc* – Alan Sillitoe, from his own novel *ph* – Freddie Francis *ed* – Seth Holt
a.d – Ted Marshall *m* – Johnny Dankworth 89 mins.

Albert Finney (*Arthur*), Shirley Ann Field (*Doreen*), Rachel Roberts (*Brenda*), Hylda Baker (*Aunt Ada*), Norman Rossington (*Bert*), Bryan Pringle (*Jack*).

My main concern was to show that, while in one sense a certain section of those who worked in factories had their earthly bread, they by no means had been shown any kind of worthwhile spiritual bread . . . Having been some time out of England, I didn't know of Hoggart's *Uses of Literacy* – which pointed out more or less the same thing . . . Those who see Arthur Seaton as a symbol of the working man and not as an individual are mistaken. I wrote about him as a person, and not as a typical man who works at a lathe. I try to see every person as an individual and not as a class symbol, which is the only condition in which I can work as a writer. (Alan Sillitoe, *Daily Worker*, 28 January 1961)

Saturday Night and Sunday Morning is completely a director's film . . . Alan Sillitoe's novel gives a powerful expression to a brand of romantic anarchism, destructive and passionate, but perhaps lacking a clear sense of direction . . . The film, on the other hand, places Arthur at a certain distance and encircles him with sharply observed minor characters . . . The difference between the film and the novel amounts to no less than a difference between a romantic and a rational approach to a similar theme. (Boleslaw Sulik, *Definition*, no.3, p.17)

Here at last is a film which not only in the contemporary fashion is about the working class but of and for the working class . . . It shows uncompromisingly that Arthur's weaknesses – and his developing strength – spring not from selfishness and irresponsibility but from the oppression and sheer frustration of being a worker under the present social set-up. (Nina Hibbin, *Daily Worker*, 29 November 1960)

I still think that Mr Sillitoe, on the evidence of this film, has little to say except that a good wage, accessible sex and a telly are not everything. Any Sunday-school teacher could have made the point in fewer words. (Majdalany, *Daily Mail*, 25 November 1960)

It undoubtedly creates an impression that the young men of our industrial towns are a lot of ill-behaved, immoral, drunken Teddy Boys . . . The principal character could hardly be less typical of the young men of Nottingham . . . We produce as good a type as anywhere in the country, who work the best of their ability from Monday morning to Saturday noon. Many work through the weekend as well. (Lieutenant-Colonel John Cordeaux, Conservative MP for Nottingham, quoted *Daily Herald*, 6 February 1961)

Today's new fashion is tomorrow's formula and the difficulty which the much heralded *Saturday Night and Sunday Morning* has to face is that these youths, the Midland or North-country heroes of John Osborne, John Braine and, now, Alan Sillitoe, begin to wear a familiar look. The theme of the young and angry begins to be a formula . . . and young anger is no longer enough in itself. (*Manchester Guardian*, 29 November 1960)

THE WIND OF CHANGE (1961)

Cert – A *dist* – British Lion/Bryanston *p.c* – Bryanston *p* – John Dark *d* – Vernon Sewell *sc* – Alexander Doré, John McLaren *ph* – Basil Emmett *ed* – Peter Pitt *a.d* – Duncan Sutherland 64 mins.

Donald Pleasence (*Pop*), Johnny Briggs (*Frank*), Ann Lynn (*Josie*), Hilda Fenemore (*Gladys*), Glyn Houston (*Sgt Parker*), Norman Gunn (*Ron*).

The film, as its pretentious title implies, takes too much upon itself . . . The vitriolic nastiness of the white thugs is over-stressed, while the apparent nobility of the Negroes seems implausibly saintly. But underlying the slickly treated violence and ritual teenage trimmings – coffee bar jive sessions, guitar-twanging and tough talk – the situation is a genuine one. (*Monthly Film Bulletin*, April 1961, p.51)

SPARE THE ROD   (1961)

Cert – A   *dist* – BLC/British Lion/Bryanston   *p.c* – Bryanston/Weyland
p – Victor Lyndon   *d* – Leslie Norman   *sc* – John Cresswell, from novel by Michael Croft   *ph* – Paul Beeson   *ed* – Gordon Stone
a.d – Jimmy Komisarjevsky   *m* – Laurie Johnson   93 mins.

Max Bygraves (*John Saunders*), Donald Pleasence (*Jenkins*), Geoffrey Keen (*Gregory*), Richard O'Sullivan (*Harkness*), Betty McDowell (*Miss Collins*), Eleanor Summerfield (*Mrs Harkness*), Claire Marshall (*Margaret*).

The novel *Spare the Rod* was first published in 1954. It is about the problems of teaching in a tough, badly run secondary modern school and it's an attack on corporal punishment . . . Max Bygraves knew the book backwards. It was his own schooldays, he said. He believed in the story and he wanted to play a dramatic part . . . I took him at his word and sold him the option . . . Leslie Norman (the director) threw out the original script because it was too 'heavy'. The new writer gave the teacher-hero a wife but got caught up in the problem of whether she could have children or not and was promptly dropped . . . The new man, John Cresswell, went straight back to the book, and I stuck my nose in whenever I could. I persuaded them to drop the endless problems of married life, but couldn't talk them out of the incredible riot at the end or the scene where the sexy schoolgirl tries to get Max into bed – 'After all, you must have Entertainment, old man'. But they kept to the theme of the book and the message just about gets through. (Michael Croft, *Observer*, 4 June 1961)

The film has too little time in which to make any genuinely constructive criticism; and beats a painful retreat into rosy unrealism with a finale of discomfited villain, comforting heroine, grateful negroes and Christmas. (*Monthly Film Bulletin*, July 1961, p.96)

FLAME IN THE STREETS   (1961)

Cert – A   *dist* – Rank   *p.c* – Rank/Somerset   *p/d* – Roy Baker
sc – Ted Willis, from his play *Hot Summer Night*   *ph* – Christopher Challis
ed – Roger Cher   *a.d* – Alex Vetchinsky   *m* – Philip Green   93 mins.

John Mills (*Jacko Palmer*), Sylvia Syms (*Kathie Palmer*), Brenda de Banzie (*Nell Palmer*), Earl Cameron (*Gabriel Gomez*), Johnny Sekka (*Peter Lincoln*), Ann Lynn (*Judy Gomez*).

One of those well-meant, earnestly tailored pieces about life as it is in the headlines. (William Whitebait, *New Statesman*, 30 June 1961)

The British sociological film . . . is now firmly established: recipe plain-to-stodgy, final taste perfectly predictable; progressive but 'sensible', and all points of view given an airing. First and foremost, it has a Problem (intolerance, colour, crime), and the people are there to illustrate it. Then you can expect good acting, with energy and conviction down to the smallest parts; plain, 'tough' direction that isn't really going to offend Aunt Edna, a plain 'tough' script that ditto, and a lower-middle-class background. The family will live in a mean, small street and the interiors will all look carefully right, half-heartedly comic relief being provided by the older members, who sit in corners smoking enigmatically. It is advertised as searing, thought-provoking, blisteringly outspoken; but its impact is mild. (Isabel Quigly, *Spectator*, 30 June 1961)

VICTIM (1961)

Cert – X *dist* – Rank *p.c* – Parkway *p* – Michael Relph *d* – Basil Dearden *sc* – Janet Green, John McCormick *ph* – Otto Heller *ed* – John Guthridge *a.d* – Alex Vetchinsky *m* – Philip Green 100 mins.

Dirk Bogarde (*Melville Farr*), Sylvia Syms (*Laura Farr*), Dennis Price (*Calloway*), Nigel Stock (*Phip*), Peter McEnery (*Jack Barrett*), Donald Churchill (*Eddy Stone*), Anthony Nicholls (*Lord Fulbrook*).

A serious and sympathetic study of men in the grip of a compulsion beyond their control . . . a sobering picture of the way homosexual inclinations make a permanent nightmare of private lives. (*Daily Worker*, 2 September 1961)

What seems at first an attack on extortion seems at last a coyly sensational exploitation of homosexuality as a theme – and, what's more offensive, an implicit approval of homosexuality as a practice. Almost all the deviates in the film are fine fellows – well dressed, well spoken, sensitive, kind. The only one who acts like an invert turns out to be a detective. Everybody in the picture who disapproves of homosexuals proves to be an ass, a dolt or a sadist. Nowhere does the film suggest that homosexuality is a serious (but often curable) neurosis that attacks the biological basis of life itself. (*Time*, 23 February 1962)

The film portrays the screen's first homosexual character to choose visibility and thereby challenge the status quo. The issues of repression and enforced invisibility were equated, for the first time, with the law's relegation of homosexuals to a lawless subculture in which they became victims of their own ghostly status . . . An acceptable hero to some liberal audiences because he admits that homosexual acts are wrong and refrains from acting on his urges, Farr becomes a hero in the gay perspective because he is willing to lend a little dignity to his homosexual relationship by fighting to legitimize its existence. (Vito Russo, *The Celluloid Closet*, New York, Harper and Row, 1981, pp.129–31)

THE KITCHEN (1961)

Cert – X *dist* – British Lion *p.c* – ACT Films *p* – Ralph Bond, Sidney Cole
d – James Hill *sc* – Sidney Cole, after play by Arnold Wesker
ph – Reg Wyer *ed* – Gerry Hambling *a.d* – William Kellner
m – David Lee 74 mins.

Carl Mohner (*Peter*), Mary Yeomans (*Monica*), Eric Pohlmann (*Mr Marango*), Tom Bell (*Paul*), Martin Boddey (*Max*), Sean Lynch (*Dimitri*).

In theory *The Kitchen* is exactly the sort of British film we have been looking for for years. It is an adaptation it is true . . . but at least it is an adaptation from something eminently worthwhile. The play has not been adulterated; it is boldly presented with its full, original text, in its single, claustrophobic setting of a big restaurant kitchen. The setting is realistic, and the personages in it are real people doing real work. So what is wrong? . . . The difference is that while the play succeeded in being at once documentary and intensely dramatic, the film hesitates somewhere between . . . In John Dexter's stage production the drama and mechanics of the kitchen were entirely fused, here they are divorced . . . *The Kitchen* is probably one of the most honest, sincere and thoughtful British films since the war, and so its failure is all the sadder. (David Robinson, *Financial Times*, 14 July 1961)

A TASTE OF HONEY (1961)

Cert – X *dist* – Bryanston *p.c* – Woodfall *p/d* – Tony Richardson
sc – Shelagh Delaney and Tony Richardson, from Delaney's play
ph – Walter Lassally *ed* – Anthony Gibbs *a.d* – Ralph Brinton
m – John Addison 100 mins.

Rita Tushingham (*Jo*), Dora Bryan (*Helen*), Robert Stephens (*Peter*), Murray Melvin (*Geoffrey*), Paul Danquah (*Jimmy*), David Boliver (*Bert*).

Shaken by the eloquent fact that the last Woodfall film showed a bigger profit than *Hercules Unchained*, the Wardour Street money-bags are now busy asking one another whether Tony Richardson's *A Taste of Honey* is a second *Saturday Night and Sunday Morning*. In the crude arithmetic of the front-office, I suppose that an illegitimate Negro baby plus a homosexual may well be equal to an attempted abortion plus a beating-up. The point of view was repellently summarised to me the other day by the head of a British production company: 'It's the dirt that brings in the cloth cap and muffler trade.' No doubt the same contemptuous man could even design a salacious poster for *A Taste of Honey*. It would be like painting a leer on to the mouth of a Cranach nude. Apart from the fact that it is a triumph, and also clearly a money-maker, *A Taste of Honey* is no second *Saturday Night*. Karel Reisz's film was heroic; Tony Richardson's is poetic, full of a hard, glowing realism that any film-goer bred on bogus British naturalism will rise to like a kite. When one meets the word 'poetic' in a notice of a British film, one is generally all too right in inferring a travesty, probably about children and certainly involving the sort of studied photography that is called 'a joy' in the sedate Press; the purity and compression of the genuinely poetic have not figured much in British films. But *A Taste of Honey* is the real thing. Like Shelagh Delaney's original stage play, which she has adapted with Tony Richardson, it is marvellously expressive and invigoratingly direct. It is also moving, funny, packed with imagery and Lancashire fortitude, and emotionally without a false note. (Penelope Gilliatt, *Observer*, 17 September 1961)

I have always had a sneaking idea that . . . Miss Delaney had one of those electronic playmaking machines. Into this she fed the most singled-out for discussion topics she culled from the reviews of the then contemporary proletarian drama – 'teenage rebel', 'unmarried mother', 'colour prejudice', 'homosexuality', 'basic insecurity of the unloved'. (Eve Perrick, *Daily Mail*, 14 September 1961)

PETTICOAT PIRATES   (1961)

Cert – U   *dist* – Warner-Pathé   *p.c* – Associated British
p – Gordon L.T. Scott   *d* – David MacDonald   *sc* – Lew Schwarz,
Charlie Drake   *ph* – Gilbert Taylor   *ed* – Ann Chegwidden
a.d – Robert Jones   *m* – Don Banks   87 mins.

Charlie Drake (*Charlie*), Anne Heywood (*Ann*), Cecil Parker (*C-in-C*), John Turner (*Michael*), Maxine Audley (*Superintendent*), Eleanor Summerfield (*Mabel*).

Though hardly as rollicking as it might have been *Petticoat Pirates* is at least a reasonably jolly farce, and a film without any subtle overtones or undertones . . . As any successful farce must be, this one is founded upon a genuinely ridiculous idea – that of women taking themselves in deadly seriousness as naval units. (Alan Dent, *Sunday Telegraph*, 3 December 1961)

As British naval farce the piece is middling to dim, and for men who have a built-in aversion to women in uniform, it was virtually insupportable. (James Breen, *Observer*, 3 December 1961)

ONLY TWO CAN PLAY   (1962)

Cert – X   *dist* – BLC/British Lion   *p.c* – Vale   *exec.p* – Frank Launder,
Sidney Gilliat   *d* – Sidney Gilliat   *sc* – Bryan Forbes, from the novel *That
Uncertain Feeling* by Kingsley Amis   *ph* – John Wilcox   *ed* – Thelma Connell
a.d – Albert Witherick   *m* – Richard Rodney Bennett   106 mins.

Peter Sellers (*John Lewis*), Mai Zetterling (*Liz*), Virginia Maskell (*Jean*),
Richard Attenborough (*Probert*), Kenneth Griffiths (*Jenkins*), Maudie
Edwards (*Mrs Davies*).

In fact *Only Two Can Play* functions partly as a vehicle for Peter Sellers,
expert mimic rather than Amis rebel, and partly as another in the present
'tough' school of British films, earning its X certificate by its love scenes and
keeping up a steady fire of sex jokes, lavatory jokes and jokes about people
being sick. Bryan Forbes' script, and direction which keeps the film bustling
along after the Boultings' manner, are calculated to pull in the audience.
(*Monthly Film Bulletin*, February 1962, p.21)

There is an old English film convention which says that adulteresses, even,
as in this case, would-be adulteresses, must be either foreign or absurd . . . or
both; and that if they can be left unsatisfied so much the better. Forbes has
funked it and gone along; one might have guessed it from the title . . . This is
British film-making at its most nannyish and cowardly. (B. Partridge, *Time
and Tide*, 18 January 1962)

A KIND OF LOVING   (1962)

Cert – X   *dist* – Anglo Amalgamated   *p.c* – Vic/Waterhall
p – Joseph Janni   *d* – John Schlesinger   *sc* – Willis Hall, Keith Waterhouse,
adapted from a novel by Stan Barstow   *ph* – Denys Coop
ed – Roger Cherrill   *a.d* – Ray Simm   *m* – Ron Grainer   112 mins.

Alan Bates (*Vic*), June Ritchie (*Ingrid*), Thora Hird (*Mrs Rothwell*), Bert
Palmer (*Mr Brown*), Gwen Nelson (*Mrs Brown*), Malcolm Patton (*Jim
Brown*), Pat Keen (*Christine*), David Mahlowe (*David*), James Bolam (*Jeff*).

A Kind of Loving belongs to our new 'industrial realism' school. It is simpler
and even truer to life than *A Taste of Honey* or *Saturday Night and Sunday
Morning* . . . You will be shocked by this highly moral film only if you are
shocked by life. (Felix Barker, *Evening News*, 12 April 1962)

Although he was aware that the social background of the story was
important, he was also aware that what happened in human terms was more
important still. What mattered most . . . was the human drama that was
being played out against this background of job, family, class distinctions,
social conventions, etc.; and for me the human drama always comes through
in the film. (Gene D. Phillips, *John Schlesinger*, Boston, Twayne, 1981, p.50)

The sad thing is that, with just an ounce more courage, it could have been a genuine, affronting original: for if it had the candour to say so its real theme is not social discontent, like the other two [*Room at the Top*, *Saturday Night and Sunday Morning*] but the misogyny that has been simmering under the surface of half the interesting plays and films in England since 1956. (Penelope Gilliatt, *Observer*, 15 April 1962)

TERM OF TRIAL (1962)

Cert – X *dist* – Warner-Pathé *p.c* – Romulus *p* – James Woolf
d – Peter Glenville *sc* – Peter Glenville, based on the novel by
James Barlow *ph* – Oswald Morris *ed* – James Clark
a.d – Anthony Woolard *m* – Jean-Michel Damase 130 mins.

Laurence Olivier (*Graham Weir*), Simone Signoret (*Anna*), Sarah Miles (*Shirley Taylor*), Hugh Griffith (*O'Hara*), Terence Stamp (*Mitchell*), Roland Culver (*Trowman*).

Too many reminiscences of other kitchen-sink movies confuse a basically old-fashioned vision. Oh, that gratuitous beating-up (from every American picture), that brick through the windscreen (ex – *The Angry Silence*), Signoret amorous near a fuming geyser (ex – *Room at the Top*), Sarah Miles being all gawk (sort of Rita Tushingham), those love scenes with passionately thrumming trains (from any forties English picture), and that little sequence (ex – Free Cinema) of modern youth's Nice Time, all leather-jackets, dirty bookshops, and films with sex and violence, both qualities in which *Term of Trial* is not conspicuously deficient. At least Glenville seems aware of some of his hero's shortcomings . . . Nonetheless, we seem to be expected to applaud Teacher's 'courageous' stand before all those frightening boys and girls. Even those working-class kids who have a longing for higher things remain a rabble . . . It becomes an attack on the working-class for being disgusting . . . We have been persuaded that only a thin chalk line has been holding proletarian savagery at bay. (Raymond Durgnat, *A Mirror for England*, pp.43–4)

LIFE FOR RUTH (1962)

Cert – A *dist* – Rank/Allied Film Makers *p.c* – Michael Relph,
Basil Dearden *p* – Michael Relph *d* – Basil Dearden *sc* – Janet Green,
John McCormick *ph* – Otto Heller *ed* – John Guthridge
a.d – Alex Vetchinsky *m* – Muir Mathieson 91 mins.

Michael Craig (*John Harris*), Patrick McGoohan (*Dr Jim Brown*), Janet Munro (*Pat Harris*), Malcolm Keen (*John Harris' father*), Megs Jenkins (*Mrs Gordon*), John Barrie (*Mr Gordon*).

It is seldom indeed that the cinema successfully attempts one of the highest of the theatre's functions – that of making people seriously debate about reason and reality, not to say matters of life and death. It does so here. This is . . . the best-argued, best-made, best-directed, and best-acted film in an interesting week. (Alan Dent, *Sunday Telegraph*, 2 April 1962)

The problem in *Life for Ruth* is the refusal of a father to let his dying child have a blood transfusion because of his fundamentalist religious beliefs. The problem seems a marginal one but it touches on very important matters like a parent's responsibility to his children and the value of conscientious objection in a society. The way that Relph and Dearden have turned all this into a conventional 'entertainment' reveals an appalling vulgarity and insensitivity. (Alan Lovell, *Observer*, 2 September 1962)

SOME PEOPLE (1962)

Cert – A *dist* – Anglo Amalgamated *p.c* – Vic *p* – James Archibald *d* – Clive Donner *sc* – John Eldridge *ph* – John Wilcox *ed* – Fergus McDonell *a.d* – Reece Pemberton *m* – Ron Grainer 93 mins.

Kenneth More (*Mr Smith*), Ray Brooks (*Johnnie*), Annika Wills (*Anne*), David Andrews (*Bill*), Angela Douglas (*Terry*), David Hemmings (*Bert*).

James Archibald, the producer, was approached by the Duke of Edinburgh Award Scheme to make a picture for them. They wanted a picture which brought the idea of the scheme to the attention of what the sociologists call the 'unattached teenager'. He and I went on a tour with the scheme's deputy director which was aimed to show us a cross-section of young people throughout the country. As a result we decided that in order to give them the film they wanted, we would have to make an entertainment picture (not a didactic documentary, because it wouldn't reach the audience it was intended for) and one in which there was no aspect of people being got at. There was obviously a propaganda requirement. The sponsors said they wanted their point made good and strong. We said they wouldn't achieve anything by being blatant about it. It would be foolish and dishonest to pretend that it wasn't there, but it would have to be there very much in proportion to the other activities – as it would be in life if this subject were to come up: the kids would talk about it, in the coffee-bar scene for instance, for two or three sentences and then get on to talking about Helen Shapiro. (Clive Donner, quoted in V.F. Perkins, 'Clive Donner and Some People', *Movie* no.3, 1962, p.23)

With its vitality and feeling for the idiom of youth, it avoids any hint of sanctity . . . What comes across is a harsh, strident picture of British youth – the rowdies with leather jackets, roaring motorbikes, and no sense of purpose. (Felix Barker, *Evening Herald*, 19 July 1962)

211

Not without charm and showing, for the most part, a nice attention to detail, this teenage film (the profits of which go to the Duke of Edinburgh Award Scheme) is transparently well-meaning and made with obvious affection. Unfortunately, it has nothing to add to that now painfully familiar delinquency formula which combines a liking for coffee-bars, motorbikes and guitars with an inability to talk reasonably to Father. (*Monthly Film Bulletin*, September 1962, p.128)

THE BOYS (1962)

Cert – A *dist* – Gala *p.c* – Galaworldfilm/Atlas *p/d* – Sidney J. Furie
sc – Stuart Douglass *ph* – Gerald Gibbs *ed* – Jack Slade
a.d – John Earl *m* – The Shadows 123 mins.

Richard Todd (*Victor Webster*), Robert Morley (*Montgomery*), Felix Aylmer (*Judge*), Dudley Sutton (*Stan Coulter*), Ronald Lacey (*Billy Herne*), Tony Garnett (*Ginger Thompson*), Jess Conrad (*Barney Lee*).

Is it unfair to condemn these youngsters without a second glance? To associate them with trouble when to all intents and purposes they are peaceful young citizens with high spirits and youth on their side? This is the important question which . . . *The Boys* poses. It is a question as relevant as nuclear disarmament, as modern as the conquest of space. More so, because it touches all of us every day. It is part of the society we live in, the framework of our modern economic system. (Publicity material)

The zest, urgency and passion of much of *The Boys* make it the most worthwhile British film for some time. (Derek Hill, *Topic*, 15 September 1962)

When the point of the film for the first two hours has been that it is wrong to suspect all teenagers of being juvenile delinquents, especially when they have more gaiety and originality than any other group in the country today, it seems woolly minded to introduce the final twist that the boys are vicious murderers after all. It confirms every suspicion the Tory witnesses ever had. (Penelope Gilliatt, *Observer*, 16 September 1962)

Why is *The Boys* given an A certificate when the delinquent teenagers whom it is meant to discourage and shame will revel in it with no shame at all and no feeling of disagreement? (Alan Dent, *Sunday Telegraph*, 16 September 1962)

THE LONELINESS OF THE LONG DISTANCE RUNNER (1962)

Cert – X *dist* – BLC/British Lion/Bryanston *p.c* – Woodfall
p/d – Tony Richardson *sc* – Alan Sillitoe, from his short story
ph – Walter Lassally *ed* – Anthony Gibbs *a.d* – Ralph Brinton,
Ted Marshall *m* – John Addison 104 mins.

Tom Courtenay (*Colin Smith*), James Bolam (*Mike*), Avis Bunnage (*Mrs Smith*), Michael Redgrave (*Governor*), Alex McCowen (*Brown*), Joe Robinson (*Roach*).

The war between the classes has never been joined in British films as openly as it was this week. In the forties the working classes were idiom-talking idiots, loyal or baleful. In the fifties they grew rightly articulate and angry. Now we get what may be the prototype for the sixties: Colin Smith, borstal boy hero of *Loneliness of the Long Distance Runner*, a youth beyond anger, almost beyond speech, joining battle. (P. Williams, *Sunday Telegraph*, 30 September 1962)

Loneliness of the Long Distance Runner . . . is a British film very much in the fashion. It is a film of youth . . . it is realistic in theme and setting and it is concerned with the problems and difficulties of those who find themselves on the wrong side of the law . . . Nevertheless, it would be a pleasant change if all this elaborate apparatus of mockery at the expense of the existing order of things were put into action on behalf not of discontented youth, the spoilt darlings of the age, but of the ill, the solitary, the virtuous old. (*The Times*, 26 September 1962)

A piece of skilful but specious pleading for the British proletariat . . . The hero is too prolier-than-thou, his case too obviously rigged. (*Time*, 26 October 1962)

Sillitoe and Richardson by stuffing 'poetry' in, with little innocent idylls of the fun of pinching a car, and wandering hand in hand at the beach with a playmate girl have destroyed the true poetry of the original conception – which was in the singleness of vision: a terrifying view of modern life, a madman's view that forces us to see how mad we are. . . . The pity is that the movie audience which might have been upset, forced to think out some of its attitudes towards theft and property and work and social organization, is instead reconfirmed in its liberal complacency. (Pauline Kael, *I Lost it at the Movies*, Cape, 1966, pp.258–61)

THE WILD AND THE WILLING   (1962)

Cert – X *dist/p.c* – Rank *p* – Betty Box *d* – Ralph Thomas
sc – Nicholas Phipps and Mordecai Richler, from the play *The Tinker* by
Laurence Dobie and Robert Sloman *ph* – Ernest Steward
ed – Alfred Roome *a.d* – Alex Vetchinsky *m* – Norrie Paramor 112 mins.

Virginia Maskell (*Virginia Chown*), Paul Rogers (*Prof Chown*), Ian McShane (*Harry Brown*), Samantha Eggar (*Josie*), Catherine Woodville (*Sarah*), David Sumner (*John*), John Hurt (*Phil*).

The indefatigable producer-director team of Betty Box and Ralph Thomas are not to be outdone on any score. *The Wild and the Willing* is their answer to the new wave of films with sociological themes and working-class and provincial settings . . . They excel all their predecessors in ripe language and bold sexiness; but, predictably, their approach to a socially motivated theme goes no deeper than the naughty words themselves. It is just another old Pinewood melodrama in which regional accents and working-class accents are no more than fashionable trappings. (David Robinson, *Financial Times*, 19 October 1962)

The Wild and the Willing shows, all too clearly, some of the hazards lying in wait for proven commercial expertise (in this case, that of the Box-Thomas équipe) when it ventures into the areas of the new British realism. One doesn't doubt the film's good intentions: the seeking out of a promising location, with Lincoln standing in for red-brick provincialism; the use of an eager and largely untried team of young actors (among whom John Hurt and Samantha Eggar show the most promise); the resolute excursions into the 'X' certificate dialogue, pub scenes and bedroom scenes which have helped to equate this kind of realism with box-office. But the film, from Virginia Maskell's frustrated don's wife, swigging whisky out of the bottle and seducing her husband's students in the kitchen, to the extravagantly self-conscious heartiness of the roistering in pubs, looks either slightly off-key or hilariously so. Harry may have seemed a plausible character in the original play; here he becomes a walking compendium of jaded Angry Young Man attitudes, while the film leans so far backwards in its determination to integrate Reggie, the coloured student, into the group that it achieves a kind of desperate self-consciousness about him. Ralph Thomas directs in a manner more restless than brisk; but the restlessness is hardly that of urgent youth. (*Monthly Film Bulletin*, November 1962, p.152)

THE MIND BENDERS (1962)

Cert – X *dist* – Warner-Pathé/Anglo Amalgamated *p* – Novus
p – Michael Relph *d* – Basil Dearden *sc* – James Kennaway
ph – Denys Coop *ed* – John D. Guthridge *a.d* – James Morahan
m – Georges Auric 113 mins.

Dirk Bogarde (*Dr Henry Longman*), Mary Ure (*Oonagh Longman*), John Clements (*Major Hall*), Michael Bryant (*Dr Tate*), Wendy Craig (*Annabelle*), Harold Goldblatt (*Professor Sharpey*).

Dearden and Relph have, as usual, contrived to snatch a plot out of the headlines, though the 'secrets' Sharpey has disposed of seem to be of a kind familiar to any popular science magazine. In fact, and having got on to the fascinating theme of personality changes and the techniques of manipulating the human mind, Dearden and his scriptwriter, James Kennaway, have pulled it all down to elementary Jekyll and Hydism. Jekyll Longman, the happy family man whose children, in the old North Oxford tradition, are given such names as Piers and Persephone, goes into the tank, screams and gibbers through a sci-fi sequence, and emerges as Hyde Longman, whose unlikely recreation (offscreen) consists of hiring an Amsterdam prostitute's window to show off his wife in it. With a screaming of gears, the film changes up (or down?) for the childbirth sequence of the depressing order known as 'frank', and back comes Jekyll Longman, proudly nursing another candidate for a whimsical Christian name. (*Monthly Film Bulletin*, March 1963, p.32)

THE L-SHAPED ROOM   (1962)

Cert – X *dist* – BLC/British Lion *p.c* – Romulus *p* – James Woolf, Richard Attenborough *d* – Bryan Forbes *sc* – Bryan Forbes, based on the novel by Lynne Reid Banks *ph* – Douglas Slocombe *ed* – Anthony Harvey *a.d* – Ray Simm *m.d* – Muir Mathieson 142 mins.

Leslie Caron (*Jane*), Tom Bell (*Toby*), Brock Peters (*Johnny*), Cicely Courtneidge (*Mavis*), Bernard Lee (*Charlie*), Avis Bunnage (*Doris*), Patricia Phoenix (*Sonia*).

On the screen these days, realism usually means unmarried mothers, abortions, prostitutes, homosexuals, lesbians and what Mr Somerset Maugham has taken to calling 'sexual congress'. (Harry Weaver, *Scene*, no.10, 15 November 1962)

Bryan Forbes takes two and a half hours to knock the last nail in the social realist coffin. (Derek Hill, *Topic*, 17 November 1962)

THIS SPORTING LIFE   (1963)

Cert – X *dist* – Rank *p.c* – Independent Artists *p* – Karel Reisz *d* – Lindsay Anderson *sc* – David Storey, from his novel *ph* – Denys Coop *ed* – Peter Taylor *a.d* – Alan Withy *m* – Roberto Gerhard 134 mins.

Richard Harris (*Frank Machin*), Rachel Roberts (*Mrs Hammond*), Alan Badel (*Weaver*), William Hartnell (*Johnson*), Colin Blakely (*Maurice Braithwaite*), Vanda Godsell (*Mrs Weaver*), Anne Cunningham (*Judith*), Jack Watson (*Len Miller*).

It is easier to say what a film is *not* about. *This Sporting Life* is not a film about sport. Nor is it to be categorised as a 'North Country working-class story' . . . I suppose that the film is primarily a study of temperament, it is a film about a man. A man of extraordinary power and aggressiveness, both temperamental and physical . . . Flying in the face of fashion, we have tried to make a tragedy. Much as I admire many of the experiments made by the young French directors and particularly their adventurous breaking away from the outmoded conventions of cinematic 'style' . . . I think that even in their work there is apt to be a terrible lack of weight, of substance and human significance. Their very brilliance seems to trap them in facility and vogueishness . . . For all of their scorn of artistic conventions, their films do not *disturb*. The case of the new British school is rather different . . . Here the achievement has been the opening up of new territories, both of subjects and of the social backgrounds in which they are set. But it could also be restrictive if we make films for too long with an eye on what is representative – films about 'working class people' looked at objectively, almost with a documentarist's vision. (Or a sociologist's, which is worse). Of course, too, it must rule tragedy out; for tragedy is concerned with what is unique, not what is representative . . . No doubt I shall be accused, or congratulated, for having deserted the ranks of 'commitment'. Both accusations and congratulations will be misplaced. All works of art have political implications: but they have political implications because they are works of art, not vice versa. (Lindsay Anderson, *Films and Filming*, vol.9, no.5, February 1963, pp.16–18)

Lindsay Anderson's *This Sporting Life* is a stupendous film. It has a blow like a fist. I've never seen an English picture that gave such expression to the violence and the capacity for pain that there is in the English character. It is there in Shakespeare, in Marlowe, in Lawrence and Orwell and Hogarth, but not in our cinema like this before. Lindsay Anderson's films before this have been documentaries, but his first feature certainly isn't a documentary about Rugby League. Nor is it a sociological study of a kind of contemporary man. Frank Machin cõuld have lived at any time, and he is not anyone's representative; the film is about a unique man who suffers an absolutely personal kind of pain. (Penelope Gilliatt, *Observer*, 10 February 1963)

It is not, surely, the North Country scene that's exhausted, nor the realistic style, but the convention that a sex relationship must be at the centre of a film, to be flogged, as here, for more than it's worth. (Patrick Gibbs, *Daily Telegraph*, 9 February 1963)

You can feel . . . the determined efforts cf the director . . . to cut off character from social roots. The producer, Karel Reisz, showed when he directed *Saturday Night and Sunday Morning* the essential relationship between character and society. But the two people in *This Sporting Life* are rotten because they are rotten. There is nothing to explain them or make you care. (Nina Hibbin, *Daily Worker*, 9 February 1963)

THAT KIND OF GIRL (1963)

Cert – X *dist* – Compton-Cameo *p.c* – Tekli *p* – Robert Hartford-Davis *d* – Gerald O'Hara *sc* – Jan Reed *ph* – Peter Newbrook *ed* – Derek York *a.d* – William Brodie *m* – Malcolm Mitchell 77 mins.

Margaret-Rose Keil (*Eva*), David Weston (*Keith*), Linda Marlowe (*Janet*), Peter Burton (*Elliot Collier*), Frank Jarvis (*Max*), Sylvia Kay (*Mrs Miller*).

There is much padding and surplus material before the film arrives at its main theme – the dangers, through ignorance, of VD. Directed to adolescents, the propaganda element is reasonable enough, even if the medical profession is depicted in rather too glowing and sympathetic terms; but the story is sheer melodrama, running the weird gamut of anti-nuclear demonstration, striptease, pre-marital intercourse, rape and improper use of the telephone – scarcely a digestible mixture. (*Monthly Film Bulletin*, May 1963, p.70)

THE LEATHER BOYS (1963)

Cert – X *dist* – BLC/British Lion/Garrick *p.c* – Raymond Stross
p – Raymond Stross *d* – Sidney J. Furie *sc* – Gillian Freeman, based on
the novel by Eliot George *ph* – Gerald Gibbs *ed* – Reginald Beck
a.d – Arthur Lawson *m* – Bill McGuffie 108 mins.

Rita Tushingham (*Dot*), Colin Campbell (*Reggie*), Dudley Sutton (*Pete*), Gladys Henson (*Gran*), Avice Landon (*Reggie's Mother*), Lockwood West (*Reggie's Father*).

The notoriously long delay in putting this film into the cinemas has made it the proto-martyr of the crisis in the British film industry. The fact that it has only one star and touches, however, delicately on the subject of homosexuality, presumably outweighs the wit, feeling and artistry that have gone into the direction, acting and photography. (*Monthly Film Bulletin*, February 1964, p.21)

The implication of this film seems to me brutally anti-feminine: that what makes men turn to men is women. (Thomas Wiseman, *Sunday Express*, 26 January 1964)

HEAVENS ABOVE! (1963)

Cert – A *dist* – BLC/British Lion/Romulus *p.c* – Charter *p* – Roy Boulting
d – John Boulting *sc* – Frank Harvey, John Boulting, from an idea by
Malcolm Muggeridge *ph* – Max Greene *ed* – Teddy Darvas
a.d – Albert Witherick *m* – Richard Rodney Bennett 118 mins.

Peter Sellers (*Rev John Smallwood*), Cecil Parker (*Archdeacon Aspinall*), Isabel Jeans (*Lady Despard*), Eric Sykes (*Harry Smith*), Bernard Miles (*Simpson*), Brock Peters (*Matthew*), Ian Carmichael (*The Other Smallwood*), Irene Handl (*Rene Smith*).

The Boultings have not lost their satirical sting, but they direct it not so much at the Church as at its parasitical hangers-on and the petty snobberies, tyrannies and jealousies they engender. The result is the brothers' most human picture. If it is not as outrageous nor as consistently uproarious as we have come to expect, it still has some glorious moments. (Cecil Wilson, *Daily Mail*, 22 May 1963)

Heavens Above is a dingy and ill-made farce . . . The only people it is likely to offend are those who care about good films. (Philip Oakes, *Sunday Telegraph*, 26 May 1963)

BILLY LIAR   (1963)

Cert – A   *dist* – Warner-Pathé/Anglo Amalgamated   *p.c* – Vic Films
p – Joseph Janni   *d* – John Schlesinger   *sc* – Keith Waterhouse and Willis Hall, based on the novel by Keith Waterhouse, and the play by Waterhouse and Willis Hall   *ph* – Denys Coop   *ed* – Roger Cherrill
a.d – Ray Simm   *m* – Richard Rodney Bennett   98 mins.

Tom Courtenay (*Billy Fisher*), Julie Christie (*Liz*), Wilfred Pickles (*Geoffrey Fisher*), Mona Washbourne (*Alice Fisher*), Ethel Griffies (*Florence, Grand-mother*), Finlay Currie (*Duxbury*), Gwendolyn Watts (*Rita*).

Billy's society is a society of conformity . . . There is the captivity and lack of communication in his relationships with his family, and the dullness of the routine of his work . . . He hates it all but ultimately he doesn't have the courage to break away from it . . . The problem is universal. (John Schlesinger, *Films and Filming*, May 1963, p.10)

I still can't decide whether this screen version of the Keith Waterhouse-Willis Hall play is the funniest film of the year or the saddest. But there's one thing I am certain about: it's brilliant. (Margaret Hinxman, *Daily Herald*, 16 August 1963)

The story of Billy Fisher . . . should come over with a convincing realism. But it doesn't. One reason is that in some ways we've seen it all before – 'A Taste of Loving on Saturday Night at the Top'. We've seen the dreary town, Billy's useless defiance, the office where he works and the men who bully him. We've seen his girlfriends and his parents and we have got a pretty good idea of what they are going to say next. (Ian Wright, *Guardian*, 13 August 1963)

In *Billy Liar* one feels at a cross-roads in cinema. The sad-faced boy who stays behind and conforms, a rebel only in his dreams, has been passed by the new type of girl swinging confidently and joyously out into a future that is part and parcel of an affluent generation's life-style centred on youth, dreams and metropolitan delights. With Julie Christie, the British cinema caught the train south. (Alexander Walker, *Hollywood England*, p.167)

A PLACE TO GO   (1963)

Cert – A   *dist* – BLC/British Lion/Bryanston   *p.c* – Excalibur
p – Michael Relph   *d* – Basil Dearden   *sc* – Michael Relph, based on
the novel *Bethnal Green* by Michael Fisher   *ph* – Reginald Wyer
ed – John D. Guthridge   *a.d* – Bert Davey   *m* – Charles Blackwell 86 mins.

Bernard Lee (*Matt*), Rita Tushingham (*Cat*), Mike Sarne (*Ricky*), Doris Hare
(*Lil*), Barbara Ferris (*Betsy*), John Slater (*Jack Ellerman*).

The film is very much concerned with the wind of change which is blowing
through the East End of London, a wind which is sweeping away the close-
packed street of drab little houses and bringing new, shining modern flats in
their place. The trouble is that this wind blows too fast for the old but not fast
enough for the young. (*Daily Cinema*, 25 July 1963, p.30)

An anthology of every British 'new wave' backstreet cliché, including pub
sing-songs, flick-knife fights, loneliness in the new tenements, eviction from
the old street, Dad forever on the dole and Mum just as eternally laying the
table for high-tea. (Alexander Walker, *Hollywood England*, p.250)

THE PARTY'S OVER   (1963)

Cert – X   *dist* – Monarch   *p.c* – Tricastle   *p* – Anthony Perry
d – Guy Hamilton   *ph* – Larry Pizer   *a.d* – Peggy Crick   *ed* – John Bloom
m – John Barry 94 mins.

Oliver Reed (*Moise*), Clifford Davis (*Carson*), Ann Lynn (*Libby*), Catherine
Woodville (*Nina*), Louise Sorel (*Melina*), Mike Pratt (*Geronimo*).

The Party's Over, in fact, has a moral theme; melodramatically moral. But
everything in it is disjointed, implausible, absurd. (Dilys Powell, *Sunday
Times*, 4 May 1965)

Possibly the most outspoken and controversial film ever made in Britain.
(John Ardagh, *Observer*, 27 October 1963)

THIS IS MY STREET   (1963)

Cert – A   *dist* – Warner-Pathé/Anglo Amalgamated   *p.c* – Adder
p – Jack Hanbury   *d* – Sidney Hayers   *sc* – Bill MacIlwraith, based on the
novel by Nan Maynard   *ph* – Alan Hume   *ed* – Roger Cherrill
a.d – Alex Vetchinsky   *m/m.d* – Eric Rogers 94 mins.

Ian Hendry (*Harry*), June Ritchie (*Margery*), Avice Landon (*Lily*), Meredith
Edwards (*Steve*), Madge Ryan (*Kitty*), John Hurt (*Charlie*), Annette Andre
(*Jinny*), Philippa Gail (*Maureen*).

This highly moral tale bears all the hallmarks of a serial from one of the not-so-glossy women's weeklies. Weak on characterisation and over-loaded with sub-plot, it forms a very flimsy base for a screenplay. Bill MacIlwraith has supplied some snappy dialogue, Sidney Hayers uses the Battersea locations intelligently and keeps up a cracking pace, while slightly flashy editing adds to the general impression of slickness. But the glossy surface only emphasises the emptiness of the writing. (*Monthly Film Bulletin*, March 1964, p.43)

YOUNG CASSIDY (1965)

Cert – A *dist* – MGM *p.c* – Sextant *p* – Robert D. Graff,
Robert Emmett Ginna *d* – Jack Cardiff, John Ford *sc* – John Whiting,
after Sean O'Casey *ph* – Ted Scaife *ed* – Anne V. Coates
a.d – Michael Stringer *m* – Sean O'Riada 110 mins.

Rod Taylor (*Johnny Cassidy*), Flora Robson (*Mrs Cassidy*), Maggie Smith (*Nora*), Julie Christie (*Daisy Birtles*), Edith Evans (*Lady Gregory*), Michael Redgrave (*W.B. Yeats*), Jack MacGowran (*Archie*).

This is little more than a conventional act of hagiographic homage . . . O'Casey spruced up for export and audience-identification. The scenes of social and political unrest are short – in a spirit of plague-on-both-your-houses savagery. True enough O'Casey detested bloodshed: but where is the faintest hint that he was a passionate Communist and a virulent anti-Catholic? (Kenneth Tynan, *Observer*, 28 February 1965)

It is rather as if Disney had decided to make a film about Lenin guaranteed to tread on no right wing toes. (Isabel Quigly, *The Spectator*, 5 March 1965)

DARLING (1965)

Cert – X *dist* – Anglo-Amalgamated *p.c* – Vic/Appia *p* – Joseph Janni
d – John Schlesinger *sc* – Frederic Raphael *ph* – Ken Higgins
ed – James Clark *a.d* – Ray Sim *m* – John Dankworth 127 mins.

Dirk Bogarde (*Robert Gold*), Laurence Harvey (*Miles Brand*), Julie Christie (*Diana Scott*), Jose-Luis de Villalonga (*Prince Cesare*), Roland Curram (*Malcolm*), Alex Scott (*Sean Martin*).

The description and condemnation of the character of Diana, particularly in the popular press, is of an extraordinary vehemence. She is variously a bitch, a witch, a slut, a trollop, a tramp, a wanton. The foregrounding of issues relevant to women's lives is obscured by a deeper need to appropriate and contain the threat of female sexual autonomy. Through its reactionary message that permissiveness, however momentarily pleasurable, will be punished, *Darling* appears to have made a signal contribution to repressive discourses around female sexuality in the contemporary context of anxieties about the 'permissive society'. (Carrie Tarr, *Screen*, vol.26, no.1, January/February 1985, p.64)

ALFIE   (1966)

Cert – X *dist* – Paramount *p.c* – Sheldrake *p/d* – Lewis Gilbert
sc – Bill Naughton, based on his own play *ph* – Otto Heller
ed – Thelma Connell *a.d* – Peter Mullins *m* – Sonny Rollins 114 mins.

Michael Caine (*Alfie*), Shelley Winters (*Ruby*), Millicent Martin (*Siddie*), Julia Foster (*Gilda*), Jane Asher (*Annie*), Shirley Ann Field (*Carla*), Vivien Merchant (*Lily*).

When you see seven women in one film putting up the performances of their young or middle-aged careers, it is unusual enough to rouse a cheer. The fact that this happens in a British film deserves two cheers. And the fact that one man is the equal of all of them, in acting and expertise, will get three hurrahs from filmgoers of at least one sex. Lewis Gilbert's tremendously exuberant and enjoyable new film, *Alfie*, calls up such mixed emotions of artistic pleasure, national pride and sexual satisfaction in me this week. (Alexander Walker, *Evening Standard*, 24 March 1966)

I'm not going to turn up my nose at the verbal film, especially when it is very nearly at its best as here. So very nearly. The piece to my mind is fatally flawed by the central character being at odds with the theme. While the text is superficially avant-gardish, with racy dialogue and an anti-hero who appears to be successfully defying society, it is basically old-fashioned. After enjoying Alfie's anti-social antics for half the film, it is an awful let-down to be read what amounts to a moral lecture. (Patrick Gibbs, *Daily Telegraph*, 25 March 1966)

TO SIR, WITH LOVE   (1966)

Cert – A *dist* – Columbia *p.c* – Columbia *p* – John R. Sloan,
James Clavell *d/sc* – James Clavell, after novel by E.R. Braithwaite
ph – Paul Beeson *ed* – Peter Thornton *a.d* – Tony Woollard
m – Ron Grainer 105 mins.

Sidney Poitier (*Mark Thackeray*), Christian Roberts (*Denham*), Judy Geeson (*Pamela Dare*), Suzy Kendall (*Gillian Blanchard*), Lulu (*Barbara Pegg*), Faith Brook (*Mrs Evans*).

If the film pretends to social realism by its frequent allusions to race prejudice, broken homes, ill-equipped classrooms and so on, its solutions have all the facile optimism of the most utopian folk-songs. (*Monthly Film Bulletin*, October 1967, p.156)

The children have turned out to be no threat after all, they were only pretending to be independent. The audience goes home, red-eyed and consoled: in the cinema at least, the young still know their place. (Robert Robinson, *Sunday Telegraph*, 10 September 1967)

Good old-fashioned sentimental nonsense. (John Russell Taylor, *The Times*, 7 September 1967)

General Index

Other Books on British Cinema from BFI Publishing

All Our Yesterdays
90 Years of British Cinema
Edited by Charles Barr

At regular intervals in its history, British cinema has been pronounced dead or moribund. François Truffaut once said that the words 'cinema' and 'Britain' might be incompatible and the Indian director Satyajit Ray thought the British not 'temperamentally equipped to make the best use of the movie camera'. But the time has long been ripe for a reappraisal. British cinema has been rightly (if contradictorily) championed for both its realism and its rich vein of fantasy. *All Our Yesterdays* examines the diversity of British cinema, from mainstream to independent, melodrama to documentary, animation to crime movies, and establishes its links with theatre, literature, music hall and broadcasting. A perspective of 90 years of British cinema emerges which is appreciative, entertaining and often surprising.

Cinema and State
The Film Industry and the British Government 1927-84
Margaret Dickinson and Sarah Street

From the earliest days the British government played a part in the formation of the British film industry. However, it was in the aftermath of the crisis caused by American domination of the industry during World War I that the government was forced to intervene directly in order to prevent a total collapse in production. Since then, as one crisis has succeeded another, the question of what the government should do has always been at the centre of plans to rejuvenate the industry. This book, based on new research into sources in the Public Record Office and elsewhere, traces the always tortuous but often fascinating story of the role played by the State in the affairs of Wardour Street.

British Cinema Now
Edited by Martyn Auty and Nick Roddick

Following the recent wave of success, the British film industry seems once more to be out of the doldrums. Were films such as *Chariots of Fire* and *The Draughtsman's Contract* part of a genuine renaissance in British cinema or another false dawn? Does the future of the British film industry depend on international prestige productions or more modest ventures aimed at a specialist market? What effects will the relationship with television have on the industry of the future? The well-informed and lively articles in this book offer the facts and analysis necessary to understand the acute problems facing British cinema.

Humphrey Jennings
Film-Maker, Painter, Poet

Edited by Mary-Lou Jennings

Best known as a documentary film-maker and in particular for such wartime classics as *Listen to Britain* and *Fires Were Started*, Humphrey Jennings was also a writer, photographer and painter, and before he turned to film-making was actively involved in surrealism and Mass Observation – concerns that flow into and enrich his later film work. This book traces his brilliant career with the aid of many documents previously unpublished, essays by Charles Madge, Kathleen Raine, David Mellor and Dai Vaughan, and Lindsay Anderson's famous 1954 article *Only Connect*. The figure that emerges is that of a truly remarkable artist.

Portrait of an Invisible Man
The Working Life of Stewart McAllister, Film Editor

Dai Vaughan

Stewart McAllister was a fellow student of Norman McLaren at Glasgow School of Art and was editor of Humphrey Jennings' finest wartime documentaries. In the eyes of his more famous colleagues he had a talent equal if not superior to their own. Did he just never fulfil his promise, or is it the film technicians destiny always to be overlooked in favour of the more prestigious roles of producer and director? In this book Dai Vaughan, a film editor and writer, reconstructs the fascinating story of McAllister's career and offers a challenging reinterpretation of the British documentary movement and documentary in general.

Traditions of Independence
British Cinema in The Thirties

Edited by Don Macpherson

Traditionally, independent British cinema in the 1930s is remembered for John Grierson and the documentary movement. In fact there were many groups – political organisations, trade unions, the Left Book Club – involved in the making and showing of films which sought to reflect an alternative voice. This book is the first comprehensive analysis of a tumultuous decade of independent cinema in Britain. Documents of the period, witness to a lively debate about film and politics, are reprinted with contextual comment, and original essays discuss the various political and cultural questions raised by the films and their makers.

The Wandering Company
Twenty-One Years of Merchant Ivory Films
John Pym

In 1961 Indian film producer Ismail Merchant and American director James Ivory paid a visit to Polish-born writer Ruth Prawer Jhabvala, then living in Delhi, with a proposal to make a film of her novel *The Householder*. Thus was born one of the most productive partnerships in the history of the cinema, resulting in such films as *Shakespeare Wallah, The Europeans* and *Heat and Dust*. Many of the films have been concerned with the meeting of cultures; all of them are marvellously evocative of time and place. Author John Pym has talked to all three film-makers and James Ivory has added his own comments. The result is a fascinating insight into the experience of film-making.

Scotch Reels
Scotland in Cinema and Television
Edited by Colin McArthur

Scotland and the Scots have been appearing on the cinema screen since the turn of the century, and Scotland has had its own distinctive cinematic institutions since the 1930s. Yet to date these activities have never become a focus for debate. This book is an attempt to map the field of Scottish film culture. The essays contained in it cover topics such as the influence of Tartanry and Kailyard on Scottish culture generally, the image of Scotland in mainstream cinema and the inadequacies of Scottish television. All the essays are unashamedly polemical in intent, their purpose to provoke an urgent inquiry into the means by which cinema and television in Scotland can be revitalised.

Projecting Britain
Ealing Studios Film Posters
Edited by David Wilson

Film posters are by their nature ephemeral, and very few of them deserve to be preserved. But the marvellous posters produced by Ealing Studios are an exception. Specially commissioned from such artists as Edward Ardizzone, John Piper, Edward Bawden, Ronald Searle and John Minton, these posters were as distinctive and idiosyncratic as the films – *Kind Hearts and Coronets, Passport to Pimlico* – which they advertised in the 40s and 50s. Sixty of these posters are reproduced here in full colour as a tribute to their designers and to the film company which had the imagination to commission them.

Powell, Pressburger and Others

Edited by Ian Christie

A guide to the work of Michael Powell and his many distinguished collaborators. Specially written sections deal with Powell and Pressburger's challenge to orthodox realism, the wartime propaganda apparatus and the 'scandal' of *Peeping Tom*. Important critical articles are reprinted, and an extensive chronology traces Powell's progress through 50 years of British cinema.

Launder and Gilliat

Geoff Brown

Frank Launder and Sidney Gilliat were key figures in British cinema for 50 years, working with Hitchcock, Walter Forde, Carol Reed and Anthony Asquith and writing and directing such films as *Millions Like Us, Waterloo Road, The Rake's Progress* and *The Happiest Days of Your Life*. This extended survey of their careers, fully documented and including much comment by Launder and Gilliat themselves, is a revealing account of several generations of British film-making practice.